Praise for the previous edition:

This is a biography written in blood, love and tears in the tradition of Gosse's *Father and Son*.

Philip Howard, *The Times*

Have you ever wondered how even the most dedicated anti-Semite could stay an unashamed Jew-baiter once the 1946 newsreel footage of the concentration camps, with their corpses piled up like firewood, had been seen. Trevor Grundy's touchingly honest memoir goes some way towards answering that question.

Maurice Gran, *Financial Times*

In Trevor Grundy's household Oswald Mosley was a god and antisemitism a religion. Fifty years on, he tells how he escaped his hateful upbringing and how he discovered his mother's terrible secret.

Murray Armstrong, *The Guardian*

Trevor Grundy's childhood autobiography is a chilling confession which is bound to cause ripples. It reminds us how the corrosive influence of Fascism dripped through British society from the House of Windsor to the proletariat.

Julia Pascal, *The Independent*

Young Grundy was fed on a diet of antisemitism, race hatred and the belief that all would be well when Mosley became Britain's leader. Grundy describes his early years and escape from the shackles of Mosley's Union Movement (the racist party he founded in 1948) with insight and humour. The surprise is that he can write about this with sanity and honesty.

Stephen Boyd, *The Sunday Times*

With both parents now dead, Trevor Grundy has at last been able to let in the light. He has written a remarkable book, an understated very English example of how evil and corruption in a family and a political movement were finally defeated by decency and truth.

Anne Chisholm, *Times Literary Supplement*

Memoir of a Fascist Childhood is a salutary reminder that ordinary people – star-struck women, spellbound children – were affected by what, for Mosley's languid friends, often seemed like an upper-class game.

Ben Pimlott, *The Guardian*

Trevor Grundy was once a bright young hope of British Fascism. At the age of 17, he spoke at a meeting in Trafalgar Square on behalf of the Fascist movement and its leader Sir Oswald Mosley. How he got into this predicament, and then how he escaped, is an extraordinary story, revealing and pitiful at the same time.

David Pryce-Jones, *The Evening Standard*

The very fact of his being able to write so dispassionately and so well about such strange beginnings is a kind of victory for the human spirit.

Robert Hanks, *The Independent on Sunday*

This book is compelling and moving. You can get books that tell you more facts about Fascism. But nothing else offers the colour and texture of the times and the people.

Francis Beckett, *New Statesman*

Trevor Grundy's survival is remarkable. And his book is salutary, because it is often funny and tells effectively of Fascism as farce. Accounts solely of gruesomeness have been told often enough and can encourage what they aim to defeat.

Nicholas Mosley, *Daily Telegraph*

It is as if someone brought up in the asylum eventually got over the wall to bring the world tales of lifelong derangements, dangerous obsessions, malevolent stupidities and the crippled soul of permanently damaged inmates. Grundy's account of this is simply written but is clearly propelled by anger at a life so distorted. His journalistic skills are employed to great effect to produce a crisp, no-frills memoir of shocking intensity.

David Nathan, *Jewish Chronicle*

LOVE, HATE AND THE LEADER

Love, Hate and the Leader is a memoir of growing up in a Fascist family in post-war Britain.

For Trevor Grundy and his family, Fascist leader Oswald Mosley was a God and antisemitism was a creed. His father was a Fascist brawler, his mother obsessed with Mosley and Grundy himself dreamed Mosley was his father and grew up to be the youngest member of the Fascist Union Movement to speak at Trafalgar Square. But, after her death, Grundy learnt that his mother was Jewish. The book features additional material from its original 1998 edition with more detail on Fascist figures in Grundy's childhood as well as his life after leaving the Fascist movement.

This book will appeal to those interested in British Fascism, far-right history and family memoirs.

Trevor Grundy is an English journalist who lived and worked in Central, Eastern and Southern Africa from 1966 to 1996.

Routledge Studies in Fascism and the Far Right

Series editors

Nigel Copsey, Teesside University, UK and Graham Macklin, Center for Research on Extremism (C-REX), University of Oslo, Norway.

This book series focuses upon national, transnational and global manifestations of Fascist, far right and right-wing politics primarily within a historical context but also drawing on insights and approaches from other disciplinary perspectives. Its scope also includes anti-fascism, radical-right populism, extreme-right violence and terrorism, cultural manifestations of the far right, and points of convergence and exchange with the mainstream and traditional right.

Titles include:

The Rise of the Radical Right in the Global South
Edited by Rosana Pinheiro-Machado and Tatiana Vargas-Maia

Global Identitarianism
Edited by José Pedro Zúquete and Riccardo Marchi

The Politics of Memory in the Italian Populist Radical Right
From Mare Nostrum to Mare Vostrum
Marianna Griffini

Love, Hate and the Leader
A Fascist Childhood
Trevor Grundy

Memory in Hungarian Fascism
A Cultural History
Zoltán Kékesi

For more information about this series, please visit: www.routledge.com/Routledge-Studies-in-Fascism-and-the-Far-Right/book-series/FFR

LOVE, HATE AND THE LEADER

A Fascist Childhood

Trevor Grundy

LONDON AND NEW YORK

Designed cover image: The author on a bicycle, Oswald Mosley speaking, and the author's mother sat at a table © Trevor Grundy.

First published as *Memoir of a Fascist Childhood: A Boy in Mosley's Britain* (London: William Heinemann 1998)

Revised edition published 2024
by Routledge
4 Park Square, Milton Park, Abingdon, Oxon OX14 4RN

and by Routledge
605 Third Avenue, New York, NY 10158

Routledge is an imprint of the Taylor & Francis Group, an informa business

British Library Cataloguing-in-Publication Data
A catalogue record for this book is available from the British Library

Library of Congress Cataloging-in-Publication Data
Names: Grundy, Trevor, author.
Title: Love, hate and the leader: a fascist childhood/Trevor Grundy.
Other titles: Memoir of a fascist childhood
Description: Revised edition. | Abingdon, Oxon; New York, NY: Routledge, 2023. | Series: Routledge studies in Fascism and the far Right | "First published as Memoir of a Fascist Childhood: A Boy in Mosley's Britain (London: William Heinemann 1998)."
Identifiers: LCCN 2022061802 (print) | LCCN 2022061803 (ebook) | ISBN 9781032451732 (hardback) | ISBN 9781032451374 (paperback) | ISBN 9781003375722 (ebook)
Subjects: LCSH: Grundy, Trevor – Childhood and youth. | London (England) – Social life and customs – 20th century. | British Union of Fascists – Biography. | Fascists – England – London – Biography. | Grundy, Trevor – Family.
Classification: LCC DA676.8.G78 A3 2023 (print) | LCC DA676.8.G78 (ebook) | DDC 942.1/084092 [B] – dc23/eng/20221223
LC record available at https://lccn.loc.gov/2022061802
LC ebook record available at https://lccn.loc.gov/2022061803

ISBN: 978-1-032-45173-2 (hbk)
ISBN: 978-1-032-45137-4 (pbk)
ISBN: 978-1-003-37572-2 (ebk)

DOI: 10.4324/9781003375722

Typeset in Bembo
by Apex CoVantage, LLC

For Jane

If you don't stay bitter
and angry for too long
and have the courage to go back
you will discover that the autumn smoke
writes different more hopeful messages
in the high skies of the old country.

– Charles Mungoshi

CONTENTS

PROLOGUE

London, April 1991

My father's body lay in the funeral parlour at Rayner's Lane a bit longer than is usual because he died just before the Easter weekend of 1991. The day after his death, I flew to London from Zimbabwe and the following morning arrived on the doorstep of his council flat. My stepmother, Peggy, opened the door, which had a brass name-plate on it. It was the first thing you saw when we lived at 40 Blandford Square, Marylebone, after the war and it read 'S. Grundy. Photographer.'

Peggy stood back when she saw me, like a woman about to be mugged by someone she knows. Then she took a step forward and raised her arms as though she was going to put them round me. Finally, she withdrew and put her hands firmly down by her side like a soldier. She had been a Wren in the war. My father laughed at her and said she'd been doubly stupid, serving the Jews *and* Winston Churchill.

'Am I pleased to see you, Trevor Grundy. I wondered if you'd ever come.' She looked at me carefully. 'I'm sorry but for a moment, in that light, you looked just like your dad.'

My father was in his eighty-fourth year when he died of heart failure. On the Saturday morning, I went to say goodbye to him.

The funeral assistant was indifferently efficient. He removed the lid of the coffin before I went into the room, which was decorated with spring flowers in baskets and pots. There were lots of daffodils, my father's favourite flower. I was with him only two or three minutes. I wasn't able to kiss his face, though I felt for a moment that I wanted to. I said softly, like a prayer before his shiny black coffin, 'I did try and love you, Dad.'

The following Tuesday at the crematorium we were welcomed by the young Australian vicar who was finishing a three-year secondment at a church close to Rayner's Lane. 'Good morning, Peggy, how are you? And this, of course, must be

DOI: 10.4324/9781003375722-1

Jane, Trevor's wife. There's a couple of your dad's old friends inside the church. Friends of yours, too, Trevor.'

James and Peter had telephoned to say that they'd be there. 'For old time's sake, old members of Union Movement and all that,' James said. 'On behalf of Friends of Mosley. Your dad used to come to the annual dinners right up until the end. Lady Mosley still gets across from Paris. Alexander brings her.'

Most people called him Jimmy, but I always called him James from the day I'd met him, when I was eleven in 1951 and he was in his late teens. James had been a bit in love with my sister, Lovene, like most of the young men of his generation in the Mosley Movement.

The chapel could hold a hundred people. There were seven of us, eight with the vicar. No order of service had been printed, and there were no hymns, but the vicar had been told a little about my father when he came to see us at the flat.

'Tell me about your dad,' he said. 'I never had the pleasure of meeting him, so we get someone close to him to recall what he was like, what he most liked doing, and then I read out a bit during the service, which, I hope, gives the impression that I really knew him.'

In the chapel on that cold springtime morning, he read, 'Sidney Grundy was eighty-four when he died, a good man with a loving family. He was much-loved by his wife, Peggy, his son Trevor and his wife, Jane, and Benjamin, who is one of Lovene's sons. Lovene lives in America and unfortunately could not be with us today.'

'Mr Grundy was born on January 12, 1908 and Trevor told me that when his father was young it looked as if he was going to become a vicar, but for some reason he didn't end up with a dog collar round his neck. Perhaps he was lucky. I'm told that Mr Grundy loved music and could play the piano beautifully. His favourite composers were Beethoven, Mozart and Wagner.' He pronounced Wagner with a W. 'Well, each to his own but I can't help thinking of what Mark Twain said about Wagner, that his music was better than it sounded.'

Silence met the joke.

'I'm afraid one of the biggest blows to hit the Grundy family was the sudden death of the first Mrs Grundy in 1970. Trevor and Lovene's mother died very suddenly and tragically but we don't have to go into that today. Mr Grundy was an extremely fortunate man because he married again and enjoyed more than twenty years with his second wife, Peggy, who was his first cousin and a lady who loved her husband very much and looked after him so well and with such love during the years he was ill.'

Peggy had her head down.

'I think Mr Grundy must have earned a lot of respect during his life and Trevor told me that when his father was a London taxi-driver he volunteered to take disabled children to Brighton for the day.'

I thought: 'Without this well-meaning Australian man of God, my father would just slip away.'

'In the name of the Father, and of the Son and of the Holy Ghost.'

We bowed our heads and my mind drifted to another time, another place, another father figure.

Eleven years earlier, Mosley's death in Paris had intruded sharply on my life in Zimbabwe. Sir Oswald was eighty-four when he died at his home outside Paris, in a house called Le Temple de la Gloire, which had been built in 1800 for General Moreau, who was one of Napoleon's marshals.

He died almost the same time as a mentally disturbed American, with a copy of Salinger's *The Catcher in the Rye* under his arm, killed John Lennon. I searched *Time* and *Newsweek* magazines, which carried front-page pictures of Lennon and eventually found a tiny obituary on Mosley, which quoted one of his sons, the novelist Nicholas, who wrote, 'I see clearly that while the right hand dealt with grandiose ideas and glory, the left hand let the rats out of the sewer.'

It took me close on a decade to gather any further information about Sir Oswald's funeral. I'd written to several people who might have been invited, but no one replied. One day in 1990, I received a letter with a Winchester postmark. It was un-signed and contained the briefest description of the formal event. I had no idea why the letter was sent like some secret communique. But the Mosley Movement bred secrecy.

The service had been held at the crematorium on the hilltop above the famous Pere Lachaise Cemetery, which contains Oscar Wilde and Jim Morrison of 'The Doors.' There was no religious leader, but there wasn't a chance of Sir Oswald Mosley just slipping away. It was a freezing day, and there was nothing for the congregation to do but stand around. There were no hymns to sing, no vesicles to respond to, and no prayers to say 'amen' to. Although there were over two hundred people at the service, only three or four of Mosley's Fascists had been invited. One of them was a Welsh schoolteacher named Jeffrey Hamm.

A grand professional choir, hired from a local opera company, sang excerpts from Verdi's 'Requiem,' 'the Sanctus and Agnus Dei' from the plain song Requiem Mass, some bits of Bach, Cesar Franck, Mozart's 'Ave Verum,' Handel's 'Hallelujah' chorus and finished with an organ recital of Handel's air to the song 'See the Conquering Hero Comes' from Judas Maccabeus.

Between the musical items, there were readings by three of Mosley's sons, Nicholas, Max and Michael, of extracts from Goethe, Nietzsche, Valery and Swinburne.

I imagined the speeches, the choir, the music, especially 'See the Conquering Hero Comes,' which, ironically, was dedicated to one of the great folk heroes of the Jews.

Mosley's funeral, like one of his great orations in the 1930s, must have reached a crescendo of sound and colour, reminding some of the onlookers of the tragic squandering of his talent.

A hand touched my shoulder and brought me back to the present moment. Peter whispered, 'If you want one of us to take the vicar outside for a moment you can do the salute over the coffin. It's often done at funerals of old members. It'll only take a second and the vicar won't see.'

I must have made some gesture of understanding because James smiled at me and reached across and patted my shoulder.

The vicar continued. 'Trevor told me that before the service ends, he'd like to say a few words. When I met him last week for the first time, he said he thought the words St Paul spoke to the Corinthians were the most beautiful he'd ever read, so it's appropriate that he should read them at the funeral of his sadly missed father.'

My hands were shaking. When I found the right section, I looked at Peggy. 'I don't have much to say because the vicar has already said most of it. I want to try and remember the good things about my father, just as you do.'

I felt the eyes of James and Peter bore into me. The last time they had heard me speak was at Trafalgar Square, shortly after my seventeenth birthday, thirty-four years before.

'St Paul was talking to his disciples about what really matters.'

For a moment, I paused.

'Though I speak with the tongues of men and of angels, and have not charity, I am become as sounding brass, or as tinkling cymbal. And although I have the gift of prophecy, and understand all mysteries, and all knowledge; and though I have all faith, so that I could remove mountains, and have not charity, I am nothing. And though I bestow all my goods to feed the poor: and though I give my body to be burned, and have not charity, it profiteth me nothing.'

I took a deep breath and looked up to see the vicar smiling brightly to encourage me. I read slowly.

'When I was a child, I spake as a child, I understood as a child. I thought as a child but when I became a man, I put away childish things. For now, we see through a glass darkly, but then face to face: now I know in part, but then I shall know even as I am known. And now abide faith, hope, charity, these three; but the greatest of these is charity.'

As we left the chapel, the vicar shook my hand. 'Well done,' he said. 'You read that beautifully.'

James frowned at me and asked, 'Why did you read a piece which gave the impression that your father was involved in something childish?'

A three-course lunch awaited us after the service.

'Your dad left money for everything,' Peggy said.

James and Peter collared me. 'Never thought we'd see you drinking non-alcoholic beer.' I said to Peter this morning – 'Well, if we're going to see Trev Grundy it's going to turn into a right old piss-up, but don't suppose now is the right time.'

'We're a respectable lot now. Company directors. I'm sure you know that Max is one of the best-known men in the motor industry. Still married to Jean. And Alexander is a publisher in France and neither has anything to do with politics, right-wing, left-wing, any wing at all, though Max did try and get selected as a Conservative MP, can you imagine?'

'Every year, the Friends of Mosley have a dinner near Victoria. Alexander sometimes brings Lady D across. She's frail and stone deaf but still beautiful and dignified and Alexander is such a good-looking bloke, grey hair now, married to some beautiful young girl called Charlotte, He's tall and imposing like his father but he's never had anything to do with the Movement or Friends of Mosley, just sits there politely with his mother making sure that she's okay.'

'But whenever he's been across, he asks about you and said to your father last time, "And how are Trevor and Lavinia, Mr Grundy?" Always calls her Lavinia. And people say: "Whatever happened to Sid Grundy's boy, the one who spoke at Trafalgar Square? See, you're famous, but you've never been back once."'

'But we're not going to let you go this time. On Friday night, we are going to have a bit of a do for your father at my house.'

He gave me his card. It had on it a Bethnal Green address.

'I'm not sure how many people will turn up, probably a couple of hundred. You know what the Movement's grapevine is like. It would be our way of saying goodbye to your father. There's a set of drums up in the attic and we bring them down now and again. Funnily enough, the neighbours don't seem to mind. Secret supporters, perhaps. Well, no one has complained yet.'

'Will your wife come? I mean, she knows about OM and the Movement?'

'She knows,' I said.

In front of the two middle-aged stalwarts, I stood up as straight and tall as I could, like a new recruit on the parade ground and imagined I heard, 'Buttons need shining, hair needs cutting but under the circumstances the new recruit looks promising enough, sir!'

But I was no new recruit.

After the meal, James and Peter got into their car. One of them turned on a tape and I heard marching music and drums. James smiled. I thought he was going to wave at all of us but instead he looked only at me and raised his right arm in a half-salute, the sort Mosley did after the war when he was respectable, no longer a Fascist.

Without thinking, I returned the salute and caught Jane's eye. Later, I told her what I'd done and she said, 'No one knew. I thought you were just waving. Why are you so upset? It's not important. You always turn things into such a drama.'

1

40 BLANDFORD SQUARE, MARYLEBONE, LONDON, 1948

My mother said at supper, as if she was starting a fairy-tale, 'If you want to know the truth, listen to what I tell you.' It was the summer of 1948 and I was eight.

'You were in your pram and I was pushing. Your father was walking along holding Lovene's hand when we turned the corner and there they were. The Special Branch sitting in a car. One got out and asked, "Are you Sidney Grundy of 11 Buckingham Street, Brighton?"'

'They let your father pack a few things and took him away. Before he left, he said, "Is this the right thing, Edna?" And I said to him, "We'll never betray The Leader." And they drove away with your father looking at me through the back window.'

I looked at my mother and wanted to burst with pride. Nothing could ever destroy this woman, this magnificent mother who was like a goddess. What courage when everyone else was going off to fight a Jewish war.

I had seen pictures of the men in tin hats in *Picture Post*; they were always smiling and smoking. Usually, the women were crying or waving or giving the V-sign like Mr Churchill.

My father hadn't been so stupid as to go. Churchill had organised the war to get power. Churchill was Jewish, but that was a secret only a few people knew. My mother, my father, Lovene, me and, of course, The Leader.

My mother put aside her knife and fork and acted out the parts.

'They let your father come home after six months. I never found out why. They stood him in front of a tribunal of old men, church people. I listened from the gallery and sent out vibes so he'd be strong and not weaken.' One man said, 'Doesn't your conscience prick you, Mr Grundy, you safe in prison while everyone else is being bombed and everyone you went to school with fighting the Germans? Do you still object to fighting a man whose evil hordes are invading neutral countries, Mr Grundy? *Neutral* countries!'

DOI: 10.4324/9781003375722-2

I stopped eating and stared, knowing exactly when the earthquake would occur. My mother looked at me and turned her eyes into dark brown balls. My father called it her 'Mosley look.'

'Then your father stared at me from the dock and said as loud as he could in front of all the church fuddy-duddies in Brighton: "As long as my Leader is in prison without trial, I will also stay in prison without trial."'

She mimicked – 'Take him away!' said the magistrate. 'Take him away and lock him up until he sees sense. Next case!' and she banged her fist on the table making the fish cakes jump. 'Next case!'

She banged the table even harder. Bonnie, our wire-haired fox terrier, whom my father had bought at a pet shop opposite the Classic Cinema in Baker Street, wagged her tail and barked.

After we'd eaten, my mother continued: 'Two months after you were born, The Leader was arrested. And later his wife Diana, who'd just given birth to their second son in April was picked up by the police.'

When Mummy told how Max, the baby, was separated from his mother, I gripped the edge of the wooden kitchen table. I felt that Max was my brother because we were the same age. My father went to prison almost exactly the same time as his. But Max was a bit better than me, even though he was one month younger, because his father was The Leader.

My mother said – 'Lady Mosley was feeding him when a Special Branch man came and pulled Max off her breast. They hauled her off to prison. The two boys, Max and Alexander, were left without their mother and father and had to go into a home with a nanny,' and my mother's dark eyes flashed with anger.

She told us these stories often, sometimes with very little or no emotion in her voice but when in full-flood, she acted it all out with great feeling. I would try to hold Lovene's hand under the table but my beautiful dark-haired, brown-eyed sister who was five years older than me, pushed me away. Just before my mother turned round from the sink, Lovene mouthed the usual word which never failed to fix me in my chair.

'Weed.'

My mother told us that one night, not long after the sirens had started and people in Brighton and elsewhere were digging holes four feet deep as bomb shelters and covering them with tin roofs, the Special Branch men came to the Grundy flat.

As she spoke, my mother touched the top of her head and with both hands patted the sides of it, like a woman about to go on stage or deliver an important charity appeal.

'I asked them what they wanted and one of them said, "You've got to leave Brighton."'

'Why?' I asked.

'Because you're a security risk. The Germans might invade and you could go down to the beach at night and shine a torch.'

'I haven't got a torch,' I said.

'Have you ever heard of matches?' he asked and I said, 'Rubbish. Mosley told us all to do nothing to damage England even though we're at war because of the Jews.'

We knew the story by heart but Lovene and I always behaved as if it was the first time.

'So, the three of us left Brighton for London by train.' She leant forward with her full lower lip resting on top of her crossed hands, which were already beginning to show the small lumps and bumps that signal the start of arthritis.

'Our new neighbours in London said to me: "So where's your man?" and I said that your father was on special duties and I had been told not to tell anyone because of the Official Secrets Act. And then I asked, "And where's *your* man?" and one of them said, "He was killed at Dunkirk." I wanted to say, "You fools, if only you'd listened to Mosley."'

'Before he went to prison your father taught Lovene to speak a bit of German. What was it, Lovene? *Wir sind Freunde* . . . we're your friends.' She laughed. 'That was all your father could say in German. That and *Sieg Heil*.'

I was two when we moved, Lovene seven and my mother thirty-five, a strange little fatherless Fascist family heading for the London blitz. My mother said that the police found the flat for us, one room in a house, 66 Loudoun Road, midway between St John's Wood and Swiss Cottage.

Lovene attended a local primary school in the mornings and in the afternoons stayed with me while my mother went out on her own for long walks. Once or twice a week my mother would slip something sweet-tasting into my mouth when she was washing me. She told me that American friends gave her chewing gum and sometimes fruit sweets which tasted of real oranges or pears. Once I was clean, she'd stick a pink, prickly embrocation called thermogene onto my chest, wrap sticking plaster over it and button up my shirt. It made me look overfed, even fat. She told Lovene, 'Trevor's like Uncle Rolly, he's got a weak chest. If I don't take care of him, he'll turn into a sickly child dependant on me for the rest of his life, or die of TB like his uncle.' She always made me wear a jacket and striped tie and even when it was hot, I had to wear a thick overcoat because of my weak chest.

Sometimes I watched her staring out of the window when it was raining, which was most of the time. Even then I thought her an extremely beautiful woman with her auburn hair, perfectly shaped Roman nose, dark eyes, lovely soft skin and full figure. I remember that when we went across to the shops on the opposite side of Loudoun Road, people treated her with respect. The butcher and the greengrocer let her pay 'next week,' though I can't remember her ever having any money in her purse.

When I turned four, I heard women in the shops say that soon the war would be over. 'Then we'll show Mr Hitler who's the boss,' laughed a big fat woman with red cheeks and blonde hair. She put her arm round my mother; I thought, 'How unusual. I've never seen anyone touch my mother.' My mother winced as if she was in pain.

'It'll be nice to have 'em back again, won't it, luv?' said the woman. My mother said nothing but pulled me along back to the flat as if I were a puppy on a lead.

At night, my mother opened the door of a small wooden cupboard next to the lavatory. When we heard the planes, she woke us and we squeezed into the cupboard. She put her arms around us and the three of us would make a unit, a single cuddle. The doodlebug was right overhead and we heard it whine, then silence and my mother counted – 'Nine, eight, seven, six, five, four, three, two one and . . .'

Afterwards, she told us that if you could hear the explosion, you knew you were still alive. Once she explained that a very great and good man called Hitler was trying to rescue Daddy and The Leader. After Hitler won the war, both would be released. Then the Jews would be for it.

Towards the end, the bombing became so bad that a worried neighbour knocked on the door of our flat in her nightie. My mother left us alone in the cupboard.

'You shouldn't be here on your own in there with two kids, missus. Your old man's out there fighting for you and yours but this is taking a risk without reason. Come down to the shelter at the end of the road, we'll fit you in.'

At the shelter, while the bombs piled onto London, my restless and frightened nine-year-old sister turned over in her top bunk and fell onto the concrete floor. She badly split her top lip and when the Germans flew away, she was taken to Great Ormond Street Hospital.

When we went to visit her, the nurse asked my mother, 'Can't you send the children away somewhere, Mrs Grundy?'

My mother said she would write to her mother and father, who lived outside Newcastle but several months later we were still at 66 Loudoun Road.

In September 1944, a letter arrived. My mother read it slowly to herself and then told us to sit on the bed with her. I knew it was terribly important because on the back of the envelope there was a crown. It was from the King. She read it aloud, without a hint of drama in her voice.

Sir,

I am directed by the Secretary of State to inform you that the Restriction Order made against you under regulation 18A of the Defence (General) Regulations, 1939, have now been revoked. I am, Sir, Your obedient Servant

'Only a civil servant could lock you up for four years and sign himself, *Your obedient Servant*,' my mother commented. 'So, your father will be home soon,' she added, gazing out of the window at the black and leafless trees.

She put the letter on the mantelpiece next to the clock and a very small picture she had of The Leader, with his dark hair combed back and his fiercely intelligent eyes staring down a long Roman nose, just like my mother's.

She showed me a picture of my father wearing a black shirt before the war. His head was turned slightly sideways, revealing a very large nose, and his hair swept back and heavily greased in the style of the time. My mother said he had lovely pale blue eyes but that his lips were much too thin, 'Just like his Scottish schoolmarm mother's.' My father's most outstanding feature, said my mother looking down at the small photograph which she kept in an envelope in the drawer, were his hands. 'He had the most beautiful hands and if he had been properly trained could have been a concert pianist. His father, your Grandfather Grundy, was the church organist when we got married.'

Lovene and I had never seen our grandparents on either our mother's or father's side. She told us her maiden name was Maurice and that it was spelt M-a-u-r-i-c-e and not M-o-r-r-i-s, the way Jews spelt it.

I asked her, 'What are Jews?'

She said, 'You'll find out soon enough.'

My father returned. He picked me up and looked me full in the face. 'My God, Edna,' he said, 'he's the double of Uncle Jamie.' I didn't know if that was a good thing or a bad thing and wondered if he also had a weak chest.

He put me down when Lovene came into the room. He cuddled her and kissed her face. He clearly adored her. He kept kissing the stitches on her upper lip. 'My poor, poor darling,' he said.

He proudly announced to my mother that he had given up smoking in prison. 'That's why I've put on a few pounds.' My mother said that he'd soon lose them once he started working and got us somewhere decent to live.

That night I heard the bed creak and listened to them talking. I snuggled up to Lovene and whispered, 'What are they doing?' and she nudged me and said, 'Keep quiet and go to sleep. You always want to know everything.' I remember thinking that even though he was my father he had no right to be in bed with my mother, making a noise like that.

In the morning he looked through the newspapers, searching for a job. Occasionally, while he was reading, he would pull me towards him without looking up and I sat on his knee. 'You don't really know who I am, do you?' he said. 'But I've been away most of your life, haven't I, so we'll have to get to know each other.'

Not long after that the rows started. Angry words were exchanged in the tiny kitchen, but at lunch, or supper, they would pretend that nothing had happened. My mother said that Lovene and I were too sensitive and that all mothers and fathers had rows. 'Trouble is, you're both Pisces. You were both born in March and you're both fish swimming in opposite directions. It's a watery sign and Pisceans usually end up drunks.'

Lovene and I would find the stars column in the *Evening News, Evening Standard* or *The Star* and look for the double fish sign. It always said that we were nice people to know but too easily influenced by those around us. I said to Lovene, 'I'll never drink beer like Daddy because Mummy says I'll turn into a drunk like the man downstairs.'

On Victory Day every child in Loudoun Road and the adjoining area was invited to a large street party. Tables were set up in the middle of the road, and there were bottles of lemonade; red, white and blue cakes; pictures of Mr Churchill doing the

V-sign and at least six Union Jacks hanging from shops opposite where we lived. A dozen or so yards from the table was a large bonfire and on it a stuffed effigy of a man with a moustache and a lank lock of hair falling over one side of his forehead. I had seen this effigy of a human being slumped next to the potatoes and cabbages in the greengrocer's shop and women coming and going said, 'Morning, Adolf! Not feeling much like bombing us today, are we?'

The day before Victory Day my parents had a gigantic row. Lovene and I stood on the landing listening to the shouting.

'They'll stick a Union Jack on his head and tell him lies about Hitler!' screamed my mother. 'What did you go to prison for if you're letting your only son be paraded in front of a burning Hitler?'

My father opened the flat door and told us to come inside. They both calmed down. They looked like Catherine Wheels that had stopped spinning. As if to officially end the row, my mother made a cup of tea and then sat staring into space. My father went out to buy an evening paper, and Lovene and I played another instalment of a radio programme called *The Way to the Stars*. I was an RAF hero and Lovene was my girlfriend. Then, we took it in turns to scrape the condensed milk tin and my mother said that we would both die of tin poisoning.

My future was bleak. I'd become a drunk like the fat man with the bald head who lived in the basement or suffer a slow, lingering death from tin poisoning.

On the morning of the celebration, my father took me to the wash basin and combed my hair flat against my head, with a parting on the right which some of the kids in Loudoun Road said was the girl's side. He put me into a pair of grey shorts and knotted my tie. At eleven o'clock, he took me downstairs into the road and we joined a party of boys of my own age. A large woman with an enormous bust put her arm around my shoulders and pulled me towards her. 'You from 66 are you, luvvie?' She put a paper Union Jack shaped like an upside-down ship on my head and someone took a photograph. My father walked away but turned several times to check that I was safe. Within a few minutes, I was standing on my own holding a sticky bun and a mug full of lemonade.

'Where's your sister, luvvie? What's her name again? Something foreign?'

'Levy something,' said a man lifting an accordion from the back seat of a small car. 'I think your dad must have made a few lady friends in France during the war to come up with a name like that.' They laughed and I remembered that my mother hadn't said a word about Lovene attending the Victory Day Parade. I wondered if it was for boys only but, no, there were plenty of girls Lovene's age in the street that day.

After our lemonade and cakes, the vicar said that we were gathered together on this wonderful day in 1945 to celebrate the end of the war and to praise God for making sure that good had once again triumphed over evil. He turned to the man with accordion and said, 'I think . . . *now!*'

The bonfire was lit and a vast orange flame leapt into the air and started to lick the face of the man with the moustache, who crackled, leaned forward and exploded. After a while he disappeared, to the cheers of the children and the roars of approval from mums and dads, the greengrocer, the butcher, the postman and a couple of policemen who looked old and tired in their dark blue uniforms and helmets. The vicar beamed at the man with the accordion and later pretended to conduct an orchestra. Everyone was singing but I sat silently on my own.

Hitler has only got one ball
Goering has got one very small
Himmler has something similar
But poor old Go-balls
Has no balls at all.

I laughed and clapped with everyone else and then the Union Jack cake was cut. I kept the icing for Lovene in my pocket and told myself to remember the words of the song because I was good at that. I would sing the song to my mother when I got back home.

That would cheer her up.

In early 1946 my father got a job with Kodak, packing and loading films and photographic paper and other equipment into lorries.

We left the flat in Loudoun Road. My father signed a lease with the London North Eastern Railways (LNER) and became the landlord of a tall, badly bombed Victorian house in Blandford Square, behind Marylebone Station.

Although he did not own the house, once it was repaired – at his expense – he could make money by letting flats. My father banged the table and laughed and said before he signed the lease some old colonel type in a tweed jacket and school tie asked him what he did during the war and my father said it was too secret to say and the colonel said – 'Quite right, Mr Grundy. Quite right. That's the spirit. Less said the better. You never know who's listening. Mum's the word.' My mother was overjoyed when told she would be the landlady. She emphasised the word *lady* in the same way she always emphasised the word *Sir* when she spoke about Mosley.

Our house, number 40, was large. It consisted of a basement, ground floor and three storeys above that. The front of the house looked upon what had once been a perfectly proportioned square, now spoilt by a tall railway building. At the end of the square, there was a brick wall which looked onto the back of Marylebone Station. Immediately opposite in Harewood Avenue was St Edward's Convent, a grey and black stone building with towers and mysterious windows. From the outside, it looked like a castle for ladies and their knights, rather than a home for nuns and their pretty but skinny Irish novices.

Our flat occupied the ground floor of the house and consisted of a fairly large front room which doubled-up as a bedroom for my parents. My father said we shouldn't call it the living room. It was the *lebensraum* and we had to practice saying the word with a German accent. When I was a child, until about the age of eleven,

I slept in a single bed in a corner of that room. A thin wooden partition divided the front room from my sister's room, with its bed, wardrobe, table, record player and books that were mainly about Vincent van Gogh, the Impressionists and great musicians. Later, I was moved downstairs into the cold damp basement. My parents said it wasn't right that I should sleep in their room and so a small room was whitewashed, a bed was installed along with a table and chair, where I could do my homework. In the summer it was cool, like sitting inside a refrigerator. In winter, it was deathly cold and I'd stay upstairs in the front room after school until it was bedtime, when I descended into the ice-box below.

Two flights of stairs up from our flat was the only bathroom in the house. Everyone used it. To get hot water you put pennies in a gas meter. Out of a large copper geyser flowed boiling water, until the money ran out and then it went icy cold. All the water pipes were outside the house and they usually froze over at Christmas time. Plumbers came to the house and seemed to take it over for days on end. With their blowlamps and tools, they made the water unfreeze and run again, so that the lavatory could be flushed and baths run once more. And if that failed, the residents of number 40, with many others from Blandford Square, could be seen walking off to Seymour Place, towels under their arms, heading for the public baths at the council swimming pool.

By the time we moved to Marylebone, the word 'square' was inappropriate because three sides of the square had been amputated to make way for the station. My father spotted a picture of Blandford Square, a crayon drawing, in a book called Great Houses of London. It delighted my mother, the land*lady*. My father told us that between 1860 and 1865 a woman called Mary Ann Evans, better known as the novelist George Eliot, had lived at 16 Blandford Square. Artists and writers had lived in and around the square until the station had been constructed, when they'd deserted the area for the more salubrious air of Hampstead and Highgate.

Behind Blandford Square was Sherborne Place, a maze of tiny houses converted into flats, where, my mother said, the 'poor people' lived. She told us that in its glory days, Blandford Square had been protected from the eyes of the poor and envious by high and locked gates and only those rich enough to own houses in the square were allowed keys. The 'fancy people' lived in Blandford Square and their coachmen, servants and families lived in Sherborne Place. People who lived in 'squares' would one day support The Leader, my mother said, but people who lived in 'places' were nearly always Jews and Communists.

At number 33, Mr and Mrs Tredworth lived with their son, Timothy, who was six months younger than me. He never stopped blinking. He was my first friend in Blandford Square, and he was always being punished for something or other. Sometimes Tim wasn't allowed out of the house for days. He'd lean out of the top-flat window, wave and giggle. Then he'd be pulled back inside by his father, the window went down and the curtain closed.

My parents bought me a second-hand two-wheeler bike. I sat on it and pedalled carefully in case I wobbled, fell off and was called *Weed* by my sister. Tim waved frantically when he saw me. Once he opened the window halfway and shouted: 'I can come out tomorrow.' But as fast as it opened, it closed again.

When Tim was allowed out of the house, we would go and play football with a tennis ball in Harewood Avenue, using the doors of the convent as goalposts. When we kicked the ball over the smoke-blackened stone wall, a pretty young Irish nun would come to the gate, look through the grille and smile and frown at the same time. 'This is the last time I'm giving you the ball back today, now do you hear me you naughty boys!'

Most Saturday mornings Tim and I went by bus to Swiss Cottage Odeon. For sixpence we watched Tom Mix and Roy Rogers, saw newsreels about the last days of the Germans and a vast range of cartoons. Before the show, we sang the Odeon Saturday Morning Club song, which came up on the screen and as an organ rose from the bowels of the earth. A white ball bounced over each word and we yelled out –

We come along on Saturday mornings
Greeting everybody with a smile.
We come along on Saturday mornings
Knowing it's all worthwhile.
As members of the Odeon we all intend to be
Good citizens when we grow up
And champions of the free.
We come along on Saturday mornings
Greeting everybody with a smile
(That's right!)
Greeting everybody with a smile.

At the end of the show, Tim and I stood to attention to stop the other children pushing past us, children who did not want to waste time standing up for the King. My mother said the King was there to protect people from Communists and Jews.

One Saturday morning before lunch Tim and I went to Bell Street. He found a very old Bible on one of the stalls. Tim believed that anything old was expensive. He opened it at King's and I pointed out an illustration. Tim said – 'She looks just like your mother.' The colourful figure showed a dark woman in a shawl. Standing next to her in the kitchen was a small boy who looked ill. Next to the mother and son was a tall shining man in white with a long grey beard. His name was Elijah.

'A very great prophet,' I told Tim, who said he had never heard of him. 'Don't you know about the miracle at Zarephath?' I asked. My mother had told me about it and said that if I knew the Bible I couldn't go wrong in life.

I said to Tim, 'She looks a bit like her but not really. Everyone in the Bible is Jewish and my mother isn't.' Then I added before we went our separate ways, 'And she'd be furious if she knew you'd said that. Furious.'

In 1946, my parents decided to send me to school at St Paul's about a hundred yards behind Swiss Cottage Underground Station where Lovene was in the top class. At my interview, I met Mr Walker, the school headmaster, who was a giant of a man with short iron-grey hair. He wore a tan-coloured Harris Tweed jacket and trousers, which made him look like a mountain bear.

His assistant, Mr Simon, was a sharp-faced man who rarely smiled. He wore a sports jacket and wire-rimmed glasses clung to the end of his nose. During the interview, he told my mother that he was well-qualified to teach at a grammar school but didn't want to. 'I want to teach the children of the working class.'

She flinched.

Mr Simon said that he liked Mr Atlee, the Labour Prime Minister, but his personal heroes were a man called Morrison and another called Bevan, who came from Wales. My mother kept remarkably quiet and listened to him with her Mosley face. She told Mr Walker that she was a land*lady* in Marylebone and that her personal hero was St Paul, which made Mr Walker look at Mr Simon and grin. He asked her why and she said, 'When he found Jesus he never turned back and those are the people who get things done in this world, Mr Simon. Men of action. Not ditherers.'

My father said he was delighted that I had got into a decent school at Swiss Cottage. But he warned me never to go to sleep on the bus because I'd get into big trouble if I ended up at Golders Green and didn't have a passport.

That night before I went to sleep, my father kissed my forehead and said a 'prayer' I knew well.

Him – And the Lord said unto Moses
Me – *All the Jews shall have long noses.*
Him – All except Aaron
Me – *'Cus he shall have a square 'un.*

Later that week to celebrate my entry to St Paul's, the four of us went to an Indian restaurant off Regent's Street, called Veraswamis. My father told us that he'd won money doing the Pools.

My mother said with a broad smile on her face – 'Your father has been at it again – stealing paper from Kodak. But I like things that don't taste like Oxo and Yorkshire Pudding.'

At the entrance to the restaurant was a dark wooden chair shaped like an elephant and an Indian waiter told me that if I could pick it up, I could take it home with me. 'Indians are nice with kids,' said my father on the way home. 'Yes,' said my mother, 'but they'd be even nicer in their own country.'

The next morning and for the next three years, I put on my green school blazer with its red 'SP' on the breast pocket, my school cap and picked up my satchel. I turned at the end of Blandford Square and waved to my mother, who was standing on the front doorstep. She called out my name, stood to attention and flung her right arm up into the air in a full Fascist salute. I returned it. 'PJ' she shouted, which was Mosley – speak for 'Perish Judah.' I shouted it back and then ran down Harewood Avenue, past Marylebone Station, through Dorset Square and past the Abbey National building in Baker Street, where I joined a queue of people waiting for number 13 or 113 buses to St John's Wood, Swiss Cottage, Finchley Road and Golders Green.

I often asked myself what I would do if I fell asleep on the bus and woke up in Golders Green and a stern-faced conductor put his hand out and said, 'Passport, please! Passport!'

Once the floors were repaired at 40 Blandford Square, potential tenants came to see the shell of empty flats. They were delighted to move into a house so central, close to Baker Street, with a prestigious NW1 address and an 'Ambassador' telephone number. In reality, Blandford Square wasn't much more than a bombed-to-pieces slum with a prestige name attached to it.

A man who described himself as Colonel Felstein from the Free Polish Army moved into one flat with his effervescent French wife and grown-up daughter. Above them lived a single woman who my father said was the spitting image of the dancer Margot Fonteyn. In one half of the basement was a Scottish woman who had a different husband for every day of the week. She played the radio very loudly and ate bits of garlic as if they were peanuts.

In the other half of the basement lived a man who my mother said was one day going to be as famous as St Paul. His name was Jeffrey Hamm. My father didn't charge him rent because he was one of Mosley's most loyal followers and, with other leading members of the British Union of Fascists, had been in prison on the Isle of Man right through the war. Mr Hamm was tall and thin and always wore the same jacket and trousers. He was planning to form a non-political organisation for British ex-servicemen, even though he had not fought in the war. He lived with his wife, Lily, in a single room and shared an outside lavatory with the garlic eater, but they never complained about anything.

My father said he had the most unfortunate name because Haman in the Book of Esther was the great enemy of the Jews. Then he'd laugh – 'And I suppose the word "Ham" offends their bloody silly dietary regulations. The silly buggers have a different rule for every minute of the day. The most rule-bound people on earth. That's why they're all lawyers and clever at fiddling things.'

Mr Hamm sometimes spoke to me. He said that the future was with Britain's youth and that one day I might hear the greatest man England had ever produced speak. My father said that Mosley was a great man but he would never get anywhere in British politics because he had crossed swords with the Jews, who would never forgive him. But Mr Hamm said, 'The Leader's not looking for forgiveness. We were right, Mr Grundy. We *were* right and we *are* right.'

It was around this time that my father started bringing home maps from South Africa House in Trafalgar Square. On the best room, wall maps of Central Europe came down and maps of Central and Southern Africa went up. Even though he was making good money for the first time in his life selling and stealing photographic equipment, he thought England was finished. 'There's a big world out there. So, what's keeping us in this dump with Atlee and the Yids running the place?'

One room in the house was full of photographic paper and hundreds of rolls of black and white film, which my father sold for Kodak at the week end to people he knew all around London. I was told not to tell anyone what was in the room.

Then after quite a short time at Kodak, my father came home one night with two Leica cameras and told my mother that his days of working for other people were over.

He had secured a pitch at Hampton Court and would take souvenir pictures of couples reunited after the war as they walked by the River Thames. 'I may as well make something out of the war.' He laughed and my mother, the land*lady*, agreed to clean out a room in the basement for him to use as a darkroom. A prison friend had taught my father how to develop and print pictures and now he had a brass nameplate made for the front door and a rubber stamp, which he used to smack down on the back of his prints. *S. Grundy Photographer, 40 Blandford Square, Marylebone, London, NW1. Telephone Ambassador 1515.*

One afternoon as the school bell rang, I saw my mother standing at the gate.

It was 1948 and Britain was recovering from a bitter winter during which the lake in Regent's Park had frozen over. Despite the cold, my mother was bubbling with excitement. She told me that Bill Dodds, a good-looking man with dark hair and a moustache who looked a lot like the young Oswald Mosley, had been twiddling the knobs on his powerful new radio set and had heard Hitler speaking in German. Hitler had not killed himself in the bunker in 1945 but was alive in South Africa, or was it South America? Bill Dodds was not sure because there had been some static interference caused by Jewish technicians at the BBC, which had banned mention of Hitler or Mosley after the war.

She told me that we were going to live in South Africa. She would show me where it was on the map when we got home. The town was called Johannesburg, which meant 'City of Gold,' and the whole place was under the control of a man called Dr Malan, who had supported Hitler and was a close friend of The Leader. We were going there with the Peronis and Dodds. There was a good chance we would be joined by a famous Mosley speaker called Victor Burgess, perhaps even by Jeffrey Hamm and others who had been in prison on the Isle of Man.

'Your father has been promised a good job. It's warm. The schools are good and there are servants because most of the black people don't have jobs. Your father insists on calling it Jewburg. But most of the whites there are decent people like us and have no time for Jews. But you and Lovene will have to learn Dutch.'

The following morning, I told my girlfriend Maureen Fenn that she would have to find a new boyfriend. Tears filled her eyes when I told her about South Africa.

But I also told her that my mother had promised we would come straight back to England when Mosley came to power no later than 1955. By then we would be fifteen, almost old enough to get married.

But it was The Leader himself who stopped our plan to leave England and go to South Africa.

One freezing night in February 1948, Jeffrey came up the stone basement stairs and knocked on the kitchen door. He had on his usual light sports jacket. My mother made him some soup and he ate it quickly with almost half a loaf of bread and margarine. He nervously pushed back his hair and sat perched on the edge of his chair. He told us that he had some exciting news from Ireland, where Mosley had gone to live after his release from prison. Mosley was returning to Britain to start his new political organisation. It was to be called Union Movement. Jeffrey Hamm had done much of the spadework by helping to set up bookshops which were distributing some of Mosley's pre-war books, his defence of his position and a new book called *The Alternative*.

Jeffrey said he had heard about our plan to move to South Africa but hoped that would not happen now because Mosley needed every man, woman and child, and with a smile on his Welsh face, which appeared irresistible to women, he looked at me.

I looked at my mother and father and then at Lovene, who was thirteen and mildly interested in a new life in South Africa but not wildly enthusiastic. She said she felt sorry for the blacks in that country.

My mother leaned back in her chair and rested her head. My father stood up and for some reason I thought he was going to hit Jeffrey, but he didn't. Instead, he saluted him and went to a long, low, oak sideboard, which he had bought at an auction for a few pounds the week before. The cupboard had several drawers, some of them locked. My father returned with a bottle of whisky and poured a substantial amount of the golden liquid into three glasses. The adults stood up and raised their glasses, and I stood up pretending I had a glass in my right hand.

My father said 'The Leader!' and we responded, 'The Leader!' I put my hand to my mouth and knocked back my imaginary drink.

'The Leader,' I said.

It was a moment of great meaning and passion. I remember thinking that it must have been like this when the disciples were together in the locked room, when crowns of fire settled on their heads and they went out and spoke in tongues to people who were amazed. But Jesus was dead and Mosley was still alive. There he was on the mantelpiece, looking at me, rather thin-lipped, I thought, but with piercing eyes and a large right fist which looked as if he had just thumped the table and made the fish cakes bounce. It was signed 'O. Mosley' and was my mother's most precious possession. I watched her dust it at least three times a day.

Sometimes I would stand next to the mirror and try to imitate the Mosley look, placing my small fists in front of my chest to look aggressive and determined, a man you wouldn't play around with.

'The Leader.'

I looked up at Jeffrey whose glass was being refilled and then at my mother whose eyes were shining and whose voice sounded like music. The three were laughing and clinking glasses. There was a knock on the door and Lily Hamm came into the warm room looking pale and nervous, but after a while she too was laughing and drinking whisky.

They came up the following evening with the dummy of a new newspaper which would be published and sold in London, a paper called *Union*, which would be edited by one of Mosley's important followers, a man called Raven Thomson who had written a book about Superman. The newspaper and the movement would be called 'Union' because Mosley's new policy was the unification of Europe, which would end centuries of division between the English and the French, the French and the Germans. Once united, the Europeans would pool their resources so there would be one vast European Empire, which would be bigger than the British and Roman Empires put together.

'The Leader!'

To the right of the mantelpiece from which Sir Oswald glared out at the world, there were three seagulls: my mother told me that when the great man Rudolf Hess flew to Scotland from Germany to try to stop the war, three seagulls flew alongside his plane. Next to the birds on a table was a picture of the Mosley family at the home in Ireland: Sir Oswald, his wife Diana, Max and a shoeless Alexander. Mosley was wearing a corduroy jacket and he looked fit, even a little fat. Max was very small but happy looking. He had obviously recovered well after being pulled from his mother's breast by the man from Special Branch. I wondered if he also had a weak chest. I was certain that if we met, Max Mosley would be my best friend. My almost brother.

Before I went to bed that night, I asked my mother, 'Why is Mr Hamm like St Paul?'

She kissed the side of my face, and I breathed in the smell of lipstick and her favourite face powder, which was called Cream Puff Tempting Touch, which she bought at a chemist's shop in an arcade opposite the Lost Property Office in Baker Street.

'Because when Jesus died, the disciples gave up and Peter denied him three times. It took Paul to get them all going again and that's what Mr Hamm is doing. Getting them going again.'

She kissed the top of my head.

'But if Mr Hamm is St Paul, who is Jesus?'

She said, 'Mosley.'

Then she told me something which I must never forget.

'You're not to tell people what we talk about in this house. It's all secret. People outside the Movement would never understand and then there's trouble. Just think that you and Lovene live in two worlds. This one in Blandford Square and the other one which is everywhere else.'

I discovered that living in two separate worlds when you are eight years old is not easy.

The day after my mother's bedtime instructions, the lesson at school was about great battles and great men. We had been told to ask our parents for their opinions. Mr Walker and Mr Simon sat in on the class. Most of the children said that the greatest man of all time was Winston Churchill. Mr Walker smiled; Mr Simon looked grim, but he applauded when a boy called Hardy stood up and said that the greatest man in the world was Stalin because without him, Adolf Hitler would have won the war.

Most of the children said that the greatest battle of all time was the Battle of Britain.

The boy called Hardy stood up again. 'My father was killed flying a Spitfire.'

At the end of the discussion, Mr Walker stood up in his tweed suit and said that he thought the greatest battle of all time was Agincourt and that one day we would read about it in William Shakespeare's play *Henry V*. It was great, he told us, because it showed English people could easily beat foreigners if they stood together and showed fight.

Mr Simon rose and said, as if he was addressing a rally of factory workers, that the greatest battle of all time was the Battle of Stalingrad, where Hitler's soldiers had been defeated by Russian peasants.

At the end of the lesson, I raised my hand and said that I thought the greatest battle in history was fought at Cable Street in October 1936 when Oswald Mosley marched through the Jewish areas of the East End and where a man called Tommy Moran knocked out twelve Communists before he was beaten to the floor by Jews.

The three teachers, Mr Walker, Mr Simon and another called Miss Hill, were stunned into silence. None of the children knew what I was talking about, but I remember going beetroot red because I had betrayed my mother's instructions never, whatever the circumstances, to reveal what was spoken about at 40 Blandford Square.

Miss Hill blew a referee's silver whistle and the school was dismissed. Before I left the classroom, Mr Simon said, 'Trevor Grundy, come here. Who told you . . .' then he stopped. I stood looking at him in silence, feeling the red in my face. Then he waved his hand and I was dismissed.

We went to the playground and put on our coloured team bands for a game of football which included the girls. In our team, the blues, was a pretty dark girl who stayed outside with the wet overcoats during morning prayers. Her name was Vilna, and she looked a little like Lovene. She knew Maureen was my girlfriend. Maureen hated Vilna and said she was trying to make me her boyfriend.

A couple of days later Vilna came up to me and said, 'My father told me that the greatest man the world has ever seen was Moses and that the greatest battle ever fought was when the Jews fought the Romans at Masada.'

I thought, 'This is how my mother talks.'

'The Romans surrounded the Jews but they refused to give in so they killed the women and children and then the men killed themselves. My father told me that even though the Jews were beaten they weren't really because they kept their honour and dignity.'

When I told my mother what Vilna had said, she didn't look up from the frying pan. She was cooking sausages for supper. She said that with a name like Vilna the girl must be Jewish and that Jewish parents made their children say things like that. 'Always boasting,' she said. Then she did look up and said quite fiercely, which was strange because she hardly ever told me off, 'I told you never to repeat a thing you heard in this house about anything to do with the Jews.'

It had been snowing, so I put on my galoshes over my normal school shoes but my feet were still freezing.

'I'm cold, Beamie.' It was my private name for Lovene.

'You're so weedy,' she said, buttoning up her school mackintosh which was about three sizes too small for her. 'When Mummy had you, she told me I was getting a big brother. I don't know why she told me that. Look what I got,' and she towered over me.

My mother was dressed in a fur coat which my father had bought her when the tenants had paid the final quarter of their annual rent a few days before Christmas. He was in a long, dark wool coat. Both wore flash and circle badges on their coat lapels. My father wore a simple silver badge symbolising the 'flash of action in the circle of unity.' Mr Hamm said Jews said it was just a flash in the pan and one day they'd pay for saying that. My mother wore a far more flamboyant design which incorporated the Roman *fasces*, the symbol of unity and power in the ancient world, on a Union Jack with the letters BUF on it, British Union of Fascists.

The four of us walked to Baker Street Underground Station, where an elderly man who owned the shop where my mother bought her expensive face powder lifted his hat and said, 'Good evening, Mrs Grundy.'

A few paces down the road, my father stopped and turned. 'How do you know him, Edna? *A Jewboy*.'

First, we went to Oxford Street, where we climbed up the escalators, which were not working because of the weather, and caught a bus to Trafalgar Square. For a few minutes, we stood waiting in the cold outside the National Gallery until a small van stopped and the driver said, 'In you get. Evening, Mrs Grundy. These two your nippers, are they then, Sid?'

We drove past Saint Martin-in-the-Fields and the enormous column with Nelson on the top looking towards Parliament. I thought – 'Sir Oswald will one day be in charge of that horrible building, though he might decide to do what Daddy praised Hitler for doing – burn it down and start again somewhere else.'

We were driven to a derelict part of the East End, where I overheard the driver talking to my father. 'This was some of the worst damage, Sid. The whole area around dockland was a write-off, but at least it's forcing this bloody government to do something about housing.' He was providing a guided tour and I heard him say,

'That's where the Old Man spoke in '36' and, then – 'Ridley Road, Sid, Ridley Road on the left.'

He turned to us in the back seat and said, 'Great days, you two. Great days. Not long to wait. Great days and it's your turn next.'

When he dropped us off, he told my father to catch another bus. Cars went past and I felt a wave of icy water hit my legs. Lovene glared at me so I said nothing.

My mother bent down to me and said, 'Soon you'll see The Leader.'

Then a black van stopped in the road about ten yards from us. 'Sid!' someone shouted. We got in, but this time there were a dozen or so people in the back, and some were drinking from Watney's brown ale bottles and smoking cigarettes. We all got out when we reached a grey stone building and walked across the playground where some fresh snow had fallen on top of the black slush. My father stopped several times to greet people he knew as we moved into the main school hall.

Suddenly there were hundreds of people, most of them laughing, slapping one another on the back and talking very loudly about 'Commies,' 'Yids,' 'the good old days' and the great days to come now that the Old Man, OM, The Leader, was back.

I noticed that while my father threw himself into the thick of things, my mother stood to one side with Lovene and me, politely saying 'good evening' to East Enders, who wanted to take a closer look at her badge.

One old man knelt down and breathed straight into my face. 'Gonna do a bit of Jew bashin' when you're older then are you son?'

There were Union Jacks and several flags with flash and circles on them set against a blood-red background. My father said, 'It's unbelievable, Edna. At least a thousand people. Where have they all come from?'

Beside the stage were men with cameras and flashbulbs and every now and again, as one of them took a picture, silence descended, then cries of jubilation, shouting and a lot of laughter would swell up again.

Someone cried out:

Two, four, six, eight
Who do we appreciate?

And then the thunderous answer:

M-o-s-l-e-y
MOSLEY!

And then from another part of the room:

One, two, three
Four, five, six
Who will stop those Jew boys' tricks?
M-o-s-l-e-y
Mosley!

And then time and again:

The Yids, the Yids!
We gotta get rid of the Yids!

Someone put on a scratched 78 RPM record. It was a song about Mosley and how he was the leader of thousands. Very few people seemed to know the words but I'd heard the record played so often at 40 Blandford Square.

Mosley! Leader of thousands!
Hope of our manhood we proudly hail thee!
Raise we this song of allegiance
For we are sworn and we shall not fail thee.
Lead us!
We fearlessly follow
To conquest and freedom
Or else to death!

The reporters, still in their hats and coats, took notes. One said, 'Thank God the numbers are down a bit. Before the war it was "Mosley! Leader of *millions*."'

Suddenly the room was filled with the sound of a hymn which instantly froze the audience.

Cameras clicked and the room turned white under the flashbulbs.

After a few bars of music, I tugged my mother's sleeve, 'The Horst Wessel Song. Daddy's favourite.'

She had her eyes closed. Next to her a woman was crying, and several of the men around us raised their right arms. I had never seen my father look so stern. He made his left hand into a fist and placed it over his chest, his English lips moving to this German song –

Comrades, the voices of the dead battalions.
Of those who fell
That Britain might be great.
Join in our song for they
Still march in spirit with us
And urge us on
To join the Fascist state.

When the word 'Fascist' was sung, the room went white again.

They're of our blood
And spirit of our spirit
Flushed with the fight
We proudly hail the dawn

See over all the streets
The Flash and Circle waving
Triumphant standard
Of a race re-born.

At the end of it, Lovene said to me, 'I've got to be at school in the morning and at this rate Mosley won't be here until midnight.'

'But, Beamie,' I replied, 'Mummy says this is the greatest night in the whole of history.'

Close by, I heard a man with a camera say, 'Yes, I agree but Mosley wasn't a *real* Fascist, not a Fascist like Mussolini or Hitler. I'd say he was a *quasi*-Fascist. I mean, it was the time, wasn't it? Intelligent people were either Communists or Fascists, with not much between.'

A man in a trilby hat with the word 'Press' printed on a piece of cardboard on it had a cigarette dangling from his lips, but it didn't stop him talking quickly and aggressively.

'It's the same old Mosley. Still the same old Mosley, the Jew-baiter. You won't change that one. He's probably worse. They should never have let him out. He'd still be inside if he wasn't a friend of your mate Winston Churchill. I tell you, I went to a lot of this man's meetings before the war and you've never seen anything like it. Anyone who asked a question got thumped, got set on. Mosley not anti-Jewish? You must be bloody joking!'

A brilliant flash of white light came again, but this time it was accompanied by a thunderous roar which must have been heard all over the East End. Mosley entered the room through a side door and walked towards where we were standing, smiling and half-saluting at the same time. As he passed, my mother reached out and touched him. He moved quickly towards the microphone, which was set on a wooden stage more used to morning service and nativity plays. Mosley was smiling, nodding and raising his arm; smiling and holding his head high and then almost bowing to his followers who were chanting, screaming and yelling their souls out of their bodies as he smiled and lifted his head in acknowledgement once more.

'I touched him. Now I've got the strength to carry on,' my mother said. 'The last time I heard The Leader was at Earl's Court in July 1939. It was the biggest rally for peace the world has ever seen and you were conceived that night.'

Mosley spoke to a hushed audience. Sometimes there was a flash but no-one took any notice. The photographers pressed forward to the front of the hall to be closer to Mosley, who looked down and signalled to his supporters to move aside so the journalists could move around more freely. He was a giant of a man, or so he seemed to me, and he pawed the air, a lion in a grey suit. Sometimes he snarled at the microphone. At other times he moved towards it as if he was going to deliver a kiss. Then he would put out his right arm like a boxer, using his left to defend his body.

Whenever he said the words 'International-Jewish-finance,' there was a roar of approval. He repeated the words again, emphasising all the syllables, '*inter-national*

Jew-ish fi-nance!' and he froze at the end of the sentence as the lights flashed and the audience went wild.

Mosley told everyone that night that Britain had been betrayed by the old men of the old parties, and it didn't matter whether Labour or the Conservatives were in power because it was the same difference as being run by Tweedledum or Tweedle-dee. His generation had gone to war against the Germans in 1914 and millions of British lives had been lost. When the survivors returned home, what did they find? The old men of the old parties in soft leather chairs, men who had made a fortune out of a war which had brought Britain to her knees.

Close to the end of the speech, which marked Mosley's return to British politics as the leader of the Union Movement, he dropped his voice and became intimate with those listening to him. Later my mother said that he used his voice like an instrument to make wonderful music which brought Mosley and his worshippers together.

'Everyone of us knew that everything for which we thought we'd fought had proved illusion, had proved betrayal. But, my friends, when we rose from that disaster of that experience what happened then? It mattered not. We have not lost, we've gained, we've won. We've won ourselves and that's what matters.'

With those words, he lifted the roof off the East End school hall.

A group of men started to sing –

Mosley leads on.
In Britain's name.
Our revolution
Sets men's hearts aflame.

Fearless, faithful
Unto death,
Ours to dare and give

In the land that we love
And the people's rights
For Britons yet shall live

I thought – 'We must be like Vilna's Jews who were beaten but who weren't beaten because they kept their dignity and their honour. But why did keeping your honour mean you also had to kill yourself?'

When Mosley left the stage, a group of men followed him and I noticed one of them was Jeffrey Hamm, another was a little violent-looking man called Alf Flockhart and another Bill Dodds. When we got outside into the cold and dark, there were hundreds of people milling around smoking, shaking hands and beating their arms around their bodies to keep warm. Motor-bike riders returned after escorting Mosley halfway to his house in Chelsea and later rode off into the night.

We returned to Blandford Square by another circuitous route. My father said that after a meeting like that you couldn't be too careful because the Jews would be out in force, and they had formed a vicious gang with razors in their pockets. And they threw oranges at you with razor blades inside the fruit. We had to watch out for them all the time.

We drank tea before we went to bed. Lovene was exhausted and said she wished she hadn't gone. She had a headache. She told my mother that she had never seen Mosley before in the flesh and she didn't really want to again. 'He looks like a fox,' she said. My mother said she couldn't believe her ears, her own daughter saying something so appalling about The Leader on the night he returned to save Britain.

'A crafty fox,' Lovene added.

'He only mentioned the Jews a couple of times, Edna,' said my father. 'Do you think he's gone soft? I mean, he virtually condemned Fascism and said we'd gone beyond it. Beyond Fascism . . . beyond democracy. Beyond comprehension is what I say. But he still knows how to work you up, doesn't he? But I'm beginning to wonder if this is the same OM, or whether he went soft in prison.'

I climbed onto my father's knee to kiss him goodnight, something I rarely did but this was a special occasion. I told him that if he thought Mosley had changed and wasn't still anti-Jewish he must be 'bloody joking.'

In the playground the following day I called Vilna Cohen a Jewish bitch. She ran away, and Mr Simon found her crying in the cloakroom.

The next day I was placed in front of the school and caned by Mr Walker, three strokes on the right hand, three on the left. For the next week, I was kept inside at lunchtime and made to write lines. Vilna was swiftly taken away from St Paul's and sent to a school for Jewish children in Golders Green, so I couldn't have said 'sorry' even if I'd wanted to.

A week later I told my parents what had happened and tears stung my cheeks as I spoke.

My father stared at me and there was a long silence. Then he looked at my mother and said, 'We've got a right little Jew-baiter here, haven't we Edna?'

2

LONDON, 1948

Mosley's return to British politics ended our plan to go and live in South Africa and set all our lives in a different direction.

Maureen said she'd found it on the atlas, and it wasn't much to boast about because although South Africa was pink and belonged to Britain it wasn't anything like as big as Australia, Canada or India and most of it was desert.

We asked Mr Simon how long the Empire would last. He examined us with his sharp blue eyes, which looked like two of the marbles we rolled in the gutter after school. He said that all the countries that were pink on the map should be run by brown or black people. The only black man I had heard about was Paul Robeson, the man who sang 'Ole Man River' on the radio. Whenever he came on, my father twisted the plastic knob sharply to the left and the deep voice disappeared.

'BBC,' he'd say. 'Bloody British Communists.'

May 24 was Empire Day and the school was given the day off but not before Mr Walker had addressed us the previous afternoon. He told us that the Empire was one great big happy family of nations and races who shared a common purpose and that was to serve the King, the Queen, Princess Elizabeth and Princess Margaret, the British government and the Church of England.

He said that when we reached the age of eleven, boys should join the Scouts, which had been founded by a very great gentleman and soldier called Lord Baden-Powell, who had fought tyrants who had slaughtered English women and children during the Boer War in South Africa. The girls should join the Girl Guides, so they could be nurses good at making bandages.

After the Boy Scouts, all boys should join one of the junior military corps. He recommended the Air Training Corps, the ATC, because one of the greatest men who had ever lived, Colonel T.E. Lawrence, had given up a high position in the

DOI: 10.4324/9781003375722-3

British Army after the First World War to become a humble private in the Royal Air Force, which he saw as the first line of Britain's defence.

To make it simple, the headmaster explained that the Empire was exactly like our own families, which had a father, mother, children and religion. In Great Britain, the leaders were the English and their children were the Scots, Irish and Welsh. Members of a family could quarrel but before the sun went down, they would shake hands like men of honour and courage. Mr Walker said that if ever the Scots broke away from the English, or the Welsh went their own way, God would be extremely unhappy.

At the end of the Empire Day speech, Mr Simon was very bad tempered. He took off his wire-rimmed spectacles, wiped his forehead with his handkerchief and then coughed into it. Maureen and I watched with amusement as he banged the inter-locking doors before storming out of school before the bell rang.

I wondered if Mr Walker was a secret Mosley supporter because even though he caned me, my father had spoken the same way about the British Empire. I'd heard my father say to my mother that Mosley was mad if he thought the British people would ever get enthusiastic about his new policy of 'Europe a Nation – Africa the Empire. 'The silly buggers are giving away India and next it will be Africa but there's still Australia, New Zealand, Rhodesia, South Africa and Canada. Who's going to be interested in a union with the French or the Spanish? Germany, yes, but not with the Greeks or the Portuguese. They're as bad as the darkies.'

There was lots of talk about the Empire at our house at the weekends. About a dozen Old Members – people who had been with Mosley before the war – came to 40 Blandford Square, bringing with them large bottles of brown ale from the off-licence in Lisson Grove.

I sat close to my mother's feet on a woollen rug which my father had made. It had a large red sailing ship floating on a green sea. All around the ship was blue sky. My father said he'd teach me how to make a carpet one day but he never did. Lovene would usually sit on the piano stool, somehow untouched by the words and the beery drama of it all.

Lovene and her friend Yvonne – who lived at the end of Blandford Square and who my mother said looked a bit of a tart – were in love with a Wembley motor-cycle speedway star called Split Waterman. They spent hours looking at his photograph. When they found out from the Wembley Speedway Supporters' Club where Split lived, they began bicycling on Sundays to his house, which was halfway across London, somewhere near Wimbledon, in the hope of catching a glimpse of the dare-devil track star. Split had a small moustache like Mosley, and Lovene grew angry when I pointed that out. 'He doesn't look at all like Mosley,' she exclaimed. I cannot remember her ever using the words 'The Leader.'

Split had a New Zealand friend called Bruce Abernethy. He was also a speedway star. The two famous men once waved at the two teenage girls, and Yvonne said it was a wave that changed her life.

'Lovene's thinking about Split or Bruce,' I thought, as the conversation and the beer flowed in the front room of 40 Blandford Square.

When Mr Hamm spoke, he used his hands a lot and sometimes flashed his eyes like a lighthouse. Throwing his hand forward to express defiance, he said, 'The price of beating Hitler was to lose the greatest Empire the world has ever known and only those who think it was worth destroying the Germans and letting the Russians take half of Europe will smile in days to come.' Mr Hamm told the group of men, most of them East Enders, that Mosley was going to live in France because he was now a European and had to travel the world to keep up with new ideas and new trends.

Other people kept quiet when he spoke but when it was over, all of them had something to say about the state of Britain, the Empire and the Jews. Then, my mother and sister brought in some sandwiches.

The highlight of the weekend gathering was the arrival of a Fascist called Tommy Moran, the hero of the Battle of Cable Street in 1936. Before the war, he had been a heavyweight boxer in the Royal Navy but he had joined Mosley and was the man who knocked out Communists in Cable Street the day Mosley planned to march his men through a Jewish part of the East End. My father told me that the cowardly Jews and Communists had all run away and Mosley had been triumphant, so triumphant that the police had walked all the way back to his house in Chelsea with him and his Blackshirts. Tommy Moran was the most popular man in Union Movement after Mosley, my father said. But for some reason, Mr Moran could never get to see the man he once worshipped as a god.

During the annual re-living of the massive victory over Communists at Cable Street, I'd climb onto a chair and place a record on the wind-up gramophone. We had two precious records, one from Germany of a band playing the 'Horst Wessel' song on one side and an Italian marching song called 'Giovenezza' on the other. Horst Wessel was the Nazi hero who was beaten to death by Communists.

My favourite was the second record, which had a red and blue flash and circle in the middle of the hole and on it was The Leader speaking. When I put it on, everyone in the room fell silent and stood up. The voice was deep and full of passion. *'Brother Blackshirts, my comrades in the struggle.'* I would spin my head round as fast as I could to keep the flash and circle clear in my sight.

Mosley told us that he had nothing to offer his followers except the joy of being involved in a struggle, which would one day ensure that a great people and a great land would live again. At the end of it, the adults raised their glasses and toasted OM, and some would salute though that was no longer allowed in public because everyone had gone beyond Fascism.

'If the Old Man says we're not to use the salute, then I reckon we'll lose half the membership, perhaps more,' said Victor Burgess, who was a Union Movement hero because he dared attack Jews in front of a largely Jewish audience on Sunday mornings at Whitestone Pond in Hampstead Heath.

We went there most weeks. Mr Burgess had been razored by supporters of an anti-Fascist organisation called the 43 Group. He was olive-skinned, and there was a rumour that he was the son of a gypsy. He looked a lot like Dr Goebbels, whose pictures I had seen in a book that had pride of place on my father's bookshelf. The large red leather-bound volume was entitled 'Adolf Hitler' and was published by a German cigarette company in Hamburg. My father told me that after his signed copy of Mosley's book *The Alternative*, it was his most precious possession.

If I was a good Fascist, he said, I would one day own both those books.

I was certainly a good Fascist eight-year-old because whenever fighting broke out at Whitestone Pond, I pictured myself as a lone drummer boy in the Hitler Youth, ever faithful, ever true against the advance of the Red Hordes and the forces of Jewish reaction and corruption. There was a young German boy just like that in my father's Hitler book. He had blonde hair and wore a dark shirt, shorts and long socks. On the front of his circular drum was a flash, just like the one in the middle of the Mosley record. When the fighting started, I stiffened my body and hit an imaginary drum with imaginary drumsticks.

Rat-a-tat tat, it went in my head, *rat-a-tat-tat*.

A man shouted 'bloody Fascist bastards' and then there'd be a lot of yelling, shoving and pushing and one of ours would shout back 'fucking bastard Yids.' Then the police would appear and men would be carted off to a van or held down wriggling on the floor like landed fish. My mother didn't think I was old enough to be the Horst Wessel of Union Movement and dragged me away to the other side of the road.

'Grab his hand, Lovene, grab his hand! Trevor will get hurt. I've told you once and I won't tell you again. He's got a weak chest. Grab his hand.'

Later, the men would re-assemble and go to a Union Movement-friendly pub round the corner in Highgate. The adults would drink beer, while Lovene and I had lemonade and Smith's Crisps.

It was like a Sunday morning picnic and Union Movement people smiled and joked and sometimes raised their arms, tightened their fists, then unclenched them and waved them in the air, imitating their fights with the Jews and Communists. Then they'd laugh and buy each other more beer and then the whole thing would start again, because this was an amazing game for adults. It was also a secret game which I couldn't talk about when I went to school because even though it hadn't taken place inside 40 Blandford Square it was definitely connected and therefore forbidden to talk about.

At home, after we'd listened to the Mosley record and all the Old Members had left, I would go into Lovene's room, next to where my parents slept.

'Brother sister,' I said in as deep a voice as I could, 'my comrade in the struggle.'

Lovene failed her eleven plus and went to a school in West Hampstead, a secondary modern, so it was almost certain she would leave school without O levels and get a job somewhere in an office.

But she was a talented violinist and won a scholarship to the Guildhall School of Music when she was only twelve. She played beautiful music by the great German composers, Beethoven, Schubert and Schumann. Her painting teacher said she should apply to art school because she could draw extremely well. But when she came home and said she could sit an exam at fifteen to get into the St Martin's Central School of Art, my father said, 'Art school? Full of Communists and Jews. You won't be going there, my girl. The slump is coming and the best job for you is in the civil service, if they'll have you.' He said – 'I have contacts.'

At eight and a half my future seemed certain. My mother said that with my interest in the Bible, I could become a vicar. She said that because I could sing so well, I was bound to be an excellent speaker and would be able to turn the *fuddy-duddies* of the church into Mosley activists.

'You'll be the Mosley of the Anglican Church,' she told me. 'Under different circumstances, your father would have been a vicar. By now, he might even be a bishop. Instead, he married me.' Then she added, in a rare reference to the grandparents we'd never seen, 'His mother never forgave me for that and never will. And you must never forget, Trevor, that you're not a Grundy. The Grundys are mean, narrow-minded, church-going hypocrites and *fuddy-duddies* with one thought in their heads. *Do we look good in public*? Look at your father. He's so good, so holy. He should have been the vicar at Seaton Sluice. Your father isn't meant for this world. He's too good.'

So, I had a weak chest, was an easy-to-lead astray Piscean, a boy who might turn into a drunk at a moment's notice or die of tin-poisoning, who was not even a Grundy but a member of my mother's branch of the family who I knew nothing about. But how should I spell my name when I applied for a passport to go to Golders Green? Should it be Trevor M-a-u-r-i-c-e or Trevor M-o-r-r-i-s?

Towards the end of 1948, as I was approaching nine and Lovene was moving towards fourteen, my mother took us in search of a vicar who would help me get launched into an unsuspecting Church of England.

We'd arranged to meet the church warden at the side of Christ Church in Bell Street. At the front of the dilapidated grey church was a high bell tower and pillars which were partly hidden by a wooden hoarding with Bisto gravy and Players' cigarettes advertisements on it. The warden, Mr Morrison, was a pale, sickly looking man in his mid-fifties, with a small hump on his back. He wore glasses which were as thick as the bottom of a bottle of brown ale. He told my mother that he hadn't been in the war for health reasons. I whispered as we were being given a conducted tour around the cold, damp, airless building, 'If he wasn't in the war, is he one of us?'

Mr Morrison scrutinised my mother. His mouth was slightly open, his lips were wet and he kept looking at her fur coat. You could see that he wanted to touch or stroke it.

'You said you've tried other churches. What made you choose this one? St Peter's is nearer, just around the corner from Blandford Square.'

My mother said she wanted us to attend a High Anglican Church. I looked up at the ceiling, which was black with soot. It was very high, way beyond reach. 'I was brought up a Methodist in the north of England and my husband's family is High Church, Anglican naturally, so we want High Church for the children.'

She was so right. We had tried other churches.

The Sunday before, the three of us sat at the back of St Peter's. My mother insisted on seating us there in case the vicar insulted Hitler in his sermon. He did. He said that we lived in an age where Evil had revealed its true face, and it was the face of the madman Adolf Hitler who had killed six million Jews. The vicar said that no one had known the true scale of Hitler's crimes until now and that is why the Nazis had been put on trial and executed. I knew what was coming and so did Lovene. We closed our prayer and hymn books, adjusted our galoshes and stood up. We all made a point of bowing to the Cross before walking out into the cold and rain.

The man who had handed out the hymn books ran after us. 'Are you alright? Nothing wrong, is there? No one sick, I hope. Can I help?'

My mother turned. 'You can help by telling the vicar that Yes, we are sick, sick and tired of hearing about the Germans. Ask him about Bomber Harris and Dresden.'

The man stopped as if someone had shot him.

On the way home I thought, 'But why has she broken the rule and shown who we are outside of 40 Blandford Square?'

For the rest of the day, my mother was terribly angry and ordered Lovene to turn off Vera Lynn, who was singing about the White Cliffs of Dover.

'There should be a special church for people like us,' she announced to the kitchen walls. When *Family Favourites* came on the radio, she cheered up a bit and said we'd try Christ Church next time.

So that day she said to Mr Morrison, 'I'm sure Christ Church is what we're looking for. Quite sure.'

We continued our guided tour. Mr Morrison switched on a very weak light which partly illuminated a fresco above the high altar of the church. It showed the Risen Lord on a cloud blessing the world. Floating next to Him and smiling were golden angels. Below them was a small group of disciples who, I knew from my mother, had betrayed their leader. They were now waiting for baskets of fire to settle on their heads so they might speak again, but in a way that would set the world alight. They were waiting for something to make them live again and there He was looking down, and there they were looking up.

Mr Morrison told us that the fresco had been painted by a man called Thomas Cave who was born in Marylebone in 1820.

'That was five years after the overthrow of Napoleon. He was a terrible man like Hitler but the English got rid of him and made him live on an island. Did you know that, Trevor? Do they teach you about Napoleon at school?'

I felt my mother stiffen and got ready for the walk-out, but it didn't come.

At the end of our short tour, Mr Morrison said, looking at my heavily made-up mother, 'Well, Mrs Grundy, we're glad to welcome you and your family and hope that after the service on Sunday you'll come and have breakfast with us at Church House down the road. Bring some bread and rolls. We do the tea. Then, I'll introduce you to the rector, Father Christopher Spencer.' He showed us a badge and said he was also *Akela* of the Thirteenth St Marylebone Cub Pack and that I might like to join.

For the first few weeks, none of us went to Church House for breakfast. We kept ourselves in the back of the church just in case, but after a while we spoke to worshippers and a boy my age asked if my dad had been killed in the war. I told him no, but he worked on Sundays.

'So, what did your dad do during the war?' asked 'Ginger' Griffiths.

I repeated what I had been told to say so many times before. 'Special duties. He was on very important special duties.'

After a month, I was invited to join the choir. The organist and choirmaster, Mr Barratt, wore a wig, which he used to hold in place when he got excited. He would sweat and pant and his eyes would come out on stalks when he tried to make a special point about music. He told me, 'You could get a scholarship to St Paul's Choir School but your voice needs training. Do you want me to train your voice?'

One Friday night while I was changing from my choir cassock back into my shorts and blazer, my mother came to collect me and I heard her say to Mr Barratt, 'Be careful with Trevor because he's got a weak chest. You can see how pale and nervous he is when I'm not around.'

I walked home with her, choking back my tears because I was certain Ginger had heard what she said. Before we reached the door, I said, 'Why do you always tell everyone I'm weak? Ginger thinks I'm a girl. He told the others that I'm a Mummy's Boy. *And* my bike hasn't got a crossbar. You're always saying I'm like Uncle Rolly but I'm not. I'm Trevor and I'm all right even though I cough a lot.'

The following week after choir practice, Mr Barratt took me to one side. 'Let's have a look at you. I think you look fine. I don't think I've heard such a clear, almost crystal clear, voice in a long time.'

On Sundays I waited for Mr Barratt's organ cue as the congregation moved from their pews to the altar to take Holy Communion. My high soprano voice resounded and echoed throughout the almost empty nineteenth-century building.

O lamb of God,
That taketh away the sins of the world
Have mercy upon us.

O lamb of God,
That taketh away the sins of the world
Grant us Thy peace.

Lovene and my mother were confirmed into the Church of England in the crypt at St Paul's Cathedral. Every week, Lovene joined my mother at the communion rail. I saw them through my half-open eyes because I was supposed to be praying, and my heart swelled with pride as they reached out to receive the Eucharist, right hand over left to take the scared wafer that was Christ's body. Then they would gently take hold of the bottom of the cup which the rector tipped towards them, the golden cup which contained the blood of Our Lord.

Thomas Cave's fresco was clear in the morning light, even though it needed cleaning and repairing. I stared at the picture, at the face of Christ, and turned to see my mother's wonderful profile looking down and then up with utter confidence into the deep brown eyes of Father Christopher Spencer.

I went as red as a beetroot when I heard that my mother was waiting to see Mr Morrison. I had told her that three boys who had joined the Christ Church wolf cubs with me had been made seconders while I remained an ordinary cub.

At the end of the Wednesday cubs' meeting, Akela shouted out *dyb, dyb, dyb*, which was cub code for *do your best*. We shouted back *dob, dob, dob*, which mean that we would indeed do our best. The other cubs scrambled home for supper. I went upstairs with Father Spencer who I called The Rector.

I sat next to my mother in my green uniform, which had no badges on its sleeves. The three adults spoke about me as if I wasn't there, although two or three times I saw the rector look at me and frown.

Mr Morrison said that I never mixed with other boys, that I avoided games, especially games that involved touching anyone. He said that perhaps the other cubs resented me because I lived in Blandford Square, which they thought was in the posh part of Marylebone because they were mainly from council flats in Lisson Grove, Bell Street and the ones near Church Street Market. He said that I wasn't popular enough to be made a seconder.

My mother said I wouldn't be a cub any more, but I would stay in the choir because I was the best singer and that was probably why I hadn't been made a seconder.

Shortly afterwards, she took me to see Dr Norris at his surgery in Church Street. Opposite the surgery were run-down shops and bright red blocks of new council flats. On Saturday, the whole area was turned into a vast market, with barrow-boys selling everything from pop records to pins.

Mother asked Dr Norris what she could give me because I had started to stammer and was losing weight. 'He's as pale as a sheet and he'll never pass his eleven plus at this rate. He has had a weak chest since he was a baby.'

The doctor told me to undress and he examined my chest. My mother looked at him intently. The doctor put the ice-cold metal head of the stethoscope against my chest and listened, moving it carefully over the top part of my body. Then he banged the area under my knee and my leg flicked up automatically, which made me laugh.

'There's nothing wrong with his chest, Mrs Grundy and there's nothing physically wrong with your son. He's thin, yes but lots of children are thin. How old is he?' Dr Norris looked at my national health card. 'Eight and three quarters.'

'And the stammer? Why is he stammering?' my mother asked.

The doctor sat back in his wooden armchair and explained that it was a nervous condition. A child knew what it wanted to say but felt that if he or she said it there would be some form of punishment by parents.

My mother looked angry. 'No one punished him for anything in our house, although he was caned at school, but only once. I don't think his father has ever smacked him. I certainly haven't.' Then she told Dr Norris about me not becoming a seconder at cubs, again talking as if I wasn't there.

Dr Norris's partner, a Scot called Dr MacDonald who never smiled, rapped on the door and came in. 'The Irish Army's arrived. Six kids with her this time. Measles.'

For me, the doctor prescribed walks in Regent's Park and cod liver oil.

The following day, before I went off to school, my mother rubbed some of her rouge onto my cheeks and said, 'There. Now you look much better.'

When I got to the corner of the square, I turned as usual and saw her give me an extra-enthusiastic Mosley salute. I heard her say something before she smiled and waved. I smiled and waved back. 'PJ, mummy,' I said. 'PJ. Perish Judah.'

When I was out of sight, I rubbed my face as hard as I could with my handkerchief and tied a knot in it to remind me to wash it all off before school started.

The rector was quite a small man and very dark. He had lots of shiny black hair which made him look taller than he was. His skin was a dark olive colour, and he always looked as if he needed a shave. He had deep brown, almost black, eyes and a wonderfully warm, welcoming smile. When he laughed, he looked very young, like a student dressed up as a vicar. He rolled his own cigarettes and was a chain smoker who constantly dropped ash on the carpet and down his cassock, which he brushed off and rubbed into the cloth with his nicotine-stained right hand.

My mother said the rector was just how she had always imagined St John, the disciple Jesus loved. Peter was the tough one but John was Jesus's favourite. She said she liked the fourth gospel best because it told the truth about the Jews. 'When they cried out for the blood of Jesus, they condemned themselves for ever,' she declaimed like an actress.

The rector sat on the only soft chair in her tiny kitchen. We sat around him as if we'd invited a hungry prophet in the Bible into the house to eat with us. The room was so small you had to be careful when you moved. It contained a sink, a gas cooker, a mangle, a long wooden cabinet made of pine, a table and four chairs and a large picture of Oswald Mosley in a white fencing jacket on the wall.

The first time he saw it, the rector asked who it was. A sporting hero much admired by Mr and Mrs Grundy?

'That's Sir Oswald Mosley, the greatest living Englishman.'

He cut short his first visit after meeting Mosley-on-the-wall but came back the following week and then the week after that and for a long time 40 Blandford Square was his second home.

Once, when the rector had sat with us for over an hour in a failed attempt to make me understand the basics of arithmetic, my mother said, 'He's more like your father than your real father.' And added after a long pause, 'Pity he isn't.'

My father knew when the rector had been to the house.

'Damned vicar with his cigarette smoke,' he said after returning from Hampton Court, red in the face and smelling strongly of beer.

Sometimes in the summer, he wouldn't finish work until seven or eight o'clock at night, then he would go and have a few pints at the Mitre Hotel. He said that the famous Welsh boxer Tommy Farr often went in there. Farr was famous for going fifteen rounds with Joe Louis in August 1937, and he was the landlord of a famous pub in Brighton, so he and my father had things to talk about.

'Had a few pints with Tommy,' he would say when he got home. He banged the door shut. Violence came in with him.

Towards the end of 1950, his drinking got worse; rows between him and my mother grew fiercer and sometimes we saw them push one another around. Lovene and I dreaded Sunday at ten o'clock when the front door opened and his heavy, sometimes stumbling footsteps were heard coming along the corridor.

But when my father wasn't there and that was most of the time, the rector would be with my mother in the kitchen and the subject would inevitably end up being about Oswald Mosley. It was like a game of tennis between my mother and the rector, with Lovene and I the on-lookers, our heads moving from right to left, from left to right, to see and hear who was going to win the decisive match-ending point.

'He might be a clever man as you say, Mrs Grundy, but why was he so anti-Jewish? How can you be a Christian and, at the same time, be anti-Jewish? Our Lord was Jewish.'

'And look what happened to him!' she snapped back. 'Who killed him? The Romans hammered in the nails but who told them to? The Jews stirred up the mob against Jesus just like they do with Mosley.'

And then, 'Mosley doesn't hate all Jews. He always says, we don't hate them for what they are, only for what they do. He means the financiers who put money before Britain, the people who dragged us into the war against Germany because they had their money tied up in Polish coal-mines. The Jews are behind all revolutions. Did you know that about ninety per cent of the first Communist government under Lenin was made up of Jews? The Spanish Civil War was organised by Jews who encouraged the working class to rape nuns. We're got pictures. Do you want to see what they did to nuns in Spain, or will that put you off your fish-fingers?'

The rector lit another cigarette and wiped the ash from his cassock with his long brown fingers. 'Mrs Grundy, you are a puzzling woman. You're the only person at Christ Church who has cripples from the hostel round for supper and yet you hate the Jews. All those pictures, they're propaganda. I know where you get those books. From Spain. I could show you pictures far worse if I went along to the *Daily Worker* and asked for them but they'd be Fascist atrocities, not communist atrocities.'

'So, what would you do if the communists went in to Christ Church and started raping youth club girls?'

'I'd do what the founders of the Church did, Mrs Grundy. I'd be a martyr.'

'A martyr? By the time the commies finished with you, you'd be squashed – a to*martyr*.'

And they would laugh, smoke and drink tea.

Then she would look at the clock and if it was close to ten o'clock on a Sunday night the rector would say thank you for supper, brush down his cassock one more time and leave. Lovene and I would listen for our father's footsteps and a few seconds later witness the way he sniffed smoke in the kitchen air. Later, from our respective beds, we'd hear the increasingly frightening end-of-weekend row in which strange words were used which I didn't understand, words expressed with great passion and violence that sent me scurrying into Lovene's bed, where I would curl up in a ball. Then they would stop screaming at one another. Later we'd hear their bedsprings creek and my father's voice – 'There you are. Was that better than that bloody old man Lawes?'

We would squeeze and cuddle one another and later I would creep back into my own bed and wake there in the morning when everything would be normal again.

One evening, when my father had finished the Hampton Court season, the rector; his curate, Father Nick Cooper; who for some reason was always called 'Mr Cooper'; and Jeffrey Hamm and his wife Lily, all came to supper. At my mother's insistence, Mr Hamm was to give the two clerics the official interpretation of Mosley's career, which both men had asked to hear.

'Look at Sir Oswald's track record,' Jeffery Hamm said softly, with his slight Welsh accent.

'Mosley nearly lost his leg fighting for Britain during the First World War and then he served with the Royal Flying Corps in the days when the machines were held together with glue and rubber bands.'

'Like the Labour Party,' said my father.

We all laughed.

'He was the youngest MP since Pitt and when he was in his early thirties, he was one of the ministers in the Labour government made responsible for solving the unemployment problem. There were three million people unemployed and people like Mr and Mrs Grundy saw for themselves just what it had done to community life in Northumberland, where most of the mines came to a halt because of cheap coal was being imported from Poland. Can you imagine? From Poland! It was only after he'd tried everything possible to get the government to adopt the policy of Keynes that Mosley resigned. That was after he'd addressed the House of Commons following the publication of the Mosley Memorandum which even his enemies say is the greatest speech ever made there. Mosley said that unemployment could be cured if the government embarked on great road-building programmes, if it put men to work knocking down slums and building decent homes for the people lauded as "heroes" after the First World War. All the great historians today say that Mosley was the best thinker in the House and that's why his imaginative plans were rejected – they were just too far ahead of the time. But only when his constructive plans were ignored by the old men of the old parties did Mosley resign, form the New Party and finally the British Union of Fascists in October 1932. He went to Italy and Germany and saw what Mussolini and Hitler were doing for their people – building roads, clearing slums and marshes, and making people stand up straight with pride on their faces. Getting what was needed done. Yes, I admit there was violence but it was violence inspired by Communists and Jews who were in an unhappy alliance to stop progress in Britain unless it was the sort of progress approved, authorised and rubber-stamped by their paymasters in the Kremlin.'

I thought my mother would applaud, or salute. I wanted to touch Mr Hamm to get some strength for my homework.

'Leave Mr Hamm alone,' said my mother, but I managed to touch his sleeve.

'This was the man the gutter press called a traitor in the war. But he never had a trial. He was never charged. Mr Grundy was never charged. I wasn't and at least eight hundred of us were never charged. So much for British justice. *Habeus Corpus* is alive and well until it's needed. They'd have let Mosley die in prison if it hadn't been for Winston Churchill, who knew Mosley and knew he wasn't a traitor, but we'll have to wait another thirty years before the cabinet papers are released to see who was telling the truth. Thirty years, that's until 1980 until the government of the day dares release the papers which deal with Norman Birkett's cross-examination of The Leader – Mosley – in 1940. What a disgrace!'

'Well, I'm sure Mosley will be in power long before then and he'll be able to release them himself,' said Mr Cooper with a schoolboy grin on his face. Cooper was a large, open-faced man of nearly twenty-four, with a bright and breezy manner picked up from his days when he played rugby for a minor public school in southern England.

The rector laughed, but no-one else even twitched a face muscle.

'Mr Hamm,' said the rector, who was trying to light another hand-rolled cigarette. 'The foreign interests you talk about, which Mrs Grundy talks about, were being killed in their tens of thousands by the people your leader was praising so generously throughout the thirties, when atrocities in Germany were happening. Surely you haven't forgotten *Kistallnacht* in 1938 when the Nazis went on the rampage and smashed up every shop owned by the Jews. It was around that time that your precious leader tried to march thousands of his uniformed followers through the Jewish part of the East End Leeds and Manchester. Of course, there was violence but Mosley caused it, not the Jews. It was Oswald Mosley and we all know that.'

I waited for a sharp return drop-shot from my mother but she was silent.

He continued: 'The Jews weren't allowed to practice any of the professions under Hitler and after he came to power the greatest scientists, philosophers, religious leaders and musicians in the world fled from the land of their birth and came here or went to America or Israel.' There was a long pause, and the rector said to my father, 'Mr Grundy, how would you feel if you'd married a Jewess and then someone had come along to you and said that your children weren't British?'

There was a terrifying silence, and I felt that we were back in the cupboard at Loudoun Road, that the doodlebug was about to fall and that my mother would soon start counting backwards from ten.

My father looked at the rector. His face was red and I watched his hands. The right one formed a fist.

The rector coughed and fiddled with his Rizla roller. 'Mr Grundy, come now. It was just an example. It was an example of what might have happened, because you must admit, a great many Germans married non-German women and . . .'

My father put aside his cup of tea, stood up and walked along the corridor, opened the front door and closed it silently, with great control considering the look on his face.

The rector looked at Mr Cooper, who looked at his watch, then at my mother. He smiled and after inhaling deeply and then blowing out again said, 'Well, Mrs Grundy. Thank you for such an interesting evening.'

Jeffrey Hamm and his wife left, and later we heard music from the gramophone. It was from Richard Wagner's *Tannhauser*. My father had the full score, and sometimes he conducted it in front of an imaginary audience. I watched him through a crack in the door.

I whispered to my mother, 'If we all go into the front room, I'll ask if we can play the *Horst Wessel* song. Daddy says that when he hears the Germans singing, it makes him feel better.'

During the late summer days of 1948, a letter landed on the mat at 40 Blandford Square which changed our lives.

I took it along the corridor and handed it to my father, who was finishing his breakfast before leaving for Hampton Court. He opened it and I saw his hands start to shake. With a mixture of delight and fear on his face, he handed it to my mother and said, 'It's from Seaton Sluice.' Then like a small boy, 'It's from my mother and father.'

My mother looked at the back of the envelope and handed it to him. She was ashen-faced.

I wanted to quickly rush and tell Lovene what I had just seen and heard, but she had already left for school. Neither of us had ever fully grasped the fact that our parents had parents of their own, although we had heard short, sharp rude references about them. My mother told me about the mean-spirited Grundys. My father called my mother's mother 'that bitch of a bloody woman.'

I asked my father to read the letter. I remembered that Lovene had said to me once during one of our bedtime conversations, 'If we ever met them, what would we say? Hello, Mr and Mrs Grundy or hello Grandma and Grandpa?'

I looked at the bottom of the letter and noticed that the handwriting was almost identical to my father's. It sloped forward and was very neat. The letter was signed *Tom Grundy*. My father read it nervously.

Dear S. Grundy,

Excuse me if I am writing to the wrong person but a friend of mine was recently at Hampton Court and he told me that he had some pictures taken of him and his wife by a street photographer who looked in his late thirties or early forties. When the pictures arrived at his office in Newcastle the stamp on the back said 'S. Grundy, 40 Blandford Square, Marylebone, London, NW1.' He mentioned this to me last week when I was in Newcastle.

Perhaps I am writing to the wrong person but we had a son called Sidney Grundy and we have not seen or heard from him since long before the war. He might have been killed but there is a remote chance that this letter will reach my son.

If this is you, please write to your mother and father. Perhaps I will receive a reply and I pray it is you, Sidney.

From Tom and Elizabeth Grundy, The Hillocks, Marine View, Seaton Sluice, Northumberland.

I had never seen my father cry, but his eyes filled with tears and he left the room hurriedly. A little later, I heard the front door close. My mother was staring at the kitchen wall as if she'd just seen a ghost.

A few weeks after that letter dropped onto the mat, Lovene and I were told that we could be going to Newcastle on the 'Flying Scotsman.'

My father almost bounced around the kitchen and described Whitley Bay to us and the famous White City where the Big Dipper would take us to the top of the world. He gave us seven shillings and sixpence for spending money and promised us more as time went by. We would be away for five weeks and would be back a week late for school but that would be explained to headmasters and form masters in letters, so there was no need to worry.

Before we left for King's Cross, my mother parted my hair and plastered it down with Vaseline and dabbed some rouge onto my face with a powder puff. 'He looks so pale,' she said.

As the train pulled out of the station, Lovene took me to the lavatory, dampened her handkerchief under the tap and rubbed my face until I thought it would bleed. 'You'll be ten soon. Stop being such a weed.'

I said, crying, 'But Beamie, it's not my fault she treats me like a girl.'

I remember the journey from London to Newcastle as one of the most exciting in my life. It was our first trip together away from our parents. More than an hour passed before I realised that I wasn't missing my mother at all.

We stepped onto the platform at Newcastle station to be met by a small, bright-eyed man with ruddy cheeks, the personification of health and good humour, and his rather large Scottish wife. Lovene asked the long-researched question, 'Shall we call you Mr and Mrs Grundy, or Grandma and Grandpa.'

Elizabeth Grundy's voice was sure, but her face registered bewilderment. 'Why Grandma and Grandpa of course, pet.'

We travelled by bus from Newcastle to Whitley Bay, and there glimpsed the White City for the first time with its sparkling dome and the Big Dipper, high as the sky. We changed to another bus, which took us along the coast road to Seaton Sluice. The bus stopped outside a hotel called the 'Astley Arms,' and we walked back a few yards and came to a two-storeyed house called 'The Hillocks.'

Lovene was given a large room at the top of the house, and I had a much smaller one next to her. I opened the window and a wonderful breeze blew the smell of the sea into my face. My grandparents' house overlooked a wide expanse of grass known as The Links, which led down through the dunes to a sandy beach. To the left, I could see Blyth Lighthouse shimmering in the sunlight.

'That's Whitley Bay,' said Lovene, pointing in the opposite direction. 'That's where Mummy's sisters and parents live.'

Our grandparents wanted to know about our lives in London, had we seen the King and why was I so pale? 'Doesn't he get any fresh air or sunshine, Lovene? His father said he takes him to the park and plays football and cricket with him but there's not much sign of that.'

After only a couple of days, I said to my sister, 'I don't want to go back to London. We could live here.'

On Friday night, while Lovene was playing the violin accompanied by her grandfather on the organ, my grandmother appeared in the bathroom with her sleeves rolled up. 'Now,' she said, 'I don't want to see any more of that muck on your hair. I don't know what yer mam does to you in London but she's not doing it here in my house.'

She soaped my hair until I was dizzy.

Afterwards, she showed me some photographs of my father when he was my age. He looked so sad and serious. 'He was going to be a vicar until he met yer mam. He had a lovely singing voice and was in the choir, just like you. Your grandfather plays the organ beautifully. Listen.'

It was Hymn 167 I said, 'O Worship the King all glorious above. That's my favourite.'

'And that's more like it,' said my grandmother who gave me her first kiss on the cheek.

I said, 'I'm going to be a vicar, otherwise the Jews will take over the Church of England. My mother says that she'll live with me in the vicarage but I don't know what will happen to Daddy. Can he live here? He always says that he likes the north much better than the south and he loves Seaton Sluice.'

She stared at me and said, 'You're talking daft and it's bedtime.'

In the mornings we were let loose. We were given sandwiches and told not to return until it was four o'clock. We bought sweets and soft drinks at the nearby corner shop from a lovely, smiling blonde lady called Mrs Vera Hall. 'My word,' she said every morning when we went in. 'Londoners have got a sweet tooth.'

I was terrified of the sea but would duck my head under the water into the waves to try and impress my sister who would shout out 'Weed. When are you going to learn to swim?'

We hired a tent for sixpence and played a game based on the film *Blue Lagoon*. A couple are stranded on an island but they fall in love. I was Donald Houston and Lovene was Jean Simmons but the game soon ended.

'How can you be in a film called *Blue Lagoon* when you can't swim?' she asked.

I became tanned and put on weight. My body began to develop and there were muscles in my arms and legs which I'd never seen before. My hair blew in the wind and I began to lose my stammer I had acquired since the caning at St Paul's.

'Do you like it here then, lads and lasses?' my grandfather asked in a singsong voice.

'We love it here, Grandpa,' I sang back. 'We don't want to go home again.'

'But you're going to have to because you don't belong to us,' he said.

One day when we walked to a small rocky bay to go climbing on a rock called Charlie's Garden, a boy in long trousers appeared and shouted to us, 'Do you want any help?' He was easily identified as a local because of his strong accent, and Lovene had been told to be careful about boys from the village. I shouted back, 'I'm okay' wondering how he could tell I was a weed without having met me. He came over to talk to us. 'I meant, does your sister want help?' His name was Eddie Turney and he hoped to play football for the local side, Blyth Spartans. He was sixteen, had loads of brothers and sisters and his father was a miner.

That night, I heard my grandmother say, 'Well, Lovene, a nice boy he might be and I'm sure he is. But the Turney's are Catholics and that's just not good enough because of your grandfather's position as warden and church organist. And I'm responsible for you while you're here.'

Later, I heard Lovene crying in her room. I went in to comfort her. 'Go away,' she said. 'You're too young to understand about love.'

Towards the end of our first holiday up north, we were put on a bus to go and see our other grandparents, Grandpa and Grandma Morris and Auntie Dora. They lived in Whitley Bay in a tiny council house. We ate cake with them and I played with Dora, my mother's older sister, who was the same height as me. My mother had told me, 'Auntie Dora is a dwarf. So be nice to her.'

My grandmother wore a black dress and had a black veil. My grandfather said very little but showed me how to cut up tobacco and put it into a pipe using a small silver penknife with a large star on it.

The room was in darkness and most of the furniture was a dark colour. On one of the small tables was a large book like a Bible but when I examined it there was no Matthew, Mark, Luke or John or the Acts of the Apostles in it. When Dora saw what I was looking at, she took my arm and said we should go outside and play.

When we returned to The Hillocks, Grandpa Grundy said, 'Well, who do you like the best, Your Grandfather Morris or your Grandfather Grundy?' And we both cried out 'Grandfather Grundy.' He put his arm around Lovene and kissed her cheek and called her his *Bonnie Lass*.

On the bus back to Newcastle, we waved goodbye to Seaton Sluice. When we passed Charlie's Garden Lovene swore me to lifelong secrecy. And if I ever told anyone, I'd get the worst Chinese burn on my arm in the history of Chinese burns. Eddie Turney had kissed her up against the rocks and was going to write to her.

We arrived back at King's Cross to be met by my mother, who said that our father had come home from Hampton Court drunk the previous night and called her a slut. She was thinking of leaving him and taking Lovene. We got onto the bus which took us to Baker Street and struggled with the suitcase up past Dorset Square and Marylebone Station, along Harewood Avenue and into Blandford Square which looked so run-down and dirty.

That night I heard my parents fighting, then a long silence and then a lot of grunting followed by 'Was that better than old man Lawes?'

I said to Lovene that I wanted to go back to Seaton Sluice.

When I was ready for school the next morning, my mother said my hair looked a mess and reached for a tin of Vaseline. Lovene turned on her. 'Leave him alone! For the first time he looked like a real boy and you're going to put more of that disgusting grease on him. Leave him alone!'

That night I overheard my mother tell my father that Lovene must be having a bad period. 'She's never like that normally.'

I passed on the message from my grandparents that I should get more fresh air and the following Sunday, my father said he'd take me a walk after evensong at Christ Church.

When I got back to the house at around seven thirty, he was waiting for me in the front room. He opened a drawer in the sideboard and got out a knuckle-duster and put it into his inside jacket pocket. I'd seen it before. It had 'Peggy' engraved on it and was kept in the drawer next to a gun in a leather case. We walked down Edgware Road, past the Metropolitan Music Hall. Just before the Blue Hall cinema, there was a shop full of armour and swords. My father always stopped there to have a look. At Marble Arch we waited by the corner where some of his friends stood. We crossed the road to Speakers' Corner, and my father told me to wait by the railings. I stood next to a policeman.

There were so many speakers on platforms and after a while it got dark, and I heard my father shout '*Jewboy*!' Some fighting broke out and the policeman walked quickly towards the crowd of scuffling men. Then my father re-appeared, took my hand and we crossed the road and walked back down the Edgware Road. We stopped at Church Street and the group of Mosleyites re-formed. They were laughing and pretending to hit one another. My father went into a pub with them but came out with a lemonade and a bag of crisps. He laughed and said he'd forgotten to put his teeth back in.

An Irish girl with beautiful eyes and bad teeth noticed me. 'Out here on your own, are you, darling? When you're a big boy, I'll take you home with me.'

The following week, my father said at supper, 'Next time Lovene and Trevor go up north, I think we should go with them, Edna. There's an awful lot of damage that needs repairing.'

Damage? I hadn't noticed any and surely Grandma Grundy would have had it fixed. She kept The Hillocks, and especially her cooking oven, spotless. Grandpa Grundy said she was the most house-proud member of the Women's Institute in Northumberland.

3

LONDON, 1951–1956

Mr Simon told the class that only a handful of pupils had passed the eleven plus. In 1951, a three-tier system existed at secondary school level, with the brighter children going to grammar schools, the middle-bright going to secondary central schools and the not-so-bright to secondary modern schools. Mr Simon read out the names and kept mine until last. I was thunderstruck because I was hopeless at arithmetic.

At lunchtime, Maureen went home crying. She was going to a secondary central. Most of the class were destined for secondary moderns. After lunch she said, 'My father says that a secondary central is just as good as a grammar school and better in some ways because the children who want their O levels work harder.'

It was the end of a four-year love affair.

My mother was overjoyed when I told her my exam results and immediately made two telephone calls. The first was to the rector at Christ Church, whose support, she said, was needed to get me into the right kind of Church of England school. The second was to Alf Flockhart, the secretary of Union Movement at 302 Vauxhall Bridge Road.

Later, she said, 'The rector says that he'll do is best to get you into the right church school and Alf said he'll telephone The Leader in Paris with the good news.' She stroked my cheek. 'If Max passes his eleven plus, you'll both be grammar school boys. Wouldn't it be wonderful if you both end up in the same school?'

I was enrolled at a south London grammar school, despite a bad interview.

When asked to spell the name of the school, I wrote Tennyson's. 'You are an unobservant child,' said the headmaster, who was a small, spiky man who looked like the drawing of Punch in that famous magazine. His name was Dr Percy Robinson.

Archbishop Tenison's Grammar School had been founded in 1685 in the crypt of St Martin-in-the-Fields. Now the top floor of the red-brick school building

DOI: 10.4324/9781003375722-4

overlooked the famous Oval, home of Surrey Cricket Club, and we were allowed to play two matches a year against other London schools on that sacred turf.

I was placed in the 'c' stream of form one, which meant that unless I could work my way up to the a or b stream by the time I was thirteen I would not learn Latin, so essential for my future career as a vicar.

As soon as my beautiful royal-blue blazer was brought from the school shop in Buckingham Palace Road, I went walking with my mother to the 'Jewish' end of Regent's Park. My mother loved parading around that end of the park, looking at the ducks and swans but also watching the Jewish women with their French or Scandinavian *au pair* girls. She was on nodding terms with several women and pointed out to them the mitre on my school badge. '*Archbishop* Tenison's was founded in 1685 by the *Archbishop* of Canterbury.' I went red and prayed she wouldn't also tell them that she was a land*lady*.

One woman who we'd seen walking with her poodle in Dorset Square said to my mother while I was being displayed like a turkey at Christmas, 'Why aren't you sending him to one of our schools?'

My mother smiled and we walked on into Queen Mary's Gardens to admire the fountain.

'What did that lady mean, one of *our* schools?' I asked.

My mother looked delighted. 'Oh, I think some of those silly women think that I'm Jewish. Your grandmother's mother was Spanish and that's why Lovene and I have such dark eyes. Jewish women think they're paying you some sort of compliment when they say that.'

She laughed. 'If only they knew.'

And together we said 'PJ.'

Then, as always, I was conscious of receiving my mother's undivided attention. Shared and secret moments such as this reinforced my belief that, as long as she approved, I could do anything. That night, she hung up my blazer and placed it in the wardrobe next to her fur coat. 'Never let me down, Trevor,' she said, without looking at me. 'You're never to let me down because all my hope is on you . . . you and The Leader.'

Lovene was now sixteen. She had left school in Hampstead the year before and gone to work in the typing pool at the Ministry of Local Government and Housing.

She went to night school and started to learn shorthand and German. She played her violin only rarely, mainly because my father was a complete dictator when it came to music.

One evening, with a crowd of Union Movement people in the *lebensraum*, he insisted Lovene play for them. She bit her lip and said that she'd been learning a piece by Mendelsohn.

My father broke the room's eerie silence.

'Mendelsohn! That Jew boy! We won't be playing any Jewboy music in this house.'

A voice said, 'Your father's right, Lovene. We don't want to listen to Jewish music. It stinks. They all do. Yidos.'

Lovene left the room and went to her friend Yvonne's basement flat. My father went looking for her and she came home crying. He shouted, 'You're a disgrace.'

She never touched the violin again.

In October 1951, at the start of Mosley's winter campaign, Lovene was asked to present Lady Mosley with a bouquet of flowers at the Movement's annual dinner, which was held at a dining room at The Albert pub.

There were about two hundred people in the room when she made the presentation and Lady Mosley, playing royalty, smiled and thanked her. The Leader looked on and beamed and just about everyone in Union Movement under the age of thirty fell in love with Lovene, including a good-looking public schoolboy called John Wood, who was about to do his National Service in the Suez Canal Zone of Egypt.

From the moment that I entered Archbishop Tenison's, I excelled at religious studies. Although I only got ten or at the most fifteen for arithmetic, I regularly came top in religion, with ninety sometimes ninety-nine per cent and became the favourite of the religion and music teacher, Mr Burton.

At the end of the first term, my parents were invited to meet the house masters and teachers and my mother, dressed to the nines, told Mr Burton that I wanted to be ordained.

The following day, Mr Burton announced that to the whole of Form 1c, most of whom came from the council flats around the Oval or from Brixton. I was one of the few boys from north of the Thames, which already made me odd, without having the added label of 'the vicar' hung round my neck. I had also started playing the violin, which probably increased my alienation from my rough-tough peer group.

My mother told me that the earliest I could be ordained was twenty-three and the question was, should I go straight from Archbishop Tenison's to university, or to theological college? The subject would be frequently discussed by what my father called the 'god-botherers,' who assembled on a regular basis at 40 Blandford Square when he was working at Hampton Court. They were made up of Father Spencer, Mr Cooper and the organist and choirmaster, Mr Barratt.

'University,' suggested Mr Cooper. 'Trevor needs the chips knocking off his shoulder and university is the place for that.'

'What chips?' asked my mother aggressively. 'Trevor hasn't got any chips on his shoulder or anywhere else. What do you mean?'

The rector changed the subject. 'A theological college is just as good, Mrs Grundy, but Trevor has first to be accepted by a church selection committee. He just can't be ordained the moment he leaves school.'

Clifford Barratt was a wonderful pianist. After supper he sat down at my father's piano, a Chappell, and played, note-perfect, music by Liszt, Chopin, Beethoven and Schubert. He could also perform and improvise any hymn. During a performance, which sometimes took up to an hour, sweat poured down his face. He mopped his forehead with a handkerchief and somehow managed to adjust his wig which slipped to one side, while maintaining a furious pace at the keyboard.

His great love, apart from entertaining on the piano, was playing the trombone with the Regent's Hall Salvation Army and on Sunday afternoons before he went to evensong at Christ Church. By chance, my mother had taken me there to hear the music. Afterwards she approached him. 'I knew it was you, Clifford, when I watched them playing the Dead March. Then I remembered someone said that the service was to mark the death of Colonel Barratt and I guessed he must be your father.'

'Mrs Grundy, it's not generally known as Christ Church that I play the trombone for the Salvation Army. I would be grateful if you kept the matter between us.'

My mother laughed. I knew she liked to know other people's secrets.

One Sunday evening at our house, after a virtuoso performance on the piano, Clifford Barratt was unable to contain himself any longer. He finished the Chopin and, sweating profusely, stood up and pointed at Mosley's picture on the mantelpiece. After he had adjusted his wig and stopped panting, he said, 'Mrs Grundy! How can you, as a Christian, support this man, the most anti-Jewish politician Britain has ever produced?'

My mother stood up and I thought she was about to reveal Mr Barratt's secret trombone playing, but instead she delivered her opening serve.

'Mosley's not anti-Jewish,' she said. 'The Jews are anti-Mosley.'

They stood facing each other. Then Mr Barratt sat down again on the piano stool, and she sat down next to the large, highly polished table in the middle of the room. For a few moments, it became a staring competition and the loser would be the one who blinked first.

The rector intervened. 'Come, Mrs G. Surely you have read your own leader's speeches. You're always telling me to read them in his books.' He produced a notebook, and I looked over his shoulder. It certainly wasn't his writing which was small and untidy. He said it was a telegram that Mosley sent to a man called Julius Streicher in May 1935. Streicher had congratulated Mosley on making a brilliant speech. The leader was naturally pleased and had sent back a telegram which the rector read aloud. 'Please accept my best thanks for your kind telegram which greeted my speech in Leicester. It was received while I was away in London. I value your advice greatly in the midst of our hard struggle. The power of Jewish corruption must be destroyed in all countries before peace and justice can be successfully achieved in Europe. Our struggle to this end is hard but our victory is certain.'

On the same piece of paper was written in the rector's own handwriting. It said – '. . . above the stink of oil rises the stink of the Jew' and printed alongside it, 'Mosley to Mussolini after the latter's invasion of Abyssinia.'

The rector gave me the piece of paper. 'Keep that, Trevor, because one day you will know why I'm talking like this. I know that you don't at the moment because you're too young.'

I felt terribly hurt and insulted. After all, I was eleven years old and at Archbishop Tenison's and I had read all of Mosley's books, well, not *The Alternative*, which was really hard but certainly the other books which were on the bookshelf. And my father had read sections of Mein Kampf to me at bedtime and that book by Hitler was next to the two or three children's books I had read, one of them was Anna Sewell's *Black Beauty*.

Then Mr Cooper asked my mother how, as a Christian and a regular churchgoer, she could support a man who wrote in *Tomorrow We Live* that the Jews are an alien presence in Europe. He opened his notebook and read, 'The Jew comes from the Orient and physically, mentally and spiritually, is more alien to us than any Western nation. There are many waste places on the Earth possessing potential fertility and the collective wisdom on a new Europe should be capable to finding territory where the Jews can escape the curse of no nationality.'

He passed me this piece of paper, too. I folded it and put it in my prayer book which my father had given me the day I was confirmed at St George's Chapel, opposite Lord's Cricket Ground.

It seemed that the three men from Christ Church had worked out a plan of attack and next it was the turn of Mr Barratt who asked, 'How can a man who would like to lead the people of the British Empire, with its different races, religions and beliefs, have written in the same book, Mrs Grundy, that the Jews constitute a state within the nation and,' I quote, 'set the interests of their co-racialists at home and abroad above the interests of the British state?'

'Mrs Grundy,' he continued, 'Benjamin Disraeli was a Jewish prime minister of Great Britain and one of the best we ever had. Some of our best scientists are Jews, some of our greatest musicians. They don't put foreign interests before the interests of the people in this country. What I want to know is, does Mosley really believe what he says about the Jews or does he say it because he thinks it will make him popular with a certain type of person so he can gain power by teaching people to hate minorities?'

My mother rose, gazing round the room with a studied Mosley-look on her face and replied as I knew she would. 'But he was only talking about the Jews who put their interests before the interests of the British people.' The Leader says: 'We do not attack Jews for what they are but for what they do.' She sat down, stood up and then sat down again. She looked at the three men and her eyes sparkled. Then she gave a smile of triumph first to Lovene, then to me. And I thought as I thought so many times before that she was magnificent, a goddess, a totally indestructible person.

'Did he love Hitler?' She was performing like Mosley in front of the microphone. She answered her own question. 'He did. But then you should know, Rector and you, Mr Cooper, that if you really love a man who is despised the world will hate you, perhaps crucify you. Mosley said, "Hitler was my friend" and if a man like Mosley can say Hitler was his friend, that's good enough for me.'

Mr Barratt said he could no longer listen to such nonsense. 'I don't see how you can claim to be a Christian while supporting such a terrible man, a Jew-hater and a man who has had dozens of other women while he was still married to his first wife. And a lot of people say she was half-Jewish. Everyone in your movement spends so much time covering up the past, covering up the truth. And then Sir Oswald, your beloved leader, stole Diana Guiness from her first husband when she was little more than a child, only twenty-two. What happened to her two children?' He reached for his overcoat and the two clerics rose. Before he left, Mr Barratt peered at the Christmas card on the mantelpiece. 'I love your card of Sir Oswald, Diana Mosley and their two children. But where are the children from his other marriage? What sort of example would those two set Christians in England if Sir Oswald and his black-shirted hooligans came to power?'

My mother looked at him as if he was a worm. 'When I listen to people like you, Clifford Barratt, I want to get a gin bottle and swing round the lamppost at Christ Church when you're having a service. What did Jesus say? Jesus said, "Let him without sin cast the first stone." You Clifford Barratt, do you have plenty of stones in your pocket?'

The 40 Blandford Square discussion group ended abruptly as the front door opened and my father's solid footsteps came up the stairs. He entered the room red-faced and asked whether I had done my homework.

'Play chess with your father while I make him something to eat.'

I sat opposite him at the kitchen table and heard the guests leave. There was a strong smell of beer on his breath and his face looked puffy, his eyes full of anger. The night before, he told us that he had a business partner, a fat, bald man called Charlie Watts. My father had bought him a Leica from an American who had smuggled it out of Germany. My mother said Charlie Watts was a drunk and that any money they made would disappear at one of the bars at the Mitre Hotel.

I made my usual opening move with a pawn and felt the tension rising.

'Those Christ Church people have been round again. Do they live here? Haven't they got homes? It's gone nine and I haven't eaten and probably won't now unless it's beans on toast because everything else in the house has been consumed by that bloody rector and the curate. Now the organist as well. Next week it will be the scoutmaster, the cubmaster and half the bloody congregation, including those two cripples your mother feeds and gives money to.'

'Suppers ready, daddy,' said Lovene. 'It's beans on toast.'

For a few minutes, my parents sat facing one another across the table. He complained about the smell of smoke. She complained about the smell of beer.

He asked, 'Do these people live in my house when I'm not here? Why do they leave as soon as I come in?'

She waved her hand in front of her face as if to remove a vision, or a smell. 'Because you make in unbearable. You force them to leave with your manners and you've been in The Mitre again with Charlies Watts.'

'Don't you tell me what to do, you bloody bitch.' There was a loud bang as he hit the wooden table with a clenched fist. He picked up his plate. 'Is this what you give the rector? Is it? Is this what you give him?' He moved closer as if he was going to make her eat the beans on his plate. 'Is this what you give your bloody boyfriend?'

My father saw me staring. He stopped talking and swallowed his tea, and I heard him half run down the stairs and heard the front door close.

Before I went to bed, I touched the glass which covered Sir Oswald's face. 'Please, Sir Oswald, make them stop it. Come to London and do a campaign and make them stop it.'

The following week, the same thing happened but it was much worse.

My father returned at nine o'clock. The Christ Church trio had already departed. Lovene and I left my parents alone, and my sister said something which hurt and puzzled me, 'I think they enjoy this,' she said. 'First the violence. Then what follows.'

It all started quietly. My father told my mother in a soft, gentle voice that he had lost his Hampton Court pitch. He said that the '43 Group told him if he went back again he'd be razored. 'They know me from Speaker's Corner and Ridley Road. Then he raised his voice,' We're going to be penniless again. It will be like Brighton only worse. Ten times worse.'

For a while I could not hear what they were saying but voices were raised and Lovene and I stiffened when we heard a smacking sound. I opened the kitchen door and pleaded, 'Daddy, stop it. Daddy, please stop it.'

My father stared at me. My mother had the breadknife in her hand. He was red-faced and sweating and had his hands out as if he was going to throttle her. My mother's body was frozen as if she was posing for one of his photographs.

One of the flat doors above us slammed, and my mother put the knife back in the drawer. Lovene came in and put her hands around my mother's shoulders. She was silent, like an animal about to be beaten. My father left the room and my mother said, 'Do something useful. Go and play chess with your father.'

As I set up the chess set, I tried in vain to hide the tears that were running down my cheeks. 'Why are you crying,' he said. 'Be a man. Do you hear me? Don't snivel. Be a man. Or at least try to be.'

My father lost his pitch but got a job as a darkroom assistant after writing to a box number advertised in the *Evening News*. He started work one Monday morning and was back home again in the afternoon. I heard him tell my mother that the boss was a Jew who recognised him from a fight in Ridley Road in 1948. He was immediately dismissed. My mother telephoned the company and said she wanted to leave the address of her husband who was owed a day's pay. She told us at supper that the owner was actually Irish and had said that my father knew only the basics about darkroom work and was no use to him or any big professional set-up.

After a few weeks on the dole, my father started work at Paddington Telephone Exchange as a switchboard operator. He worked mainly at night, leaving Blandford Square about five thirty with a lilo air bed under one arm, sandwiches and a heavy book about history or philosophy under the other.

When he turned the corner, there was no one to give him an encouraging Fascist salute and a mission to Perish Judah.

He said to my mother, 'It's not so bad when the supervisor goes for his supper break. Then I can switch off and read. That way, I survive until the morning. But in a way, it's worse than prison. At least in prison you know you're going to get out.'

One evening, I returned home after a violin lesson to find my father in the kitchen cleaning his bicycle, which he'd placed upside-down on the table. Bonnie, our fox terrier, was asleep underneath it. While wiping the rims with a cloth and oiling the chain, he told me that my mother and Lovene had left.

Without looking at me he said, 'I suppose they've gone to live in some dump off King's Cross or Euston. You're staying here with me, so get washed and do your homework. Get on with maths, not that religious stuff you're always doing and we'll go for a walk before supper. Don't start snivelling for your mother. We're on our own now and that's for the best, so be a man.'

I washed at the sink and sat down at the table in the front room. I heard him breathing heavily. I thought he was going to speak to me but he didn't. All he said was 'This house is filthy. Dirt everywhere from top to bottom.'

I could hear him take the bike down and push it backwards and forwards to test the brakes, which made Bonnie wake up.

'Your mother was always more interested in dressing up and parading around Regent's Park than doing the housework. And Lovene is getting just like her. How old is she, your sister?'

'Seventeen,' I called back trying to sound like a man. 'Seventeen going on eighteen.'

'And you need toughening up. You're a real Mammie's Boy. She used to put lipstick and rouge on you, do you remember that?' Then he stopped speaking, put on Bonnie's lead and said with great sadness in his voice –

'But then I was, too.'

It was a silent walk. After supper he put my black bike without a crossbar onto the table. 'I may as well sell this and get you a new one. You've had this for years.' He started cleaning, looking down, rubbing hard muttering *filthy* this and *dirty* that.

I went in to say goodnight hoping he wouldn't kiss me. He didn't but as I stood near him, I felt very afraid and felt goose-pimples everywhere.

Without looking up, he spun the front wheel of my bike and said, 'Your mother was a prostitute. She used to go with men and take money. Her rotten mother and father, those damned people in Whitley Bay, used to get half of it and that evil old bastard of a father would gamble it away on horses. He'd lost everything and they'd have been living on the street if it hadn't been for your mother being pushed to that man Lawes in Whitley Bay. She was sixteen, younger than Lovene is now and he was a city councillor or something like that, old enough to be her grand-father. He only wanted her because of her looks and dropped her like a hot potato when something better came along. Your stupid mother thought he was going to marry her, give her a position and money to say her damned parents and that dwarf. But when his wife died, he sent your mother a postcard and a pound saying he was getting married again. And your mother tried to kill herself and then those damned people let her get on a bus to London to make money. And she had nothing but looks. Nothing but her looks.'

He spun the wheel of the bike again and said, 'This wheel's wonky.'

I knelt down so I didn't have to look at him. I played with Bonnie who rolled over so I could tickle her stomach.

When the spinning stopped, I watched him through the wheel spokes.

'When she came back up north, she was treated like a gypsy and if it hadn't been for me, she'd have died somewhere on her own in a room because that's what happens when they're washed up and lost their looks. But I married *yer mam* and I sometimes think she only turned to Mosley to get revenge on her own people for doing what they did to her. What pretence! What hypocrisy. They dressed her up and put a cross round her neck. And now she's making a fool of herself with that damned rector man. She thinks that if she leaves me, he'll come running after her but he won't and I know he won't. He's involved with that woman who teaches Mr Cooper Hebrew. What's her name, Ruth or Pat Simpson or something like that. And your mother doesn't know it but Mrs Simpson used to be married to some rich hotelier and she's Jewish. She's making such a damned fool of herself.' And then a terrible smile crossed his face. 'A Jewess with a cross around her neck and a good Yiddish first name, Ruth.' And then slowly and terrifyingly, 'That should please your mother.'

He spun the wheel hard and then suddenly stopped it and spat out through the spokes, 'Go to bed. You shouldn't be listening to this.'

I went to bed and pulled the blanket up over my head and prayed that I would not wake up until my mother and Lovene were home again.

But before I went to sleep, I climbed out of bed and wrote on a piece of paper in my religious affairs exercise book the word 'prostitute.' I wasn't sure what it meant but it was something like a lost woman. Jesus had met one who loved Him and she was with Him when He died. And she was the first person to see Him when He rose from the dead. So perhaps my father was expressing love not hatred when he used that word.

4

BLANDFORD SQUARE IN THE EARLY AND MID-1950S

'Is that you, Trevor?'

I put my satchel, violin case and Bible down by the side of my bed and looked at my father through the crack in the door which divided my room from the kitchen. He was without his jacket and was slumped in a chair with Bonnie on his lap. The dog heard my footsteps, jumped down and wagged.

'Fox terriers are more loyal than people,' said my father. 'When did you see Lovene and your mother?' I said, 'I saw them in the morning before I went to school. They're staying at Church House. They sleep in a spare room above the Rector and Mr Cooper.'

'I knew it.'

He told me to get on with my maths and listen to the wireless. He said he was going to have a drink with a friend, but I knew he was lying because he hadn't got a friend. He put on his jacket. I knew where he was going and my stomach knotted.

Later, Ginger Griffiths from the choir told me what happened. Ginger was leaving Church House when my father arrived. He knocked on the door and rang the bell. When there was no reply, he banged on it heavily and, when 'Ginger' opened it, he stumbled inside but did not fall. He walked straight past Ginger and up the stairs to another door which led to the rector's flat. Ginger said he looked drunk. He rang the bell and Mr Cooper appeared.

'Where's my wife?' Ginger heard him shout. Once Ginger knew something, everyone in the choir would know and then the whole of Christ Church. When he told me the story, I went crimson with embarrassment.

Mr Cooper tried to shut the door. Ginger heard him say, 'Mr Grundy, I'll be forced to call the police' and then 'You have no right . . .' Ginger reported no further noise after that. Later, Mr Cooper was seen holding a handkerchief to his nose but he never called the police. I thought, 'Mr Cooper really believes in God

DOI: 10.4324/9781003375722-5

because Jesus didn't call the police when he was attacked by the Jews in the Garden of Gethsemane.'

A week or so later, my father returned home, put his arms round me and kissed me on the forehead. It is the only time I can remember him kissing me. 'This has been bad for you,' he said. 'Your Mam and Lovene are coming home tomorrow. Your Mam has promised. We have both promised that this will never happen again.'

Then he sat down and read the *Evening News*, as if that was that. The paper rustled and I saw Bonnie jump onto his lap. Later, he called me for supper and smiled as if he was really happy.

'Newcastle won but Sunderland . . . beaten again. I give up! Don't know why I support the silly buggers. They need a decent goalkeeper. Why can't they buy Manchester City's Bert Trautmann? There's a real goalkeeper. Ex -paratrooper with the Luftwaffe. That's what Sunderland needs between the posts but I suppose the so-called managers at Roker Park didn't touch him because he's German. As for Arsenal, lucky home win. Dirtiest team in the first division, Arsenal.'

I went next door to try and do my maths homework and cried until I could no longer see the page.

When the notice appeared on the board at school showing who had gone up to 3a and 3b, I was shocked. My name was not on the list, even though I had come third out of thirty-one in 2c. My housemaster, Mr Griffiths, said that although my maths was hopeless, I had worked hard and he was surprised I had not been pushed up a stream but there was nothing he could do about it.

On my mother's advice, I asked to see Dr Robinson, the headmaster, and as I waited nervously outside his office. I overheard his secretary say, 'Trevor Grundy, 2c' and the name 'Father Spencer.'

I stood in front of the headmaster, trembling, which was almost a tradition when you met him in the 1950s.

'You're the boy whose parents were going to divorce,' he said, as three boys from the form above me were leaving his room. 'Let me see.' He scrutinised the file without looking at me. 'Your father had applied earlier this year for you to be transferred to Morpeth Grammar School in Northumberland so that he could go and live with his father . . . your grandmother died last year. Where is that? Some tiny spot near Newcastle called Ellington Village.

He took off his glasses and peered at me as if I was an insect pinned to a board. 'You take no interest in sport. You had to be forced into joining the 766 squadron of the Air Training Corps and the only thing you're good at is religion. The PT instructor says you're unable to get over the wooden horse, stand on your head or carry the medicine ball for more than a few yards without dropping in on your foot. And you want to take up fencing. Why fencing? Because no-one else wants to do it, perhaps?'

'I have been headmaster here for twenty-five years and Tenison's has never yet had a boy pass religion at O level, yet alone A level. And you are hopeless at maths. What do you think you're going to do in life with religion, biology and history, without maths, Latin, French or any other modern language? Well, you're going to stay in the "c" stream. You're lucky to be in a grammar school. Perhaps this time next year there'll be a review.'

That night I asked my mother why Father Spencer had been to see Dr Robinson.

'He thought it might help, him being a vicar,' she said. 'He knows how much you wanted to go up a class. Well, I think your headmaster is stupid. If you're going to be a vicar, what's the best subject? Religion. And what do you want to join the Air Training Corps for? To learn how to drop bombs on the Germans? Far better you drop bombs on Mrs Simpson!'

It was the first time I heard her mention the Hebrew teacher's name.

The relationship between my mother and father appeared to have improved. There were fewer rows, none of them violent or in front of us. My father had decided that he would always work nights at Paddington Exchange and instead of sleeping during the day, learn The Knowledge, which would qualify him for a licence to drive a black Hackney cab.

'They make a fortune, that's why the Jews do it,' I heard him say. 'I know a man who makes twenty pounds a day and only pays tax on a tenner a week.'

The kitchen was turned into a sort of map command post and the limitless energy he might have put into theology when he was young now went into learning every street and public building in London. 'You should be doing this,' he said. 'When you leave that damned school, we could get a couple of cabs and form a company. Grundy and Son.'

The *Marylebone Mercury* carried a short announcement on an inside page. There was a picture of the Rector of Christ Church, the Reverend Christopher John Edward Spencer, and his intended, Mrs Ruth Pat Simpson, a widow who lectured in religion and Hebrew studies at the University of London.

In the kitchen, I sat silently next to my mother, who was transfixed by the announcement. She looked like one of the waxworks in Madame Tussauds. My father came in that morning, I thought quite cheerily. I think my mother remained in that chair, her face white and waxy, for most of the day.

After supper she said she wanted to speak to me alone, so we went to Regent's Park and walked to Queen Mary's Gardens in the Inner Circle.

'The rector has been hypnotised by this woman,' she said. 'It's what Jews do with men. How can a Christian vicar marry a Jewess? What will happen to their children? They'll be half-Jewish, or what's the rector going to do? Drain their blood?'

She showed me the letter she'd received from him that day. It was written on Christ Church headed notepaper.

Dear Mrs Grundy,

Naturally, I hope that you and Mr Grundy, Lovene and Trevor will be at our wedding. Sincerely, Chris Spencer.

She told me to ring Church House to make an appointment to go and see him, to tell him that he had betrayed Jesus by marrying a Jew and that none of us would be at the wedding. She said that she would also have to leave Christ Church and that I would, of course, leave the choir. We would attend for the final time on Sunday and if anyone asked why we were leaving, I should tell them that the rector was about to betray Jesus.

She said we should be getting back because it was my father's night off and we were going to the pictures at the Odeon in Edgware Road to see a film about Rommel starring James Mason.

I dreaded the thought of going to the Odeon with them. I knew my father would be passing comments throughout the film and with a Rector/Jewish woman wedding coming up, he would get my mother's full support.

I imagined the evening before us.

'Jewish propaganda,' he'd say at the top of his voice and when the screen credits came up at the end – 'Look at that Edna. Silverstein, Jacobs, Isaacson.'

People in the front rows would turn and look at him but that only acted as a spur. 'Rubinstein. Look who wrote the music. Isaac Wolfers My god, not an English name in sight. And this is supposed to be a film about Rommel.'

The following day, the Grundy Family received a letter from the London Diocese of the Anglican Church, which informed my mother that we had been chosen to represent Christ Church in a competition to find Marylebone's 'Christian Family of the Year.' The Bishop of London would deliver a sermon and prizes would be handed out at a ceremony in St John's Wood the following month.

My mother said she would have to write back and explain why we had decided to leave Christ Church. My father said he wouldn't have gone, because he was on nights.

Later that week, I faced the rector in his study. He had a handsome face and I loved him like a father.

He poured some tea and lit a cigarette. 'Why won't you come to the wedding, Trevor?'

'Because you're a leader of the Church. Because you're supposed to be setting everyone an example and you're going to marry a Jewess and the Jews killed Jesus.'

He put down his cigarette and stared at me. 'Trevor. Is that what you really think, or is that what your mother or Mr Hamm has told you to say?'

'It's what I really think.'

'You can't know how cruel you are being. It's terrible to hear what you have been made to say to me. You are too young to believe any of this.'

'Jesus was only twelve or thirteen when he argued with the priests about what was wrong.'

His face changed and it registered anger.

'It's high time you learnt, Trevor Grundy, that you are not Jesus Christ.'

He put his arm around me but I moved away. He said, 'You have become like a son to me. Give Pat – Mrs Simpson – give her a chance. She's a wonderful woman, very clever and I'm sure that one day, despite all this cruelty, she will learn to like you, even love you.'

I said, 'If you have children, they will be half Jewish.'

'They will be Christians, Trevor. Not gentiles, not Jews but Christians.'

I blurted it out, 'What are you going to do, Rector. Drain their blood?'

I wanted to cry. I did not want this man to leave my life. But even worse was losing my mother's approval.

And I would have to tell Mr Barratt that I was leaving the choir and that might make his wig to fall off.

That last Sunday at Christ Church, my mother sat on her own in the middle of the church. Lovene had refused to go with her and said she would definitely go to the rector's wedding, even if she had to leave home and live at a civil service hostel.

For the first time my sister and I were becoming strangers. Lovene was moving towards semi-independence and was increasingly critical of my mother's curt dismissals of those who didn't see the world her way. I was more and more an appendage of my mother. More than ever, I could not conceive of arguing with her, of losing her love and support.

As the service reached its climax, the rector and Mr Cooper prepared the bread and the wine as the server's bell rang. I looked up from the front row of the choir and studied the oil painting hanging over the altar. I thought, 'But everyone I love is here, apart from Beamie.'

Then my voice rang through the church.

O lamb of God
That taketh away the sins of the world
Have mercy upon us.

O lamb of God
That taketh away the sins of the world
Grant us Thy peace.

The confirmed in the congregation walked to the altar and knelt at the rail as the rector held the Host above his head.

When my mother returned to her seat, she looked as if she had lost not only her heart but also her soul.

My father must have been particularly grateful that Mr Cooper never called the police that night he was drunk and went to the rectory, or filed a complaint against him, because shortly after my thirteenth birthday I was escorted to the head master's office by a worried-looking housemaster.

'I don't know what you've done, Grundy, but the head is furious and there are two plain-clothes policemen waiting to see you in his room.'

I knew what I'd done. To impress the school rebel, Chas Caldwell from Brixton, I'd taken my father's Luger gun to school inside my violin case, like a Mafioso in Chicago. Caldwell had earlier dismissed me as a fiddle-playing religious twerp.

This took place soon after the Craig-Bentley case. Christopher Craig, the teenage son of a bank official, received a life sentence, later reduced, for shooting a policeman and his unarmed associate. Derek Bentley was hanged. Bentley was below normal intelligence, illiterate and an epileptic. The hanging sparked off a spate of social protest and changed the image of the police force. They were no longer beyond criticism in Britain. Caldwell said he'd love to kill a cop.

The chief witness, a policeman's son, was brought into Dr Robinson's office. He said that he'd seen me show Caldwell the gun in the biology lab, which overlooked the main hall. Frightened as I was, I wanted to laugh. Did they think that Caldwell was going to point the gun through one of the windows and shoot Percy Punch, kill the headmaster?

Dr Robinson was speechless. His main concern was that there would be no mention of the incident in the local newspaper. He greatly cared for the school's reputation as a symbol of the Establishment, and the Church of England in South London and was terrified of adverse publicity.

The detectives looked at me carefully. One said, 'Where did you get this gun from, sonny?'

I told him.

'So, it's your father's gun. Probably picked it up in Germany after the war, did he? Good job it wasn't loaded.'

'Has your father got more weapons at home?' asked the other policeman.

'No sir, I replied. Just the Luger and a knuckle-duster but he never takes them out of the sideboard or the room when he goes to Speaker's Corner, Not the gun, anyhow. He won't get into trouble, will he?'

'He will if it's not licensed,' came the reply.

That night, my father hit me for the first and only time, He was furious. 'You've made me look like a bloody fool and they've taken the gun away from me. You must have been mad, taking it to school.'

'Don't Sidney!' shouted my mother. 'It's not his fault. You shouldn't have a gun in the house.'

Later that week, a representative from Special Branch, who knew my father's political background, came to the house and had a cup of tea with us.

His job was to keep an eye on what he called 'fringe movements.' I heard him say, 'Well, Sid, I'm going to have to put all of this in your file but we've never regarded Sir Oswald or the UM people as dangerous and Sir Oswald has always co-operated. But you've got to be more careful. You should never had let your kid get access to a drawer with a bloody gun in it.'

My father was never charged and the gun was never mentioned again. But the matter did not end there.

Dr Robinson called me downstairs the following day. With him was the senior history teacher, a man called Birchenough, who had a tiny moustache and wore his hair like Adolf Hitler.

Dr Robinson looked at me. 'You have disgraced your teachers, you have disgraced me and you have disgraced Archbishop Tenison's Grammar School. Under normal circumstances, I would expel you but taking into account your recent problems, we have decided to give you a last chance.'

The following Friday, Dr Robinson went to the lectern and read from the Sermon on the Mount. As soon as he had crossed himself quickly, he read out the caning list.

My name was called and in front of the school I received six strokes, delivered by Birchenough.

Between strokes, Caldwell told me, he brushed aside his lock of hair, just as Hitler did when he got excited during a speech. I wondered how the headmaster of a Christian school could watch with a smile on his face as boys were beaten after the great sermon on forgiveness. After all, Jesus told us to forgive, not seven times but seventy times seven and the Bible said that vengeance was the Lord's and that we should turn the other cheek when attacked or wronged.

Percy Robinson obviously didn't understand that Jesus meant to the cheek on your face.

That night I told my mother that I no longer wanted to be a vicar, but I didn't tell her about the caning. If being a Christian means emulating Dr Punch, I'd sooner change my vocation.

Later, I heard her say to Lovene, 'He changed overnight. I think he's fallen for some lass. The next thing we know she'll be pregnant. And what will happen then? It will be the end of everything. Who told him about sex? It certainly wasn't your father.'

In 1955 James Dean scowled in front of the world's youth, while Marilyn Monroe sparked off frantic wanking competitions in the back row of 4c.

Before classes, or between classes, two or more boys would produce from out of their satchels magazines and pictures of Marilyn Monroe or Jane Russell and the first one to ejaculate won the bet which might amount to several shillings, most of it our ninepences for lunch money. The winner was usually a disgusting boy with blonde hair and red eyes who said he wanted to be a monk.

Boys of my age left school at four o'clock. When we got about a hundred yards from Tenison's we took off our caps and re-shaped our hair. Some tried for a James Dean look. Others, me included, went for the Tony Curtis look. All of us combed our hair carefully at the back to resemble a duck's arse, a DA. One Friday morning, Birchenough announced that if he caught anyone with a DA or a Tony Curtis he'd cane that boy every morning for a week. Dr Robinson nodded his agreement, delighted, so it seemed, at the thought of more mass canings on the school stage right in front of terrified eleven-year-olds fresh from primary schools.

Most members of my form had made up their minds to leave Tenison's soon after their fifteenth birthday. They were either going to enter the print as apprentices or join the Royal Air Force. I didn't have a clue what I wanted to do, so it seemed that the best course of action was to stay on, take my O levels and see what happened next. I might get English, history, biology and geography and if they'd let me sit for the exam, religion. Maths was an impossibility. I'd received zero during the mock exams. But as always, I tried to laugh off things I couldn't do. Asked sarcastically by one of the teachers what two and two made, I said twenty-two and was caned.

So, when school broke up during the Summer of '55, I said goodbye to almost everyone I knew. A group of 5c kids without an O level between them waited for two masters they hated to come out the front door. One shouted, 'Hey, Birch-*too*much! You can't do anything to us now!'

They turned and pointed their bottoms and DAs at him.

A smaller group shouted at another unpopular master, a man called Bates.

'Take a look at your car,' Caldwell shouted. He'd carved the word '*MasterBates*' on the side of a door.

That summer, the secretary of Union Movement, Alf Flockhart, came to the house to ask my mother if she would do Mosley a personal favour. The Leader was a friend of most of the surviving Nazi leaders, and some of them wanted their sons and daughters to travel to London to meet people of their own age and study English. Would she put up some of the young Germans? Naturally, Sir Oswald would pay my mother for doing this expensive but essential job for the Movement. She willingly agreed and gave the impression that she would host a division of the Waffen SS if that's what Mosley wanted.

After a beer or two with my father, Alf Flockhart said that it was time I did something for Mosley and Union Movement. He said that he'd been told I had a wonderful singing voice before it broke. 'If you can sing for Jesus then you can speak for Mosley,' he said, giving me the Fascist half-salute.

I asked, 'But speak about what?'

'About the aspirations, the hopes and dreams of young people. You're young, aren't you?'

I was beginning to wonder. My life seemed so sober, unexciting and cold-blooded. But then our first German house guest arrived, and it suddenly became very clear that I was as hot-blooded as Chas Caldwell.

Waltraut Skorzeny was the daughter of Otto 'Scarface' Skorzeny, who rescued Benito Mussolini from the partisans towards the end of the war. He was a master of guerrilla tactics and one of Hitler's most decorated soldiers.

Waltraut was a bit younger than me, but much taller, a honey blonde, athletically built and very tanned and beautiful. She had sparkling blue eyes, strong white teeth and a firm jaw. I'd seen pictures of dozens of girls with hoops round their waists at rallies, girls just like Waltraut.

Waltraut's English was reasonable, but it was the way she said words such as 'please,' 'thank you,' and 'excuse me' that excited me. She sort of pouted when she spoke. I told boys at school that I had met a girl who looked like Brigit Bardot.

'You don't speak any German or any other language, just English,' she said. 'You people talk about Europe and none of you have been there.' She told me that her father owned several large companies, and she was brown because she spent some of the year in Germany and some of the year in General Franco's Spain.

After I walked her around Regent's Park, showed her the ducks and swans and received stares from several Jewish women who had either seen or heard a lot about German girls like Waltraut, she said, 'Please comb your hair. I am embarrassed being in London with a small boy trying to look like a Hollywood actor.'

At night, I lay awake thinking about the girl. I found it so easy to follow the recommendation that we should love our European comrades. But she didn't stay long and didn't bother to blow me as much as an air kiss when we said goodbye at Victoria Station one Sunday morning.

The rest of the German holidaymakers arrived later that summer.

The first to arrive after Waltraut was a boy about my age but half a head taller, Klaus Naumann, son of the former Brownshirt officer, who served as under-secretary of state in Germany's wartime Propaganda Ministry, Dr Werner Naumann. He had been one of the last to see Hitler in his bunker in Berlin in April 1945.

Klaus's father had been named in Hitler's will as successor to Dr Joseph Goebbels who killed himself, his wife and children so soon after Hitler's suicide.

During the three weeks Klaus stayed with us, I didn't once see him smile or crack a joke. Alf Flockhart told us, 'He suffered so badly in 1945 because the Russian Army destroyed the family home and he and his mother had to scrounge scraps of food from dustbins. It was common to do that after the war. Most German women were raped by the Russians, sometimes by Americans and other Allied soldiers.' He said 'They should have been others in the dock at Nuremburg and not just the Germans.'

I introduced Klaus to my close friend Timothy, who was even taller than Klaus. Tim had thick curly brown hair and large facial features. He had won a scholarship to Haberdashers Askes and because of that, I saw less and less of him at weekends. But I still counted him as my best and closest friend.

Tim was a brilliant sportsman and a magnificent spin-bowler. We decided to teach Klaus how to play cricket. We used a real cricket ball and not the soft tennis ball demanded by the uniformed park keeper. Klaus swung my Donald Bradman bat around as if it was a baseball bat. He kept missing the ball and Timothy laughed at the German's antics in front of the wicket.

Klaus went red in the face. 'I don't like your stupid game and I don't like your stupid country.' He threw the bat down, walked home and the following day told Alf Flockhart that he wanted money to go back to Germany.

Klaus lacked the charm of the much older Gudrun Himmler. She appeared one day much later on at 40 Blandford Square with Jeffrey Hamm and Bob Row, a tall Lancastrian who edited Mosley's weekly newspaper *Union*.

Fraulein Himmler was visiting London for the first time, and Mosley suggested that she should meet some of his followers. Fraulein Himmler smiled but said nothing. She looked like a schoolteacher with her fair hair, wire-rimmed glasses, a tweedy skirt and brown jacket. She obviously knew that in the eyes of Mosley's followers she was a very important person. The adults went into the house and I stayed outside, too young to talk to such an important person, too old to put on the 'Horst Wessel' record or one of Mosley's speeches before the war. After about half an hour she came out again, smiled and touched my face before driving away in the same taxi that had brought her to a part of London that the Special Branch agent who visited my father half-jokingly described as 'Oswald Mosley's unofficial headquarters in North London.'

The following week or so, Timothy and I were kicking a tennis ball around opposite the convent walls in Harewood Avenue when he asked why my family had so many German friends. 'My parents are asking why you people are always with Germans. My father says it's a pity any of them are alive after what they did to the Jews during the war.'

'What did they do to the Jews that we didn't do to the Germans?' I asked, echoing what I'd heard so many times before in my mother's kitchen.

'We didn't kill Jews. My father says that Hitler and his Nazi henchmen killed millions of Jews. If Hitler had got his way, he'd have killed my mother and grandmother. They're Jews, you know. My father is from Ireland but my mother's an English Jew, so I'm Jewish because if your mother is Jewish, then you are as well.'

He picked up the ball, put it in his pocket and walked away without saying goodbye.

When I told my mother that night, she said, 'It doesn't surprise me at all. Timothy is looking more and more foreign.'

I felt sad and confused for some time. How could this person I'd been so proud to call a friend since we were six years old possibly be a Jew?

5

LONDON, 1956

The year 1956 saw two earthquakes blow their tops more or less at the same time, the Hungarian Uprising and the Suez Canal Crisis. Oswald Mosley was determined to make the most of them.

That year, he was sixty years old but looked a lot younger.

Twenty years earlier, he had been at the height of his short-lived fame. That year, he planned a huge march through Jewish parts of the East End of London. With him were about two thousand of his most hardened followers, some bussed into London from other parts of England. Around the Cable Street area, the Mosleyites were met by about one hundred thousand opponents screaming abuse and chanting the Spanish Civil War slogan, They Shall not Pass. Knowing bloodshed would follow a march, the police asked Mosley not to proceed. He complied. It was a stunning defeat for the BUF, but Mosley's propagandists turned it into some sort of victory with them claiming that the English Establishment and police had caved in to the forces of 'Jewish Communism.'

Earlier that year, Mosley had been stoned in Manchester and six of his supporters were knocked unconscious as they defended him in Hull. In September, he was assailed by a shower of missiles at Horbeck Moor, Leeds, during a meeting which attracted a crowd of about thirty thousand and at Carfax Assembly Rooms in Oxford, Mosley had taunted his opponents and caused a riot by playing the 'Horst Wessel' song on the gramophone before he started speaking.

In 1956, Mosley was still capable of arousing strong emotions. He remained a fiery speaker and an imposing figure, a six-foot three-inch tall limping Lord Byron of British Fascism. His followers said he was in 'good nick' and never asked where his deep Mediterranean tan came from and his grey campaign suit with its missing button. Yet, he also gave the impression that age had mellowed him and experience had modified his former Fascist beliefs.

DOI: 10.4324/9781003375722-6

On the platform, he continued to be a brilliant performer, a magician with words and around the dinner table of fellow aristocrats he was said to be just as fascinating at sixty as he was when he was tipped to be a future British prime minister in the late 1920s. He was considered to be one of the most intelligent and witty hosts in France, where his regular visitors included the Duke and Duchess of Windsor.

Bob Row, the editor of *Union*, said his ambition when he retired after Mosley came to power was to write a play or a book about Mosley and the Duke talking and planning together in Paris after the war. 'What a story,' he said with bouncy, boyish enthusiasm. 'The man who should have been king with the man who should have been the English Mussolini.'

Bob was a frequent visitor to 40 Blandford Square. My mother adored him. 'How's The Leader,' she asked before he took off his overcoat.

When he left, she said, 'It's like one of the Apostles visiting the Romans or Corinthians after the Resurrection.'

Union came out on Thursday nights, and Bob brought it round to our house and had supper. He'd sit for hours in the kitchen with my mother and Lovene while I read every word, hoping that one day I'd become a great writer like Bob Row.

Most of his articles told readers just how right Mosley had been to oppose the war against Germany in 1939. His stories were written in staccato sentences which often ended with an exclamation mark. With time and training and guidance, I might one day be able to write like that.

'He comes round to talk to me,' said my mother, 'but I think he quite likes Lovene and obviously thinks the world of Trevor.'

At the start of 1956, Bob told us that OM was going to make his big come-back because the Jews were trying to overthrow Nasser in Egypt.

'They'll go to war against Nasser, Mrs G. and Britain will go along with all the financial crooks because of that chinless wonder, Anthony Eden. We'll all be dragged into another Jewish war and British lives will be lost over another foreign quarrel and the Arabs will turn away from Britain and look to the Soviet Union.'

He said that one day to get rid of the Jews running Britain, Mosley would make an alliance with the Soviets just as Hitler had with the Russians in 1939. My mother expressed her amazement. Bob Row calmed her down, saying that even the Russians had found out how awful the Jews were and that before his death, Stalin planned to kill the lot of them. 'But the Jews got Stalin before Stalin got them.' And then, 'OM won't make that mistake.' He said that the Soviet Union was the headquarters of the anti-Zionist movement and Mosley's Britain would prefer to side with the Russians than be treated like poodles by the Americans. And that there were more Jews in New York than in the whole of Israel.

'They say they're Americans when they vote, Jews when they're criticised and Zionists as soon as they get to Israel.'

Then he perked up, 'So, if we attack Zionists, no one can say we're anti-Semites. And, anyhow, the Arabs are Semites and we love the Arabs. Perhaps OM's policy will be to encourage British Jews to go to Israel. Then we'll re-arm the Arabs.'

Bob tucked into his beans on toast with a Cheshire Cat grin on his face as if he'd cracked a difficult crossword clue.

Although he looked at my mother when he spoke, it was obvious that his intention was to attract Lovene. They walked around the park and went to art galleries, and Bob spent less and less time at 302 Vauxhall Bridge Road.

Meanwhile, The Leader packed halls throughout Britain, in Manchester, Birmingham, London, speaking sometimes for two hours and receiving thunderous applause. We travelled all over the country in coaches and, amazingly, there was hardly any fighting.

There was never any mention of these huge indoor meetings in the British press.

'Mrs G. We send out circulars to every news editor in Fleet Street about what OM is doing and saying but they only report him when there's been a fight. They put a D-Notice on The Leader after the war and told editors not to touch him with a bargepole. The BBC was the first to go along with that ban. Perhaps we should step up the Yid-bashing and get publicity.'

As part of the new offensive to get Mosley back into the minds of the British people, Diana Mosley had, in 1953, started a magazine called *The European*. Her upper-class friends wrote articles and poems. Henry Williamson, author of *Tarka the Otter*, made contributions and so did Richard Aldington, author of *Death of a Hero*, which Bob had given to me as a birthday present. There were articles by Ezra Pound, and several experts on his *Cantos* made contributions, including two men who appeared in the magazine almost every month, Alan Neame and Desmond Stewart.

They'd met Mosley when they were students at Oxford University after the war. Bob said that both men 'batted for the other side' but that they were close to Lady D.

Bob said, 'The Leader wants Union to win over the masses but he needs The European to pull in the intellectuals. The Leader knows that it's people like the Grundy family who make all the sacrifices and those will be the people who'll be rewarded the moment he comes to power. The intellectuals will wait and come in at the last moment when Mosley has done all the hard work. That happened in Germany, Mrs G. They waited, hung back, criticised. But the moment Hitler came to power they flattered him. But the last one in were the first one out as soon as the war started to go the other way. But Hitler knew who his real supporters were. Same thing will happen here with OM. One day, he'll be in Downing Street. Then the bells will ring.'

When Russian tanks invaded Hungary at the end of 1956, Mosley told large audiences in London that Anthony Eden had given Khrushchev an excuse to go in and put down the student uprising, because how could the West condemn him when they had invaded Egypt? At times, my mother became almost hysterical in the kitchen and said that we should drop all pretence and let people know we were supporters of the greatest man in British history who had spent his life fighting Communism, which had at long last shown its real face.

The night the tanks went into Budapest, a group of us, including a tall slim boy with golden hair, an open-neck checked shirt and blue jeans who I'd not met before, went in a van around Paddington, Marble Arch, Kensington and Marylebone and painted anti-Communist slogans on walls.

Near Edgware Road, close to where Ginger Griffiths lived, I held a bucket full of white paint while the new boy drew a huge flash and circle. I heard the noise of tyres on a wet road and then a voice.

'And what do you two little sods think you're up to, then?'

Two policemen looked down at me. One shone a torch into my face and then lit up my new companion. He squinted at the powerful light. He had a lovely face. He took hold of the policeman's torch and pointed it downwards.

'Don't shine that light in my face,' he said as if he was talking to a waiter.

I thought, 'God, we're going to be arrested,' and then, 'But perhaps it doesn't matter if my name gets into the Marylebone Mercury, because Mummy says we can stop pretending.'

The golden boy next to me said, 'This is our sign, officer. Were anti-Communist and we're protesting about students in Hungary being murdered in the streets of Budapest by Soviet tanks. We're students and all of us feel the same way.'

One of the policemen said, 'Well, you should have said.' They looked at one another and told us to beat it. 'Take that bucket with you and don't let us catch you doing this again or else there will be trouble next time.'

I turned to talk to the boy with the torch but he had gone. I went hurrying off into the night to find the others to tell them what had happened.

'That was Max, OM's son,' said John Wood who was increasingly active in Union Movement now he'd returned from National Service.

He had digs in London and often came to the house with other young Mosley supporters. They pretended it was to seek guidance from Old Members like my mother and father to hear about their days of triumph against the Jews before the war but it was clear to me that John Wood was infatuated with Lovene. My father took a strong dislike to him.

'That public school voice. I knew his mother and father. Now we've got him with his *la de da* this and his *la di da* that.' My mother snapped. 'At least his parents supported The Leader. Do you want your only daughter to start going out with boys who *aren't* in the Movement?'

The following weekend, about fifty Mosleyites joined a pro-Hungary rally in Trafalgar Square. The more experienced Movement members got to the front and said we should all go to Farringdon Street and protest outside the office of the *Daily Worker*. Hundreds followed. When we got there, bricks were hurled through the newspaper office's windows. Within minutes the police were on the spot and this time there was no tolerance or understanding about the anti-Communist nature of the attack.

One shouted, 'Get that little bastard' and half a dozen of them went tearing after John Wood, who was a skilful rugby player. He moved like lightning and we tried to keep up with him. We disappeared into the night and joined bus queues or stood looking into shop windows or walked in to the nearest underground station and then met up again at 302 Vauxhall Bridge Road to compare notes. When we came out later that evening, a plain-clothes detective said to Jeffrey Hamm, 'Try that stunt again and we'll close you down, do you hear me? One more time and . . .'

Bob told us later that OM was delighted with what happened. 'There's only one man with a consistent anti-Communist track-record in England and that's The leader. All the rest of them compromised and went trotting off to Moscow to have tea with Uncle Joe. The people are waking up. They're seeing sense at long last and turning to the one man who can save them.'

She echoed the words, 'the one man.'

Bob said the time was right for the formation of a youth wing and that I should lead it, or help form it, with other young men of my age. Until then I had kept a low profile at school, remembering that what happened inside 40 Blandford Square was one thing and what happened outside was another. But after Hungary, nearly everyone under the age of forty was anti-Communist. I taught some of the boys at school a Movement song, and they thought it was great and sang it in the corridor after morning assembly.

The red flag is turning pink,
It's not as red as people think.
With gallons of beer and gallons of blood,
We'll drag the Red Fag through the mud.

I invited a small group of Tenisonians to a Mosley dinner at Victoria. Bob said they'd get in free. A long-haired boy called Cedric Gaisford, whose only aim was to get into an art college, said he'd like to come and paint Mosley.

Gordon Lawson, who bore an uncanny resemblance to Rudolf Hess, said that he wanted to read what Mosley had written before hearing him speak.

Another classmate from 5c, Wally Walters, said that he'd like to come because he liked beer and the Nazi party started off in Munich at a beer festival.

For the first time, I felt part of a peer group at school. I was no longer the silent oddball. As Jeffrey Hamm told my father so often, 'We were right, we are right, we always will be right.'

Movement dinners were held two or three times a year at The Albert, close to Victoria Station and walking distance from 302 Vauxhall Bridge Road. The licensee supported the pre-war BUF. His wife was Italian. She hated Mosley and said that Mussolini betrayed Italy by siding with Hitler.

Dinners were attended by about one hundred and fifty to two hundred people. Bob Row told us that Jeffrey Hamm very carefully examined the list in case there were suspicious names, 'Police spies,' he called them.

I hoped that my father would not repeat at the next dinner attended by school friends what he said at a Union Movement conference the year before. The debate after Mosley's speech turned towards immigration of black people from the West Indies. Everyone said there were too many coming into the country. My father rose and said the problem was not because of blacks but because of Jews. Red-faced and with great passion he screamed, 'And if you're looking for the first man to turn on the gas taps, I'm here!' He hit his chest with a clenched fist and waited for applause. It did not come. He sat down, looked around several times and then stared at Mosley.

I watched The Leader's face. For a few moments, he stared at my father and then Jeffrey Hamm went to him with a piece of paper and announced that we'd have a short break. As we moved from our seats, a few old members slapped my father on the back. One said, 'Suppose you shouldn't have said that, Sid. Not with the Old Man here. But I would, too.'

There were two toasts at Union Movement dinners, the first to Mosley, the second to the Queen. Men who spent the war detained at the King's pleasure, stood up straight and raised their glasses to his daughter.

A collection was held at the end of the meal and as always, my father contributed twenty pounds. The money went to Sanctuary Press to keep paying for *Union* to be published, or to help fund an election campaign in the East End. Union Movement candidates always came bottom. But every failure was brushed off as just a mild set-back.

'It's twenty pounds from the Grundy family, thank you Sid and Edna.' My father got his round of applause and sat down, beaming. Alf Flockhart raised his glass and said, 'The Grundy family.' Members joined in and Mosley smiled, his small eyes beaming in our direction.

'What a man,' said my mother nudging my father. 'Look at him, Sidney. Look at him! That is what a real man should be like.'

The guest of honour in 1956 was Hans Ulrich Rudel, one of Hitler's most decorated pilots who had destroyed so many Russian tanks on the Eastern Front. He had written a book published by Mosley's publishing wing, Euphorion Books in Dublin. *Stuka Pilot* sold for twelve shillings and sixpence and it was Mosley's only publishing success story.

My Archbishop Tenison friends shook hands with Rudel. Later, Walters with a few drinks inside him laughed and sang his song – 'This is the hand that's shaken the hand that's shaken the hand of the Fuhrer.'

Towards the end of the evening, I asked if they'd join. They all said an emphatic No. Gaisford said that Mosley was a bit of a stuffed shirt and he thought it was a laugh that a party claiming to want to overthrow the establishment toasted The Queen. He said, 'They look like a collection of berks from the local council getting pissed with the mayor.' Walters stopped clowning and said his complaint was that the beer tasted like piss. Lawson said he admired Mosley's ability to state his case but that he came across as a stage actor. He said, 'He looks like Robin Hood dressed up as Errol Flynn.'

After the rector's marriage to Mrs Simpson, we moved from Christ Church to St Mark's Church, which was on the wealthier side of Marylebone Road.

Outside St Mark's during the build-up to Christmas, there was always a large notice showing a number of cars driving and people walking towards a small house with a light shining from the top floor. Underneath the words, 'Wise men worshipped Jesus – they still do.'

We were introduced to Father Crisp and his curate, Father Price. The congregation called them Price-Crispies, after the well-known brand of breakfast cereal, Rice-Krispies.

Father Crisp was a leading Anglican Church supporter of the Campaign for Nuclear Disarmament. He was a close friend of the Labour MP, Tom Driberg. He regularly visited the Marylebone flat of the Jewish gangster Jack Spot, who organised attacks on Mosleyites. Father Crisp told my mother he hoped to convert Spot to the ways of a fellow but very different Jew, Jesus Christ.

When, in his sermons, Father Crisp attacked the Nazis for committing genocide against the Jews, my mother gathered up our hymn and prayer books, replaced them neatly at the front entrance to the church and walked away, followed by me.

At St Mark's, no heads turned, no church warden ran after her to ask if someone was ill, no one cared about her sudden departure.

A church warden at St Mark's, when he heard that I might still be interested in a career in the church, told me that Father Spencer had spoken to his bishop about problems with the Grundy family.

He told the bishop that my mother was a good woman and a 'natural Christian' despite what she said about the Jews.

The bishop said that rather than lose a good but complicated Christian family, Father Crisp should contact Mrs Grundy and try and persuade her to change to another church in the area. Hence, the arrival of John Crisp in our lives.

He took no nonsense from my mother when he came to tea. And he had no interest in her appeal as a still attractive woman who had just turned fifty.

He would wrap his thick blanket-like cape around his shoulders, half hide his face in it and stare at her. The first time he came round he almost dropped his cup when he looked up and saw Oswald Mosley in a black fencing jacket looking down at him from the mantelpiece.

'Mrs Grundy. The leopard doesn't change his spots.'

'Father Crisp. Sir Oswald never had any.'

Fifteen all, I said to myself. Here we go again. Same game, different vicar.

'Therefore, Mrs Grundy, I would assume you don't see your Leader as a leopard at all. What good news. We have all been mistaken. The way he is presenting himself now certainly doesn't give the impression of having been a leopard, a lion or anything like that. Was he always so reasonable, I ask myself?'

He pouted at The Leader's picture and turned to Lovene and beamed, 'Why can't *I* be your leader?'

She laughed and said he'd look good in a black fencing jacket.

But my mother saw the chance of a drop shot. 'You could never be our leader because you lead in the wrong direction.'

'Mrs Grundy. If anyone is leading you in the wrong direction it's that man.'

The words *that man* was fighting talk in our house.

'So, what kind of man is he really, Mrs Grundy? Not what kind of *leader*. What kind of *man*? All I am saying is that if you love and follow Our Lord and take his words seriously then you must ask yourself difficult to avoid questions. Our Lord said, "Love thy neighbour as thyself" And St Paul looked to the day when there would be no Jew and no Gentile, no man and no woman, just brothers and sisters in the love of Christ. I don't think that would lead you in the wrong direction. I leave that to the man on your mantelpiece.'

I waited for a Mosley snap-back-quick reply to the vicar's words but there was silence. There was no punch-back. She said nothing. Regret and sadness clouded her face. What happened to her Mosley motto, 'Say it again. But be ruder the second time.'

Later, I heard Father Crisp say to Lovene, 'What are you doing in this family? You're it's only intelligent member and you're too intelligent to be mixed-up with this vile Mosley business. Your mother is destined to become a tragic figure and a victim of Mosley's hubris. She has Mosley muddled up with Jesus and the day will come when she sees through him. Her whole world will collapse. You and Trevor are young and can get away. But your mother. Confusing an ordinary man with Our Lord is a terrible sin, perhaps the worst of them all.'

After this confrontation, my mother's moods started to swing from intense, almost frenzied joy to moments of blank despair. She once grabbed me in the corridor before I left for school and said with desperation in her voice, 'Look at me. Look at me. I've been a clown all my life. My God, what's going to happen to me?'

As a child, I'd dreaded going home. My first question after she opened the door was, 'Has there been a row?' Now, in the middle of my adolescence, I would open the door, go along to the kitchen which she rarely left, like Hitler in his bunker, open the door and look at her face to see if she was up or down.

'Are you all right, mum?'

'Of course, I'm all right. Why do you ask? Anyone would think there was something wrong with me.'

At other times, she would refuse to say a word and turn away from me and go into a silent world sometimes for hours, sometimes for days.

'It' all to do with something called the change of life,' explained my father, who was immersed in his world of street maps. 'She'll come out of it. Your mother has never been able to do anything by halves.'

When my mother was on form, she challenged Father Crisp to attend a Mosley meeting the next time he spoke in London. 'Nicodemus went to hear Jesus,' she said.

Later that year, in Kensington Town Hall, I saw Father Crisp sit down in one of the back-row seats close to the exit. He wore a white shirt and a tie and was sunk into a black overcoat with the collar turned up to partly hide his face.

After an inspiring performance on the stage, which earned Mosley a thunderous round of applause from a cross-section of middle-class South Kensington types, there was a question-and-answer session. A tall, rather striking man in his fifties in a long brown leather coat, stood up and asked Mosley a question in German. Mosley replied, having learned the language in prison, and for the next ten minutes Sir Oswald exchanged ideas with the unknown man in a language few people in the audience understood.

Father Crisp, along with most of the audience, stood up and walked out of the hall, probably grateful that no threatening men wearing black shirts would pounce on them for insulting The Leader. But the bad old days of the 1930s were long gone, along with the shirts, leather belts and jackboots. Mosley seemed indifferent to the fact that the audience had melted away while he discussed Goethe, Nietzsche and the European Idea with a man in a leather coat.

Father Crisp spied me standing at one of the exits with a bundle of *Union* newspapers in my hands. My first contribution to that paper was inside that issue. It was an article calling for the release of Rudolf Hess from Spandau Prison. Father Crisp knew that I should be at home studying for my 'A' levels. He looked at me and shook his head.

At the end of the meeting, Mosley thanked his stewards and praised them for helping him to mount a successful campaign. He said the slump he'd long predicted was on its way and people would turn to him for leadership.

'Before the war,' Mosley said, 'Churchill was seen by the English Establishment as a monster, a man with six eyes, eight arms and twelve legs. But when the crisis came, even the strongest of Churchill's critics looked around and asked, "Who will save us now that war is here? We need a man with six eyes, eight arms . . ."' We all laughed and Mosley pushed out his jaw and sunk his hands deep into the jacket of his old grey campaign suit which had a large silver flash and circle pin on its left lapel. He flashed his eyes and made us all love him that little bit more. He sent us away with dreams in our hearts, knowing that he was right, that no force on earth could stop us.

I looked around for my embryonic youth group supporters. Les Smith, an ex-public schoolboy; Derek Ashton from Wales, who had at the last count thirty-six pictures of Adolf Hitler on his bedroom wall in the small terraced house he lived in with his mother and crippled father close to the Tate Gallery alongside the River Thames; Gordon Lawson, the tall, handsome Tenisonian who so closely resembled Hess; three other boys about my age whose parents were pre-war members of BUF and who had been told to take some interest in a new youth organisation supporting The Leader; and David Bell from a council flat near Brixton Underground Station. He told us that he heard Mosley speak and contacted Union Movement headquarters, who put him on to me. I later found out that he had been told to join by the police to find out if the Mosley Youth Group was serious, or just another five-minute wonder.

I walked out of the hall and across the road to a pub with Les, Gordon and Derek. We exchanged notes about the great victory won that night and how it would only be a matter of time before The Leader swept to power.

Having talked to the Movement secretary, Alf Flockhart and Jeffrey Hamm, I told the band of loyal supporters who were starting to worry about the last bus home, that our first full meeting would be held at my house the following week. Everyone should bring a friend and girls would be welcome if they were interested in politics. My mother and father had agreed to let us use the old darkroom in the basement as our permanent headquarters, provided no one smoked.

A few days later, as I got ready to lead young people into the future, the radio was blaring out loud at Les Smith's house in Sussex Gardens, mid-way between Marylebone and Paddington. One of his sisters had turned up the radio to hear the words of a new record. It had just leapt into the pop charts, a record everyone was playing, the words of which hardly anyone understood. It was called *Heartbreak Hotel*.

I made a mental note to say in my speech the following week, 'We, the youth of Britain, have finer, more noble things in our lives than rock and roll.' I asked Les if his sister would turn down the noise. 'If we're going to have to compete against this bloke Elvis Presley, we'll need some really powerful loudspeakers.'

The darkroom was packed. Eighteen people huddled together and, I thought, that gave the room a warm and wonderful intimacy. I had invited over thirty people but eighteen was still a good turnout. Hitler had spoken to even smaller groups at the beginning, and Mosley had formed the British Union of Fascists with only thirty-two followers. So, eighteen wasn't bad at all.

I started to speak and surprisingly wasn't at all nervous. 'We have something finer in our lives than rock and roll. I think that most of the people in this room tonight have heard about the greatest living Englishman, Sir Oswald Mosley.'

Les lit a cigarette, which was out of bounds, but I didn't want to interrupt myself.

'We are privileged to be the junior wing of Union Movement and I believe that if we take our orders from the older people in UM, I mean if we fully co-operate with them, we will be able to work miracles for Sir Oswald Mosley. He has already said that the slump is on its way and if you saw how he packed them in at Kensington Town Hall, halls in Birmingham, Manchester and other parts of England, then you'll understand how close we must be to power in England.'

'We'll start with a sales drive next week at Earl's Court to try and boost the sales of Union and then I think we'll start our own newspaper. I'd like to call it Attack, but the name hasn't been settled. It has been suggested that we start street meetings and I have been asked to address the first one in Praed Street in Paddington on Saturday afternoon at three o'clock. So, I hope you'll all come along and give me the support, maybe the protection, I need.'

I thrust my hands into my pockets like Mosley and tried to push out my jaw but that hurt because another large spot or even boil, was developing on my right cheek.

I said that the meeting that night marked something big. 'I think that we have the spirit to keep us together. You know, we don't need a uniform, although that would be great because it would help us have a way of identifying one another when we do battle with the Reds.'

One of the teenage girls from a school near Tenison's started to shuffle and said something to Gordon who had brought her along. He looked at his watch.

'So, without keeping you any longer, I would like to say that the most important thing in the world right now is to stick with the man who is best for Britain, Oswald Mosley. At the moment he might appear as the man with six eyes and eight arms, but when the time comes, people choose strong men to lead them. They did this when the war broke out and they looked to Winston Churchill and made him like the dictator of Britain. We have our own man with six eyes and eight arms, Oswald Mosley and tonight I ask you to support him and if needs be, die for him.'

My mother had supplied tea in cups borrowed from the Campaign for Nuclear Disarmament branch at St Mark's.

The girl with Gordon left the moment I stopped speaking. She'd written me a note and gave it to Gordon to pass on to me when he came back to my house after walking her to the bus stop in Baker Street.

I agreed to come along because you published it as a 'Youth for Europe' meeting. I think you should be more honest and tell people your real intensions and not encourage them to waste money on buses and tubes coming from the other side of London to get involved with Fascism, which is evil. How on earth can you be involved with someone that supported Adolf Hitler? You're far too young to know what you pretend to be talking about. I don't think you know anything about politics or economics or even religion, which you talk about so glibly. I suggest that you study hard, get your 'A' levels (if you can) and go to university and learn a bit of modesty.

I walked with Gordon to the bus stop in Baker Street, and he told me that his mother was complaining bitterly about his involvement with the Mosley Movement. 'She says it's evil and that Mosley supported Hitler for killing six million Jews.'

'Rubbish,' I said. 'Mosley never supported that and anyhow the figures are all made up. The Zionists want us to believe that Hitler was a monster to justify what they did to the Arabs in Palestine.'

Gordon looked withdrawn and I knew I was losing him.

'Trev, what the girl wrote. Read it again. There might be something in it, you know.'

He added, 'When I took her to the bus-stop she asked me if you were real or if you'd be made to talk like that. I think she's right. We're all too young for this. We weren't in the war and why should we be fighting battles for Oswald Mosley when he chose to be a Fascist twenty years ago? Why?'

On the way back to Blandford Square, I felt sad.

I heard 'Heartbreak Hotel' blaring out from a pub near Dorset Square, and the music followed me home where I heard my father playing the 'Horst Wessel' on the gramophone.

6

TRAFALGAR SQUARE, 1957 (1)

The end of 1956 saw something to celebrate in the Grundy household. My sister had become engaged to my hero, Bob Row. He was more than twenty years older than Lovene but my mother had encouraged the match, partly because she relished the idea of her daughter marrying in to the hierarchy of Union Movement and partly because it would put pressure on John Wood, who was still devoted to Oswald Mosley and in love with Lovene at the same time. My mother wanted Lovene to get married and didn't much mind if it was to Bob Row or John Wood. But John didn't have two beans in his pocket at the time and felt he was in no position to get married.

John had fallen for Lovene when he first saw her, a beautiful teenage dark-haired and brown-eyed girl in a white dress, bowing and presenting a bouquet of flowers to Lady Mosley at a Union Movement dinner.

His mother and father had been Mosley supporters before the war. His mother bore a strong resemblance to the actress, Margaret Rutherford. His father was an accountant. They were country members of the BUF who felt much more at home with Henry Williamson talking about his farm in Norfolk and otters in Devon rivers than with any of the knuckle-duster-carrying-killer-punchers who dominated Mosley's East End of London branches.

The adverse publicity Mosley received because of his speeches against Jews embarrassed them, and Mrs Wood told my mother she thought it was all nonsense.

'When Sir Oswald comes to talk to us in Wiltshire, he never mentions Jews,' she said. 'He talks about farming and very sensibly, too, I might add.'

Lovene and Bob's engagement was announced at an annual dinner that year, and I heard my mother say to Lovene, who appeared distraught, 'Well, if Johnny really wants you, he'll do something about it, won't he?'

DOI: 10.4324/9781003375722-7

Lovene rarely wore her engagement ring and though she was only twenty-one, she developed a sad, withdrawn look, which may well have increased her appeal for the two men drawn into my mother's Machiavellian marriage game.

After Christmas lunch, Bob and I went for a walk in Regent's Park. The lake was frozen over and we had taken bread for the ducks and swans, but I had eaten most of it when we reached the black ice-rimmed edge of the lake. I took him to our 'secret' tree where Lovene and I had played out childhood games and imagined we were children with lots of friends who'd never heard of Oswald Mosley.

'When OM comes to power,' said Bob, striding out like the Lancastrian farmer's son he was, 'boys like you will be groomed for leadership. You know, Trevor, the English class system stinks to high heaven. And it will go. Mosley says the first thing he'll do is get rid of public schools. He once told me that the worst days of his life were spent at Winchester College. He said the best time of his life was with soldiers in the war, the first war, that is, mixing with men from all walks of life. He said that when he broke with the old men from the old parties and formed BUF be wanted to put men into uniform to recreate war-time camaraderie, because it was the only time in his life that he'd seen men from all the different classes and ways of life pulling together for a common purpose.'

After Mosley, Bob Row was my biggest hero, a man far more important to me than Elvis Presley, or the crop of English rock singers who were popping up all over the place as 1957 approached.

Bob had two weeks holiday a year, and he walked alone in the Lake District. On holiday, he smoked thirty cigarettes a day but gave up the moment he returned to 302 Vauxhall Bridge Road. On holiday, he ate only a strict diet of brown bread and molasses. He asked me if I'd ever seen a Jew eating white bread. 'They know that all the nutrition has been taken out of white bread and that's why it's OK for the *goyim*. You know what *goyim* means? It means cattle. They think we're animals and they say that Jesus was the son of a prostitute.'

Bob earned a pittance and couldn't afford to get married but if he did, Mosley just might pay him a bit more. But living in France was expensive, and Mosley was scraping the bottom of his own barrel because he had to finance so many speaking campaigns and pay for *The European* and subsidise *Union*. 'So, there won't be any spare cash floating around just because the editor of Union wants to, get married.'

Then he'd grow serious.

'Always remember how Hitler and the National Socialists suffered before they came to power. They had no money and sometimes nothing to eat. So, we're quite well off in England and there's much to be glad about. Things will be so different when the Old Man comes to power. I'll be one of the highest paid journalists in the country. Lovene and I will ride around London in a coach. The Jews will have to pay mightily to read what I say about them!'

We went on like this hour after hour, looking up at a flash and circle-studded sky, guessing what it would be like when Mosley came to power and how we would feel when the bells began to ring.

Bob told me that The Leader was preparing for a new pre-war-style political offensive in Britain.

'Why is The Leader so convinced this is the right time?' I asked.

'The Commies want to disarm Britain so the Red Army can march into Europe from Berlin. OM is writing about this in next month's Union.'

Bob said that The Leader had been told all about my work with the youth league. He said he wanted to see me when he was next in London. The 'Leader is particularly impressed with what Jeffrey told him about your street meetings.'

The following week, I told Les and Derek and some of the boys hanging around Blandford Square that when The Leader came to power, they would be the new elite and that Mosley would send us to Rhodesia, Kenya and South Africa to show solidarity with white farmers and learn how Europeans ran things in Africa and see how better off blacks were in their own country, not here in England.

By the time I was approaching seventeen, I had spoken all over London for the youth league.

'Be careful that you don't burn yourself out before you're eighteen,' said a BUF old-timer. 'I've seen young men like you before. They burn themselves out and you never hear of them again.'

So, was this old-timer for or against The Leader, I asked Ron Clucas, who was in his late thirties. A blond-haired Hitler fanatic, he lived in a flat near Hammersmith Bridge with his mother and an Alsatian dog he called Blondi, after the name of Hitler's dog. At meetings, he wore a white shirt, a black tie with a movement flash and circle pin in it, black shoes and shiny leather shoes. His prized possession was a black leather belt with a silver flash and circle buckle.

'The old codger,' replied Ron. 'He told me that a million people had been through the BUF in the 1930s but that most of them stayed only a few weeks. They joined after hearing the Old Man speak and left as soon as they found out that nothing happened afterwards. I wish we had a few hundred now, let alone a million.'

Ron had been ordered not to wear his belt because Mosley banned uniforms, along with the right-arm Fascist salute. But that didn't dampen his enthusiasm. Every Saturday, he stood on a flimsy wooden platform in Praed Street opposite Paddington Railway Station, threw his arms out and his growing stomach and asked a handful of listeners, most of them Union Movement people, what had happened to the greatest Empire the world had ever seen.

'Where are the men who went out in little ships to unknown places across stormy seas to build a white, Christian civilisation, the likes of which have not been seen since the glory days of Ancient Rome?'

An Irish drunk outside the nearby Scotch Ale House shouted, 'They're all in here getting pissed. Wanker.'

At the end of the Paddington meetings, we would sell a few copies of Union, often buying them ourselves, and head off to a Movement friendly pub. Youth league supporters were all under age but no one seemed to worry about that.

Derek was becoming increasingly unbalanced and told me that he was a reincarnation of Horst Wessel, the Nazi martyr. The most recent tally showed that he now had forty-two pictures of Hitler on his bedroom wall and it made me nervous when he said among them, he'd stuck one of me.

The handful of Tenison boys I'd managed to interest in the Movement mostly lasted as long as Gordon Lawson who had left the sixth form and gone to live in northern Germany. He said he wanted to learn German and become a writer.

Possible recruits were told to steer clear of Mosley by angry parents who'd fought against Hitler and Mussolini during the war.

One boy I tried to recruit from the lower fifth form had been cross-examined by members of the Labour Party in Streatham. One of his inquisitors had written to Dr Robinson about my extramural activities. The name 'Grundy' began to stink at school and I was labelled 'the school Fascist,' but this time the headmaster did not call me to his study.

However, early one afternoon in a music class, I laughed out loud at something a fellow pupil has said about Beethoven being deaf. Mr Burton, whose favourite I had been during the days my mother told him I wanted to be a clergyman, abruptly turned the music off.

He fixed me with his gaze as if he was trying to make me disappear, then pulled me by the shoulder to the front of the class. I thought, 'But I'm seventeen, the leader of the youth league and not some backstreet urchin.'

He said, 'You're a rotten apple, Grundy. You're a boy who has been given every opportunity and you have thrown them all away, one by one. You are an insult to the name of the school. Get out of this class and never come back again.'

I returned to my desk, picked up my books, took my bicycle clips out of my pocket and rode towards Vauxhall Bridge. I chained the bicycle, a Norman Invader, to the railing outside Vauxhall Bridge Road and went up the stairs to see Bob Row.

'Bob,' I said, 'I can't take school anymore. I want to leave. Can't you get me a job here? I'll do anything. I know The Leader hasn't got much money but it's known I'm Union Movement at school and they're making life hell on earth for me. They're bastards. Real bastards.'

Bob Row looked weary. He'd just written another headline, 'Mosley warned the West.' It was in large type over an article about three thousand words long by a 'special correspondent' in Newcastle, almost certainly Bob Row because there were no Mosley supporters in Newcastle.

We went next door to the Café Europa for a cup of tea. Bob bought me a current cake and told me to cheer up. He said he'd find out from Jeffrey Hamm whether I could be taken on at 302 but was I really ready to leave school and work full-time for Union Movement? I would only get a few pounds a week, at the most four?

I told him, 'Yes. Definitely yes.' I would study in the evening for my 'A' levels, pass them and still go on to university, or a teachers' training college, or whatever. Bob looked at me and smiled through sad eyes.

'Do you know about Lovene?' he asked me. 'She's broken off our engagement and is going to marry John Wood. Everything has been destroyed. Everything. My whole life, all my hopes.'

I loved Bob Row, a father figure and role model. I stayed with him at his office all afternoon and when it came time to go home, I rang my mother and told her I was with Bob Row and was helping him with *Union*, always an acceptable excuse.

Around nine o'clock, I rode home past Hyde Park asking myself why life was so complicated. Why did Lovene love John more than Bob? Why had Mr Burton suddenly blown his top at me? And why were people who condemned Mosley for being intolerant, so intolerant?

Lovene's wedding took place at St Mark's Church, and I was best man in my Archbishop Tenison's blazer. We stood together for a group photograph, Lovene and John, my father and mother, myself and a few paces away, looking on, Father Crisp. Later, when the negatives were developed, we looked like a collection of Romanovs about to be taken to a wall and shot.

Afterwards, Lovene and John cut a cake which Lovene bought from a shop in Bell Street that morning. We drank some wine and Lovene played a long-playing record with Mario Lanza singing *Be my love for no-one else can end this yearning/this need that you and you alone create.*

We raised our glasses and my father made a toast – He said he liked Mario Lanza but preferred Gigli who said in 1924 that with Mussolini in power in Italy, he knew his old mother would be safe.'

He never once mentioned Lovene or John, who he detested.

That night my mother said that yes, my father did hate John. 'I think he's jealous he's married your sister, but that's your father for you. I sometimes wonder if he's all there.'

7

LONDON, TRAFALGAR SQUARE (2)

Shortly before Easter 1957, I received a telephone call from Jeffrey Hamm. He told me to go that afternoon from school to headquarters where he had something of 'great importance' to tell me. I was certain I'd got a job with Union Movement.

I was hopelessly behind with my 'A' level work, English, history and geography. Much of my time in the sixth form was free, but I spent most of it writing articles for *Union* or in Marylebone Library's reference department trying to read and understand books about Richard Wagner and Bernard Shaw, Oswald Spengler and the book that caused a sensation in 1957, Colin Wilson's *The Outsider.* The story went round Union Movement circles that Mosley had written that book but allowed an unknown man who slept on Hampstead Heath to take the credit.

At four o'clock, I rushed from school to 302 and stood in the bookshop looking up at a framed picture of Sir Oswald in his black fencing jacket waiting to hear how my life would change so gloriously.

'Come on up, Trevor.' It was Hamm's unmistakable voice. I sat opposite him and put my hands on my knees to stop them shaking.

Jeffery Hamm had taken over as the Movement's general secretary following the imprisonment of Alf Flockhart, who had been convicted for 'interfering' with an underage boy. My mother said that he'd been framed by the Jews but this was his second conviction. After he went to prison, stories circulated about night-time activities in the basement of 302, where some of the younger recruits were encouraged to beat drums in preparation for the return of the days of Mosley's great street marches. Some of the older members said that with Flockhart in charge, the Drum Corps should be re-named the Bum Corps.

After his second conviction, there were no more jokes with the East Enders saying if Flockhart showed his face again, they'd leave the Movement.

DOI: 10.4324/9781003375722-8

I was shocked to the core when I heard some of the older East End members refer to Flockhart as the Old Man's bum-boy.

Jeffrey Hamm said, 'I haven't spoken to The Leader about you joining on a full-time basis and I don't think it's a good idea because you're so close to taking you're "A" levels. Why throw away a chance of going to university? The Leader needs educated people. I know life is being made hard for you at school but stick with it. You only have a year to go there and anyhow, I have some news that will make you the envy of every right-minded boy at your school.'

He told me that Mosley would not be speaking at Trafalgar Square that year because he was tied up with a series of urgent political meetings at a place called the Lido in Venice.

'So, I have taken a decision which will surprise a lot of people.' He paused so I could take in what he was going to say. 'I will be the main speaker at this year's rally and the meeting will be opened, I trust, by a certain young man who has made an indelible impression on us all. That young man is you. This year's Trafalgar Square rally will be opened by you, followed by me as Union Movement's best-known orator after The Leader. I offer you my heartfelt congratulation for your wonderful performances all over London and sometimes beyond.'

I drifted home in a dream and left all my homework in a briefcase at 302 and didn't care if I ever saw Chaucer's *Canterbury Tales* or David Ogg's *Europe in the Seventeenth Century* or Jane's Austen's *Emma* and *Northanger Abbey* again.

I got off the train at Baker Street and walked past the café in Regent's Park, where as a child I'd eaten biscuits and drunk orange juice with Timothy. I walked past the pitches where we'd kicked footballs and flung cricket balls at one another and looked at girls in their green and grey uniforms attending the school Maureen Fenn went to in Marylebone Road.

'Now I am a man,' I said it aloud so that the ducks and the swans on the crystal-clear springtime lake could all hear me.

I continued walking around the Inner Circle, through Queen Mary's Gardens, down past Madame Tussauds and Marylebone Library, where every night I put at least one hand-sized sticker on the public notice board – Support Mosley. Europe a Nation – Africa the Empire. Mosley or Moscow.

In just two weeks, I'd be on the plinth at the base of Nelson's Column in Trafalgar Square, and everyone in the world who I loved and admired would be there, me loving them, they loving me. And I would speak from my heart and soul.

That night, I stared deep into a steam bathroom mirror. 'My friends, our task is hard but I ask you this afternoon here in Trafalgar Square, to sacrifice your all so that on this great third day of Easter 1957, Britain will rise up and Britain will be great again.'

When I told my mother, she was delighted and said that on the big day some of her make-up could be used to help disguise the spots which had started to appear in alarming numbers on my increasingly gaunt face.

So, like some teenage vicar, I retreated into my small room to prepare my speech, or sermon. My mother, melodramatic as always, said that I must speak as if it was for the last time before I died. This had to be a great memorial to Mosley, she said because while we did so little, he did so much slaving away with secret friends in a place called the Lido, which I couldn't find on my school atlas.

I now had Lovene's old room. Since her marriage to John, she had taken over the basement at Blandford Square and transformed it into an arty den, full of bright pictures, curtains, and wall-hangings and within it flowed music by Tchaikovsky, Chopin and Debussy which was, thanks to long-playing records and affordable gramophones, enriching the lives of people who hadn't money to go to theatres in London, or opera houses in Paris.

In my room, sandwiched between the front room where my parents also slept and the kitchen where my mother spent most of her days, was a large framed picture of Mosley signed by him in crayon. Over my bed were cuttings from magazines, pictures of Brigitte Bardot from a film called *And God Created Woman*, Marilyn Monroe and Anthony Perkins who had replaced Tony Curtis as the man I most wanted to look like.

Between my room and the kitchen was a cubby-hole of a lavatory. Every grunt could be heard. When summer came and the windows were wide open, it was embarrassing inviting people to my room to talk politics. I prayed that no one would use the lavatory or grunt too loudly while I was talking about Mosley.

When there were new recruits, I played records to them of The Leader speaking in the 1930s and explained how Richard Wagner, through his opera Gotterdammerung had shown that the old order of things was doomed. Hence, the need for Mosley. The new order would be an age of science and discovery, peace and harmony brought about by a man who was as indifferent to personal power as he was to personal wealth because he had been born with both, a man who had no need of gold that corrupted human beings and which was anyhow in the hands of an alien group of vile-looking dwarfs who lived at the bottom of the River Rhine.

I hadn't a clue what I was talking about but I was able to repeat, like a parrot, what Bob Row told Lovene while he was courting her in the same room with me sitting like a slave at the master's feet.

Bob said Mosley had written an article for *The European* about how he planned his speeches and how he wanted the climax to be like the soul-lifting climax of the love scene between Tristian and Isolde in the Wagner opera and how, when it worked, even his most vitriolic critics would stand up and applaud him.

But sadly, Bob Row explained, Lady Mosley said it was not suitable and replaced it with an article about Ezra Pound's *Pisan Cantos* by one of her many literary admirers, a man called Alan Neame. Bob told me he was a genius but like so many of Lady Mosley's male admirers, was as queer as a nine-bob note.

During the days before Trafalgar Square, I studied not for my 'A' levels but rather to perfect my speech that I had to memorise because no Union Movement speaker would dream of using notes.

I would make it as general as possible and beat the drum only on subjects I had heard Mosley talk about, the decline of British power, the loss of Empire because of an unnecessary war with Germany and the fact that Britain's leadership still hesitated to work towards unity with Europe, which alone would make Britain independent of the big powers, America and the Soviet Union.

In the New Europe, there would be not only a common market but a common government for a people who shared four thousand years of history. Africa would be Europe's new Empire and would provide Europeans with every mineral they required and enough space to absorb all their unemployed.

Eventually, I would say, Europeans would have the highest standard of living in the world. Then, Communism would collapse because everyone would see for themselves how well Europe was doing led by Mosley and his colleagues.

I would also talk about the lack of meaning and commitment in Britain, how young people were being asked to keep their distance from political parties that were serious. I took as my theme what Jimmy Porter said in John Osborne's play *Look Back in Anger.* In a moment of despair, Porter cried out that all the good, brave causes had been fought in the 1930s, and if the 'big bang' came and everyone died in a nuclear age it would be about as pointless, meaningless and inglorious as stepping in front of a bus. I wrote down next to that quote, 'Yes, without Mosley it would be like this.' Then I wrote, 'But there are great, brave causes left and the building of a United Europe is one of them.'

For most of the weekend, I lay next to the lake at Regent's Park scribbling notes, tearing them up and starting again. It had to be perfect and it had to be exactly ten minutes long.

On the morning of that day, my mother was in a state of nerves. 'No one disturb Trevor,' she said in a loud voice as she brought me in a cup of tea, two boiled eggs and some bread and butter cut up into soldiers.

I didn't stay at home for lunch. Les called round and we walked down to Marylebone Underground Station. I wore a white shirt and grey flannel trousers and an old school mackintosh. Les said that he would stand behind me on the plinth with a flash and circle flag.

Jeffrey Hamm arrived at Trafalgar Square with Bob Row and others from headquarters in a large van known as The Elephant. It had carried Mosley around London so many times and had iron bars over its windows. Bob shook my hand. Jeffrey Hamm asked if I was all right and repeated that I should keep the speech to ten minutes.

At the start, there were only a couple of hundred people in the square but by ten minutes to three that afternoon numbers had swollen to several hundred. There was a noisy group from the Young Communist League and a group of students carrying 'Down with apartheid' banners. One scruffy youth had a banner which read 'Don't blow up the world' and although there were quite a few policemen in the vicinity there were also a large number of curious tourists and many more pigeons.

Our flag bearers used a wooden box to climb onto the plinth at the foot of Nelson's Column and walked across to stand behind me.

At three o'clock, I took off my mackintosh, stuck a flash and circle pin in my tie and walked towards the microphone. The sequence was filmed in black and white without any sound and when I saw it later, it reminded me of a Charlie Chaplin film. I noticed that I looked nervous and walked with a stoop.

Before the speech, one old timer from BUF days advised me to concentrate on just one person in the crowd and pretend I was talking to a cabbage.

I started the usual way, welcoming friends to a great meeting in London which showed that no power on earth could hold down the truth.

There was loud booing and jeering and some laughter from the Communist part of the crowd. I took no notice and concentrated on the top of the microphone. Hamm said, 'Take no notice unless they throw something. Then we'll step in and deal with them.'

I said that the youth of Europe were waiting for the youth of Britain to lead them into a bright new age, an age without Communism, without exploitation, an age with a future.

'Last year, students in Hungary defied the entire might of the Russian war machine. Young men and women picked up stones from the streets of Budapest and hurled them against tanks and guns and those tanks and guns roared back the Communist answer to a demand for freedom. Students were shot down like dogs and that was a time when our own government, the government of Eden, saw fit to co-operate with Israel and France and attack Egypt. That, my friends, gave Khrushchev the excuse to go in. He said, "Well, if Eden can back the forces of oppression, so can I, and there'll be no one around with the moral right to condemn me." It was the great betrayal and one day our government will stand before the bar or history and be condemned, utterly condemned.'

I put my hands on my hips like Mosley. 'Some people say there are no great, brave causes left. But how wrong can they be? No great causes? What about the cause of freeing the youth of Europe and the oppression of Communism and Russian tanks? Isn't that a great and noble cause? And if we died for that, would it be as pointless and as meaningless as stepping under a bus?' I leant forward imitating Mosley. 'Look forward with hope. That's what we say in Union Movement. Not look back in anger but look forward in hope!'

I heard loud jeers and a very loud voice shouted, 'Piss off!'

I looked in the direction of the heckler. 'We know where help won't be coming from.' Our side cheered. I saw the Grundy contingent standing by one of the fountains. My mother's eyes bored into me. Nearby were James and several other people who'd been my extended family since I was ten years old. James smiled and gave me the thumbs-up sign.

'Oswald Mosley, more than any other politician in Britain, understands young people. After the First World War he returned to England and found the old men sitting in the same soft leather chairs they'd sat in before Europe went to war in 1914. In those chairs were the men who'd made million while the youth of Europe tore each other to pieces. And the get-rich-quick gang still rules this country. They dared call Mosley a traitor in 1940 when he said that if we went to war against Germany we'd lose everything we'd ever fought for – the Empire. Mosley a traitor? Mosley, the man who served in the trenches in France? Mosley, who nearly lost his leg? Mosley, who served with the Royal Flying Corps? Mosley, who crashed and was nearly killed and even today walks with a limp? And those fat old men in their soft leather chairs dared call him a traitor.'

A man shouted, 'Pity the fucker survived.'

I said he was the youngest MP since Pitt and heard 'Pit the shit' and then 'What do you know about the First World War, you spotty-faced git?'

I looked down at the voice and said, 'The youth of Britain are with Mosley. Thank God, that doesn't include you.'

Applause from our side.

'Mosley wanted to see real change in Britain, a revolution – not that you lot,' and I looked towards the Communists, 'would know how to spell the word because you're too busy killing students in Hungary. But every change, every hope of change, was thrown away in 1940 when they locked up Mosley and one thousand British patriots who opposed the war. Yet when the war was declared, my friends, Hitler was marching East not West. And until that moment Joseph Stalin had been an effective ally of Adolf Hitler so why didn't we declare war on him as well as on Hitler? We declared war on Germany not in a British quarrel but rather in a . . . rather in a . . . rather in a foreign quarrel. And had it not been for the scientists who invented the A-Bomb, the Russians would today be in Trafalgar Square and where would free speech be then?'

A man standing with a sheepdog raised his hand, and he yelled out, 'Where the hell would free speech be if Hitler and his thugs had won the war?'

He put down his hand and walked away, his large dog wagging its tail.

I looked at my watch. A minute to go. One of the Communists held up a copy of *Union*. Without taking his eyes off me, he lit the bottom of the paper with a cigarette lighter, dropped it on the floor and watched the ball of brown cinders roll towards one of the policemen standing between me and the crowd. It captured the front row's attention. I stood and watched it burn and then looked up.

'Burn a newspaper. How brave. How courageous. But my dear friend with nothing else to do with no great cause to live for, you will never burn or destroy this movement because behind us stand the people of Britain who have not spoken yet. But they will, the people who will one day turn to the only man who has never betrayed them, the man once called "traitor" but who will one day be called "hero" – Oswald Mosley, the one man who stands today between the free British people and the forces of International – *In-ter-national* Communism.'

Our lot cheered wildly. The Communists laughed and booed and then crossed the road. A large anti-apartheid demonstration was building up outside South Africa House.

Jeffrey Hamm mounted the plinth and walked towards me with a serious look on his face. My first thought was 'Should I have said International *Jewish* Communism instead of just International Communism'. But no. He had his hand out and was moving quickly towards me and suddenly it was all over, the ordeal was over and he was smiling and I was smiling and I could hear cheers and clapping and could see waving and laughing from our supporters.

'You were wonderful,' Jeffrey said, grasping my hand. 'Wonderful. That showed them. Well done . . . even when they burnt the paper . . . well done.'

For a short time, I stood on my own in the crowd and then slightly away with Les and Derek who gazed at me. I thought, 'He's going to touch me to gain strength.'

I noticed a tall good-looking young man staring at me. I tried to guess his age, probably around twenty, not much older than that. He wore a dark expensive-looking overcoat. He was very tall with brown hair and dark eyes. For a moment I thought I was looking at the young Oswald Mosley.

He approached me, put out his hand and said – 'You spoke well and you are a credit to the movement. I congratulate you.' There was a silver pin on his lapel which I recognised as the symbol of the Falange in Spain.

As he walked away, he was soon joined by a small man with long grey hair who really did look as if he'd just emerged from the bottom of the River Rhine. Alberich in person. But with him was a stunning-looking girl.

'Who's that,' I asked Freddie Shepherd, the Islington branch leader.

'Don't you know who that was, silly tart.' Freddie called all the Youth League boys 'silly tarts' and thought it was funny.

'That's Alexander Mosley. The Leader and Lady Ds elder son. He's supposed to be a genius. I've never seen him at a meeting before, though he hangs round 302 quite a lot.'

'I'm sure I know the people he's with.'

'You should do. The little bloke's Sid Proud, your brother-in-law's boss at the Spanish Travel Bureau and that's Cynthia, his daughter. Supposed to be some sort of student in Paris. Can't miss her. Not with those knockers.'

I walked towards my parents and Lovene.

When Jeffrey Hamm finished his speech about economics, Mosley's wage-price mechanism, trade unions and the coming corporate state and the end of a common European currency after Mosley came to power, he came up and again shook my hand warmly.

'Mrs Grundy,' he said looking at my beaming mother. 'Quite a performance, eh? We'll make a Mosley speaker of him yet.'

Mosley kept his promise and one Saturday afternoon, not long after my Trafalgar Square speech, I was invited to headquarters to meet him.

I put on my only casual jacket which I was buying on HP from a shop in Edgware Road with money I earned from Chiltern Stores as a delivery boy.

I got nine shillings and sixpence for four hours work (9am–1pm) and about seven and sixpence as tips from flat owners, most of them Jews in the Baker Street, Dorset Square area. The jacket was powder blue – like the one Johnnie Ray wore – and I put on dark trousers, highly polished black leather shoes, a white shirt which my mother had ironed carefully and a blue tie.

I waited in the narrow corridor by the bookshop at 302 until Jeffrey Hamm came out of The Leader's small office. He said, 'This way, Grundy' as if I was some promising cadet called in to see the general. I entered nervously and Mosley said, 'Sit down, Grundy. I hear you've been doing good work for the Movement.'

He had grown quite heavy. He was wearing his old grey campaign suit without the large silver flash and circle in his lapel. Now and again he flashed his small eyes at me and I thought, 'He's trying to hypnotise me,' and I remembered what Lovene had said so often that she hated the way he looked at you like a fox, 'like a great cunning hungry fox.'

'Hamm tells me that you want to expand the youth wing of the Movement. I approve. I want to see young people forming branches all over the country but I don't want to see any of the older members involved. I don't believe anyone over twenty- five is a youth. Twenty-one. That's the limit. Do you agree?'

Of course, I agreed and thought. 'He's saying that because of Flockhart and the Bum Corps.'

I asked him if we could call the group 'Mosley Youth,' and he said he was flattered and honoured.

'You spoke well at Trafalgar Square and Hamm said you were not fazed when a Communist burnt our paper.'

He paused and fixed his eyes on me as if I was an insect under a glass slab.

'I'll let you into a secret. Union will be re-named Action.' That was the paper's name before the war. I wanted to ask him if members could again do the salute but didn't. He said, 'And I'm pleased that you young speakers never attack Jews from the platform. No more of that nonsense. In fact, if we had some Jewish members that wouldn't be a bad thing at all.'

Was he joking? Jews in Union Movement?

He grew almost fatherly. 'How are your parents? Good people. And your mother? A fine woman. You're very close to her, I'm told. I was very close to my mother, too.'

There was a long silence. What on earth could I say that would interest this great man? He said, 'Good. Thank you for coming to see me.'

I went out and Hamm went in. The door closed and I stood in the corridor shaking.

When I reached home, exhilarated and telling myself this had really happened and wasn't just a dream, my mother opened the door, eyes shining in anticipation of what I had to tell her.

But before I could speak, she told me of her own wonderful news. The Leader's son, Alexander, had telephoned and asked to speak to me. 'He sounded just like The Leader,' she said. 'Do you want to hear what he said? He said that people in the East End said that Lady Mosley was the best advert for the Movement but that Mrs Grundy was a good second because of her dedication, leaflet bashing and canvassing and for looking after the children of top Nazis but above all for being the mother of the young man who was doing such wonderful things for the Movement.'

'He sounded just like OM. Just like him. If anything happened to The Leader, I'm sure Alexander would step into his shoes and take over.'

In the kitchen, she put on the kettle and said, 'Now tell me what happened. Did you see The Leader? Did he mention me?'

An hour or so later the phone rang again. I heard a giggle and then a pantomime cockney voice. '*Watcha* mate. Is vat the Mosley Yufe bloke? You wanna meet up and come and see Bill 'Aley and the Commies tonight with me and me big bruvver?'

Bill Haley and the Comets had just arrived in Britain from America and were thumping out 'Rock Around the Clock.' Teenagers were going mad, ripping up cinema seats and girls wetting themselves and fainting.

I realised it must be the Mosley boys and told the voice at the other end that I didn't like Bill Haley, though I thought Elvis Presley had a good voice and I also liked Buddy Holly.

'Well then, that's good, 'aint it like? We'll have to get Elvis to join the Movement, won't we? Shouldn't be difficult. Flog 'im a copy of Union before he goes on stage. (more giggles) 'Glad ya like Bloody Holly. Blue Days and Black Shirts. Bet ya like that one, eh?'

Then came another kind of voice. 'This is Max. Max Mosley. Do you know, Trevor, that there are five million teenagers in this country with an annual purchasing power of around £800 million, Could you tell me, only roughly of course, how many of them have joined your branch of Union Movement and tell me, only roughly mind you, what percentage of their incomes they're spending on Union Movement products?'

He handed the phone over and I heard more laughter. 'Do accept my apologies, Trevor. My brother has been on an advanced English language course at Limehouse and will be all right after a long lie down.'

I arranged to meet Alexander at an Italian coffee bar that recently opened next door to the Classic Cinema in Baker Street.

He handed the phone back to Max. 'Sorry, can't make it meeself, mate. Goin' dawn the 21s coffee bar just now. Gonna try and get Tommy Steele and me new mate Marty Wilde to join the Movement, so wish me luck, like.'

Max was a few weeks younger than me and I'd often told boys at school about the day his mother was arrested and how the police came and ripped her tiny baby from her breast and thrown her into prison on her own with dozens of prostitutes and women who tried to steal her jewels.

I asked my father if he'd lend me ten shillings so I could buy Alexander a cup of coffee. He gave me a pound note and said if it was for the son of Oswald Mosley, he didn't want any change.

I wandered down to Baker Street and stood outside the café recognising some of the Jewish teenagers who lived in the flats where I delivered groceries on a Saturday. There was a long queue outside the cinema which was showing Casablanca. I waited for five minutes, then ten and grew impatient after quarter of an hour because it was raining and I had neither a coat nor an umbrella. Most of the people lining up for tickets wore duffel coats and donkey jackets and around their necks, colourful college and university scarves. Some were amused and others embarrassed by the presence of a hunchback limping along the long line with his hands cupped, begging for money. When I looked closely, I saw that the beggarman was Alexander Mosley. Only then did I realise I was about to spend time with a scion of the Mad Mitfords, whose father rode around his estate and into his house to catch one of his six daughters and give her a good thrashing with a riding whip to tickle his sense of humour or appease his perverted sexual appetite.

When Alexander saw me, he straightened up to his full six foot three inches and smiled as if to say that's the sort of thing one does to amuse oneself in London when it's raining.

We went into the coffee shop and I had money to order two *cappuchinos* and two spaghetti Bologniases, which I heard a young Jew with two girls refer to as Spaghetti Bollocksnakeds. Alexander who was almost two years older than me and far taller spoke to the waiter in fluent Italian. He told me he could also speak French, German and Spanish and a bit of Gaelic from his days in Ireland after the war.

'I'm sorry Max was such a pain,' he said. 'It's all a joke to him. He finds it hard to believe that a teenager like yourself surrounded by millions of girls in one of the most exciting cities in the world spends Saturday afternoons speaking about Europe which he's never been to on a platform and Sunday evenings selling *Union* to people in some of the most run-down parts of the East End.'

It didn't take me long to see that Alexander and Max had little time for their father's Movement, or even his politics and that they both saw me as more than odd, perhaps even mentally retarded.

So why that telephone call and this meeting? What did Max and Alexander Mosley want to know about the people I knew and spent time with, the people who followed their father, the people who would save Britain from the Jews and coloured invaders from the Caribbean?

He told me that he and Max were brought up in Ireland. Sir Oswald regarded him as a stay-at-home bookworm. Max was his favourite. As a small child, he was filled with the spirit of adventure. Lady Mosley called her youngest son 'the determined one.' In his early teens, before he went to school in Germany, he would disappear for days and go riding on his own on a pony. One night, a fire broke out at the castle and no one found out who, or what, started it but precious family heirlooms went up in smoke. Alexander had been alone with his father and the two of them, plus two Irish family servants, held a large blanket while a maid jumped onto it from the top floor.

I said I knew the family had lived in Ireland because we received a card showing Sir Oswald, Lady Mosley and the two boys standing by a fireplace posing.

'We send people Christmas cards? I didn't know that. Who sends them? Surely not my mother. Christian festivals mean nothing to her or my father.'

He told me he had no wish to go to university and he didn't know what he wanted out of life. 'My father wants me to be an accountant. I want to be God.'

I told him I might become a vicar, and he gave me the Mosley 'insect under a glass' stare and stood up. I thought he was leaving. Instead, he put a coin into the jukebox and Elvis's 'Jailhouse Rock' made the girls with the young Jewish pop fan stop talking and start wriggling.

'For various reasons, this is my father's favourite. Max does a perfect imitation of Presley when the Windsors come to see my parents in Paris. They do so love the line "*you're the cutest jailbird I ever did see*" and the way Max points his hand at my mother when Elvis delivers that line.'

Alexander told me that he worked for a travel agency, the first one allowed to operate in Spain after the war. It was owned by a man called Sid Proud, who both loved and hated his father and who called Jeffrey Hamm a Pope's Nark after the secretary of Union Movement's conversion to Roman Catholicism.

I asked if he had many friends in London. He said he didn't have friends anywhere, just Max his brother though now and again he might call on me and talk to my parents about pre-war days and why they still follow his father. Perhaps he was going to write a book. He seemed clever enough to do that.

I told him how my mother had horrified the vicar when she told him how she felt when she first saw his father.

I said, 'She told him it was like coming face to face with Jesus. She said he came into a room where they were waiting before a meeting in Brighton. When he came in, they all gave the Fascist salute. She said his hair was glistening in the light because of the rain outside and that was the moment she made up her mind to follow him to the end of her life whatever happened.'

'Oh God,' said Alexander. 'She said that? Old members. I suppose it's what keeps him going, the old actor with grease-paint on his face, hungry for the final round of applause before the play ends and the safety curtain comes down.'

I was speechless.

We left the café and I walked back to Blandford Square, Alexander to his room somewhere in Chelsea. I had to get to bed early because there was always a youth meeting at Islington Market on Sundays at 11am. Sometimes I attracted a crowd as large as thirty people, plus a plain-clothes policeman with a notebook.

From Islington, we'd go in a car to Earl's Court or Brompton Oratory where we'd stand outside shouting out 'Union, the anti-Communist newspaper.'

Jeffrey Hamm often came out with Irish Catholics who were off to the pub. He said the Irish in London were a hundred per cent behind Mosley because he had condemned the Black and Tans in the 1920s.

I said to John Wood, 'But that's forty years ago.' He said, 'That doesn't matter. The Irish are like elephants They never forget.'

8

WOUNDS THAT LET IN THE LIGHT

Still spinning from Mosley's successful meetings of the previous year, 1957 was a busy year for all of us.

Coaches were hired from friends in the East End transport business and sometimes on a Sunday, we'd go to somewhere along the south coast, hold a meeting and then pack into the pub and talk about what it would be like when the bells rang after Mosley came to power. Would he be a President or a Prime Minister or just The Leader like Hitler was the Der Fuhrer and Mussolini was Il Duce? Who would be in charge of Immigration, Jeffrey Hamm or Bob Row. Would my father be made Postmaster-General because of his experience as a telephone operator at Paddington Exchange?

Once there, the beer crates would appear from the back of the coach and the drinking would begin. The usual slogans were shouted and then the old BUF song *Bye Bye Blackshirts* to the tune *of Bye Bye Blackbirds* and the Jewish song *Abie, Abie, Abie My Boy/What are you waiting for now*? The latter was about a Jewish boy who was nervous about marrying his girlfriend. When the word *Abie* was intoned, members rubbed their noses and hunched their backs to imitate what they thought was a caricature of Fagan or Shylock or even Judas Iscariot, his hands out for thirty pieces of silver.

After half a dozen beers or so, sleeves were rolled up and sometimes shirts removed to reveal flash and circle tattoos, even swastikas, along with old proudly won scars from battles against Jews and Communists at Ridley Road after Jeffrey Hamm drew crowds of thousands after the war. Voices and bottles were raised as we sang the English version of Giovenezza – Brother Blackshirts/Join your legion/Keep the flag forever flying. Some of the old-timers sang the 'Horst Wessel' song in German while passing cars were given the Nazi salute.

I watched my most loyal youth league comrade, Les, with increasing concern. I felt responsible for him, even though he was a little older than me. His parents from

DOI: 10.4324/9781003375722-9

Ireland sent him to some minor English public school when he was thirteen or so but he couldn't keep up with his peers and he failed his O levels and got a job behind the counter selling cloth and clothing to mainly wealthy Jews who lived at the right end of Edgware Road towards Marble Arch. He was caught taking money from the till, put on probation and later on met my mother who had a part-time job in a shop to supplement my father's low income at Paddington Exchange. One day he came to Praed Street, heard me speak about a new world around the corner, joined us for a drink afterwards in the Scotch Ale House and said he wanted to join Union Movement and make my dreams come true.

Les had a large and usually half-open mouth which made him look moronic. He became the effective 'girlfriend' of Freddie Shepherd, the Islington Branch leader, and they had their arms round one another in the back of the coach. Les suddenly had a lot of money at his disposal and bought everyone drinks at the pub.

One night he saw me looking at him critically and he said, aggressively, 'Don't look like that, Trevor. Freddie's got loads of money and gives some of it to me. So what? If you want to carry Jewboy food parcels up flights of stairs in Bickenhall Mansions for nine shillings, that's up to you. I don't.'

Derek always stood loyally next to the speaker's platform and would come along to the bars but never drink alcohol. He usually sat on his own reading either *Mein Kampf* or one of the picture books about life in the Third Reich. One of the books was in Gothic script. 'Can you understand all that stuff,' I asked. He shook his head and mumbled, 'No but I like the pictures.'

By the time the coach returned to 302, most of its occupants were drunk. A few papers had been sold. I'd spoken to children licking ice creams and Ron Clucas had alienated the people who saw him slap his large stomach and tell men who'd fought Hitler in the war that if there hadn't been a war Britain would be ruled by British people, not Jews, Communists, liberals. He ended his speeches delivered from the Mosley Youth platform calling on people to Keep Britain White.

Once a small group of men came up to me after one of my south coast speeches. I thought I was in for a beating. One told me I was a good speaker but should be speaking for the Labour Party, not one run by a multi-millionaire who didn't even live in England.

I said, 'Labour betrayed the working class when they wouldn't implement Mosley's plan for the unemployed in 1931.'

A man old enough to be my grandfather said, 'So you were around in 1931, were you? Mosley! Should have been hanged after the war like his playmate William Joyce, your famous Lord fucking Haw Haw.'

The week after any outing to the coast, I'd write in my weekly column in the new *Action* newspaper how a large group of dedicated teenagers won more recruits after a successful meeting in Southend, Brighton or Shoreham-by-the-Sea.

Max and Alexander were regular visitors to 40 Blandford Square.

Max sat on my bed, looked up at a large portrait of his father in his black fencing-style jacket, and said, 'The trouble is, Union Movement is made-up of a bunch of clones and clowns who aren't serious about achieving power. They just want to hang around pubs and bars and talk about the good old days when they were beating up Jews. When I told you there are five million teenagers in Britain, I was talking about the vast political power of the young. Apart from their spending power, they could change the face of Britain if they were mobilised by some political force. But where's the appeal of Don Clucas, Derek Ashton with his pictures of Hitler on his bedroom wall and all the others who are so out-of-touch with reality. The Teddy Boys would be a better lot than what you've got. How many do you have? Twenty, thirty at the very most?'

I wanted to say, 'But Jesus only had twelve' but didn't.

I told him that the lower and upper sixth forms at Tenison's had formed a skiffle group called The Harlequins and that I'd been asked to join because I knew a bit about music and played the violin.

Max's eyes opened wide.

He said that he could arrange a massive party at an empty flat that was available near Victoria Station. I could pass the word around and young people would come to an all-night party in a few weeks from now. He said, 'There must be over a hundred kids at your school over sixteen or seventeen and if each of them brought three or four friends.'

It was the time before pocket calculators were commonplace. But Max Mosley didn't need one. He had one in his golden head.

He said that having regular parties would be a way of attracting young, lively, normal people – girls as well as boys – and eventually point them towards the New Union Party without even mentioning Hitler, Mussolini, Franco, or even Oswald Mosley. And if we could attract Jews, so much the better.

He said, 'This is a new age and we're part of it.'

Both Max and Alexander were keen to meet young Jews and talk to them.

I told them about my childhood friend Timothy and how his father was Irish but his mother was Jewish. He still lived at the other end of Blandford Square and excelled at rugby and cricket but was something of an outsider at Haberdasher's. His parents did not live in a large house in Hampstead, just a tiny flat on the top floor of a German bomb-damaged former square next to Marylebone Station. And when his peer group found out that his father was a meat porter at Smithfield Market, that was the end of him.

I told Alexander and Max that I'd invite Tim round to the house and they could meet him and talk.

'Have the boys gone?' asked my mother when she heard the front door close.

'Did they enjoy their sandwiches and tea? And daddy changed cheques for them otherwise they'd have had no money for the weekend. They're a credit to The Leader, always thinking of ways of boosting the Movement and such respect for Old Members. They want to know everything about the Old Days and why we so hate the Jews. Good to see they're travelling on the same road we travelled on before the war. It's wonderful you have formed such a close friendship with them. And you and Max are almost the same age, brothers really.'

I put my arms around her and gave her a hug. She clung to me and said, 'Don't let me down, Trevor. Now that the rector has gone, you're my hope, you and The Leader are my only hope.'

While I held her, I saw she had placed a silver-framed picture of me speaking at Trafalgar Square next to the picture of Sir Oswald in his black fencing jacket on the mantelpiece and for the first time in her presence, a wave of fear rolled over me.

Listening to Max Mosley changed the way I saw myself. I became determined to become normal, a teenager in 1957, not a victim of Regulation 18b in 1940.

I joined *The Harlequins*. Practice sessions took place once or twice a week at the home of the lead singer, Frostie from 6 Arts. Having finished paying for my Johnnie Ray jacket, I opened an account with a music shop in Edgware Road and started paying every week for a steel-stringed 'Spanish' guitar.

Within a few weeks, I'd mastered all the main chords necessary for songs such as Lonnie Donegan's 'Rock Island Line' and 'Midnight Special' and other hits which included 'Aint You Glad,' 'Cumberland Gap,' and my own favourite 'Cotton Fields Back Home.'

At the start, I was uncomfortable because the boys in the group knew I was connected to a strange political set-up that they called *The Blackbelts*. But one of the boys who played the washboard with his mum's thimbles on his fingers lightened the mood at my audition. When we reached the lines which said –

I saw Peter, Paul and Moses
Playing ring around the roses

He changed them to –

I saw Peter, Paul and Mosley
Playing rings around the rosary.

And that was it. I was in. No one in the group again mentioned Fascism, Jews or coloured Invaders from the West Indies. For the first time in my life, I asked myself, 'Well, what does Fascism or Sir Oswald Mosley mean to these boys, my contemporaries, who just want to have a good time after school, who want to enjoy themselves with their guitars and washboards, their tea chests and their pretty, or not so pretty, pony-tailed girls from South London who idolise their future pop star boyfriends?'

I very much wanted a girl to sing to and a few weeks after joining The Harlequins, my long-prayed-for-Madonna came onto the scene in the shape of a twenty-something woman from Dulwich called Sonia Marchand.

When she got to know us and follow us around different parts of London, she laughed and said she was fifty per cent Scottish, fifty per cent Italian and one hundred per cent crazy about the six teenage boys from Archbishop Tenison's who she heard playing at a small coffee bar one Friday night in the late Summer of '57.

She had long black hair down to her waist, heavily made-up dark eyes, a figure like an hourglass. She wore stylish clothes like some *avant-garde* painter or novelist in a Hemingway novel set in Paris in the 1920s.

When she met us, Sonia was on the point of a divorce, having been married for two years to a French banker who wanted to move to Canada.

She wandered into a café off Wardour Street on her own but was soon joined by a good-looking man. That night we were auditioning for a regular stint so we could attract customers who'd turn into fans. Frostie said we'd play for nothing, just a coffee and spaghetti at the end of each session. 'Not asking for much then, are you?' said the man who ran the shop. 'We'll give it a go but if you're no good, you're out on your ears. Kids are queuing up to play. Where the fuck do all the tea chests come from?'

Sonia asked Frostie to join them for a glass of wine. Then she beckoned to me to come over and when the man she was with went to the lavatory she passed me a card with her telephone number on it.

'You lucky sod, Grundy,' said Micky Barrell, a school friend who left when he was fifteen to become an apprentice in the print industry. He wanted to be our business manager. 'That's about the best-looking bird I've ever seen. What does she see in you, I ask myself?'

'Must be his eyes,' said Fisher. 'Look at his eyes, all sad and sincere. Can't be his guitar playing because that's bloody awful,' and he sang –

We all realise
It must be his eyes
'cus his guitar-playing's so bloody awful.

I said, 'About as bloody awful as your lyrics,' and he threw one of his thimbles at me and we laughed.

I rapidly tired of coursework at school mainly because I was poor at geography and found it hard to tolerate our senior history teacher, Mr Birchenough, the man who terrorised my generation with his cane and who now lectured us on democratic, peace-loving England taking on the world and forming an Empire based on progress, fairness, Christianity and democracy.

Once I asked him why it was good that the British had an Empire but bad when the Germans wanted one. He stared at me and said if I hadn't been allowed, for some unknown reason, to be in the sixth form I would be caned. He said I had an un-manly reputation and after five years in the ATC still didn't know how to march properly or un-load and then re-load a rifle while blindfolded.

He must have heard in the masters' common room from Miss Fry, the senior English lecturer who wrote poems to her dead lover who was killed by Fascists during the Spanish Civil War, about the day I had to read aloud before the other students the introduction to *Pride and Prejudice* by Jane Austen. Without me knowing it, Fisher underlined the opening words in red ink and I read them out stifling laughter that became infectious –

'When Jane was sixteen, she grew her hair and longed for balls.'

Birchenough was one of the many masters who had returned from the war a lonely, embittered man who damned anyone he didn't like in history as a Hitlerite.

A handful of senior boys refused to have anything to do with the Air Training Corps and one of the brightest, who seemed bound for Oxford or Cambridge, said that all our teachers had undergone shattering experiences during the war but were unable to free themselves from the past by talking about it.

If we asked them anything about the war and what they did in, blank faces answered our inquiries and voices said that it was not their job to talk about personal issues. All they had done was their duty. Only one of them could talk intelligently to us, a tall teacher of English and French called Mr Farrell who'd been an officer with the Gurkhas in Burma. Towards the end of the war, he was posted to France where he married a French woman and where he learnt the language. I asked him after school if he believed the Germans were as bad as they were being portrayed in films, radio programmes and in books by the dozen.

'Much worse,' he said.

'But did you see atrocities or are the stories about what happened anti-German propaganda,' I asked.

'You have no idea how vile they were, Grundy and yet I'm told you sympathise with those Mosley people. How can you, an intelligent boy who might receive tertiary education one day at the expense of the British taxpayer, give support to such monsters who want to destroy everything of value and all the things we hold dear to us in Britain? Who is getting at you? I remember when you were eleven or twelve, not much higher than the desk here, saying in class that the Jews would fight the Germans to the last drop of English blood. Where on earth did you get that from?'

I looked up at the man I so admired. 'No one asked,' I said.

'You must break from them. Get away completely. One of Dr Robinson's friends was at Trafalgar Square when you spoke and was shattered when he was told you were an Archbishop Tenison's Grammar School boy. Those Mosley people will use you and then destroy you.' He shook his head. 'It's hard to understand why the French let Oswald Mosley live in their country after what the Germans did to them.'

It was only then that I realised how widespread was the knowledge that I was a Mosleyite.

I cycled to 302, chained up my bike and told Jeffrey Hamm what Mr Farrell said to me.

'That man is probably a Communist. A lot of well-meaning English people relate to France because of that country's self-praise about their respect for intellectuals, most of them Jewish Communists. But what use are intellectuals with their books and their poems and endless cups of coffee and endless calls for violence as long as they're not there when it happens and as long as someone else pulls the trigger?'

He went upstairs and came down with a book that a publisher sent to Euphorion Publications for review. It was Sisley Huddleston's *France, The Tragic Years*. Hamm said its author was no relation to Father Trevor Huddleston, who was one of the

Anglican Church's most active opponents of apartheid in South Africa. Hamm said, 'Don't be taken in by Communist schoolteachers. I was a teacher in Wales and then in the Falklands and the profession is riddled with fellow travellers. The Communists don't go in for numbers like the Labour Party and Conservatives. They make converts and then tell them to maintain a low profile and work with the trade unions and embrace popular causes, especially Christian causes. Your Mr Farrell is probably one of them. Read this (he handed me the book) and you'll understand what happened in France and how the Communists and Jews crucified the greatest Frenchman since Napoleon, Marshall Petain. That great hero of Verdun was pulled out of retirement at a time of crisis. He knew it was pointless fighting Hitler and came to terms with him to save French lives and the two men made an honourable settlement until the Jews in New York pushed America into the war. It's all in here. Read it and review it for Action.'

Before I left 302, Hamm said, 'One thing before you go. I think that music is a good thing and that it's right you mix with people of your own age who aren't in the Movement but don't forget your first duty. You have an example to set. I've been told that you spend most of your time now with a skiffle group playing Negro songs in cafes in the West End. And I saw your sales figures last week. Really bad. *Terrible* in fact.'

Somehow, I would have to arrange life so I could get two or three A levels, sell *Action* for Mosley and sing Negro songs with The Harlequins with Fisher and Frostie.

On the way home that night, I bumped into Father Crisp, who was delivering his parish paper and circulating pamphlets advertising a meeting of the Campaign for Nuclear Disarmament at St Mark's Church the following week. He saw me and stopped and said, 'You should not be doing what you're doing, Trevor Grundy. You'll fail you're A levels and where will you be then?' In a sing-song voice he said, 'You can't be a Fascist and a Christian, no you can't.' And then in case I'd missed the message first time round, it came again louder, 'You can't be a Fascist and a Christian.'

After that, my mother and I stopped attending church, and there was no further discussion at 40 Blandford Square about me becoming the Mosley of the Anglican Church.

In my room that night, I sat by the window and stared at the wall outside. I imagined it getting closer every day. I opened Northanger Abbey which was another of my 'A' level books. I read a few lines and closed it. It all seemed so silly, so meaningless. But I laughed when I remembered how Jane Austen, when she was just a bit younger than me, had longed for balls.

In the morning, I went to Regent's Park and hurled Austen's book into the lake.

'What are you going to do with the rest of your life?' I asked myself. I was no longer sure about anything, not even The Leader. Maybe I was the one who should grow hair and long for balls.

My mother opened the door. 'Come and have a cup of tea, if you're not doing your homework.'

I was struggling through the opening chapter of Gibbon's *Decline and Fall of the Roman Empire*, which I'd ordered from Marylebone Public Library which Lovene called our university.

'Some lass called Sonia Something rang and said would you ring her. She said it was to do with a music concert? Sounded foreign. Not a Jew, I hope.'

She closed the door and then opened it again, annoyed I was taking no notice of her.

'You're going to get yourself into a real mess mixing with lasses you don't know. Oh, and a friend of Freddie Shepherd's rang and said the Sunday meeting has been cancelled. And Leslie's mother telephoned. Someone has hit him and he was treated at Paddington Hospital but is home so will you ring her?'

I went to his house in Sussex Gardens, which was a mixture of a private home and a bed-and-breakfast lodge. His mother opened the door. She was Irish and a heavily built woman. I saw the face of one of Leslie's pretty dark-haired, ivory-skinned sisters peering at me from behind a door.

Mrs Rochford let me have it.

'You're a bad young man and you're a terrible influence on Leslie. He's been in trouble with the authorities before and you knew that and now look what's happened.' I thought that she would hit me. 'You've introduced him to a collection of Fascist hooligans in Islington and now he's trying to get his own sisters to join this God-forsaken Mosley Movement, whatever it's called. That Mosley man is evil and I'm saying to you, Trevor Grundy, you should stop this nonsense and leave Leslie and the rest of my family alone. Stay away! Do you hear me? You're still at school and you should be studying to make something of yourself, not standing on boxes at street corners talking about things you know nothing about. Do you hear me? Things you know nothing about!'

She said an ambulance brought her son home and he was upstairs in bed. I asked if I could see him. She said I could but for the last time.

Les was in bed and I could hardly see his eyes. They were in the back of his head and his face looked like a football that had just been kicked. 'What the hell happened to you? Who did this to you? The communists? Have you been to Islington? Does Freddie know about this?' He stayed silent. His mouth was swollen, which made his lips seem enormous. He was crying. After a long silence he said, 'It wasn't the communists.' I drew closer because his voice was hard to hear. 'It wasn't them. It was our lot.'

I drew even closer to him. 'Do you want me to tell Jeffrey Hamm? I'll go down to 302 now and tell him. He'll do something. Jeffrey Hamm won't tolerate indiscipline but you've got to tell me what happened and who did this to you. I need names.'

'Don't tell the police and don't tell Jeffrey Hamm or anyone else. And you! You can sod off! You don't ever want to know what this is all about and what's going on. They're a bunch of violent fuckers from top to the bottom. Look at me! Look! I've had it! I'm finished. Leave me alone! I don't want to see you or anyone else in that fucking lunatic asylum again.'

He sat up, violence on his face. 'Do you hear me?' Then in voice full of loathing, 'Do you hear me Trevor fucking-goody-fucking-two-shoes?'

When I left the house, Mrs Rochford slammed the door, and I turned and took a final look at the house which I'd earmarked as a good place for Mosley Youth meetings.

Later that day, I got on a bus and went to Islington and spoke to one of Fred's sidekicks, a tall, seedy-looking man in his late twenties or early thirties, someone called Greg who my father said was a special branch plant. Anyone in the Movement my father didn't like was a Special Branch plant working for M15. He was one of Fred's business partners. They had a couple of stalls at Islington Market selling second-hand clothes and shoes.

He eyed me up and down and said it was none of my business. 'Don't talk to me about that little shit. He's been taking Freddie for a ride long enough. I was late. Supposed to be at the pub with the takings. Got back late and found your little mate Les with his hands in the till. He got what was coming to him. And if you've got anything between yer fucking ears, you should keep quiet and fuck off back to where you come from. We've had enough of you little shits running round making out you're the only people what does anything for the Old Man.'

Anger was rising. His right fist was clenched but still down by his thigh. I kept an eye on it.

'Freddie said to me last night.' He said, 'Greg, these kids are burning themselves out but when they've gone, we'll still be there for the Old Man. They won't. We will.'

I said, 'Les is in a terrible state. Can I speak to Fred? On a one-to-one branch leader basis?'

'Sod off,' the angry man snarled. 'Freddie don't know nothing and if you open yer fucking trap, you'll get a bicycle pump with something not so nice in it right up where the sun don't shine.'

Sonia telephoned several times before I found the courage to walk down to Marylebone Station and into one of its many phone booths. I rang the number and a voice said 'Mrs Marchand.'

I said, 'This is Trevor Grundy. We met at the café with the skiffle group and you telephoned me and . . .'

'Do you want to speak to Sonia?' asked a voice at the other end. 'This is her mother-in-law, Eileen.'

There was laughter and then, 'It took you long enough to pick up the phone, didn't it?'

'I've been tied-up for the last couple of days and . . .'

'There's no need to be scared of me,' said Sonia. 'I just want to see you and talk. Ronnie Fisher, your sweet washboard player, lives in the same block of flats and he told me that at long last you've become almost normal. He told me you're an avid supporter of Oswald Mosley. I've read quite a bit about him in French and Italian newspapers. I'd love to talk. In short, I'd like to get to know you. Interested?'

I only had ninepence. It would be so embarrassing if I couldn't put another threepence in the slot, so I had to be quick.

'Yes. Well, I mean. Why not? That is Yes. I don't know all that much about Mosley, or anything really, but if you want to. Yes then. Why not?'

It kept going through my head – You're not yet eighteen and she told Fisher she was twenty-four. And she's married. The only girl I'd ever been close to in my life was Lovene but she was my sister. The other was Angela Watson, the fifteen-year-old daughter of Jimmy Watson, branch leader in Watford. I'd danced with her after a Movement dinner eighteen months before and kept standing on her toes.

I struggled to control a stammer. 'Yes. I'd like to meet you but not round here because . . .'

She said, 'Stop being so evasive. I'm not going to eat you. My husband, Yvan, is here if that makes you feel any better. Would you like to speak to him?'

'No,' I said. 'I'm not scared at all it's just that . . .'

'Hello Trevor' came a friendly voice with a strong French accent. 'Sonia says you are all fascinating, or should I say fascist-making. young men and that you will come and have supper with us here one evening, so please make arrangements. I hope to see you before I go to Canada.'

'There,' said Sonia. 'You're invited.' She told me how to get to the flat. 'But you know. Where Ronnie lives. They're on the second floor and we're on the third. There are buses back to the Oval every twenty minutes after ten o'clock and you can come straight after school for an *aperitif*.'

'What's that?' I asked. But the line went dead and so there was no need to insert my final threepence.

At school, Fisher told me that Sonia's husband had left for Canada. So, what sort of man would encourage anyone to go and have supper with his wife while he was away? Father Crisp was no longer in my life to ask about this. Supper alone with Sonia. I wasn't scared. I was terrified.

That night, I told Alexander Mosley what had happened. He was now a regular visitor to the house, pampered by my mother who always spoke to him about his resemblance to Sir Oswald. I saw how much that annoyed him but said nothing.

He told me in my tiny bedroom, where a large picture of his father dominated everything, 'I don't know what to make of your family. But I can see how sincere your mother is about my father. It's sad. Tragic, even.'

'Sad? Tragic? How can you say that? We're so lucky to know and support him. Think of supporting Harold Macmillan or the bloke who runs the Labour Party, those old men from the old parties.'

Alexander changed the subject while replacing one of the books on my shelf, Alexander Raven's *Civilisation as Divine Superman*. He said he was delighted to hear about Sonia and asked what she looked like.

He became wise and philosophical about a subject that frightened me, sex.

'In France, young men of a certain age and class are taken by their fathers to a brothel and left there for the afternoon. Not in the arms of some insensitive tart but probably one of their father's old lovers. They're gentle and understanding and afterwards, well, afterwards you're a man. You have balls. It makes it all so much easier later on. There's so much dishonesty about sex, all the lies, all the awful fumbling and self-flagellation.'

He said, 'You must go and see your Mrs Sonia Marchand and let things happen. How old are you, seventeen and three quarters? Well, it's about time, I'd say.'

I wished Alexander would come with me to supper and show me what to do. But the conversation had put some long-needed lead into my pencil, or so I thought.

Perhaps Sonia would accompany me to a party that Max was organising at a flat near Victoria Station. He said in an impeccable cockney accent that he'd picked up after visits – to the East End with the Movement's legendary Bailey Brothers, that it would be the biggest rock and roll gathering ever and would go on all night, perhaps the whole weekend.

I went to bed that night after playing Heartbreak Hotel which Joe, the van driver at Chiltern Stores, had lent me. Ron Fisher had telephoned and said he'd told Sonia about Max Mosley's party of the year and she said she'd be there supporting the Harlequins. Before falling into a deep sleep, I wondered what it would be like turning up and being greeted with a kiss by the gorgeous Sonia. Just for once, it might stop Max Mosley treating me like a retarded curate.

On the advice of Jeffrey Hamm, I took Derek to a greasy-spoon café in Paddington and told him to stop telling people that the real leader of Union Movement was Adolf Hitler's ghost.

Derek had become so deeply disturbed he was no use to anyone and a danger to himself. Derek took no notice and Jeffrey Hamm expelled him from the Movement. Hamm said, 'We have no room for cranks.' He admitted that the expulsion hurt him because Derek was so sincere in his beliefs but would now drift towards organisations which Hamm called 'the lunatic fringe,' outfits with half a dozen Hitlerites as members, people who labelled Oswald Mosley a 'Kosher Fascist.' Some were supporters of a man who'd once been Mosley's propaganda chief in the BUF, A.K. Chesterton, who'd written a book about Mosley called *Portrait of a Leader*. Others were followers of William Joyce, another key Mosley supporter before the war who went to Germany and broadcast against Britain and the Allies under the name Lord Haw Haw. Joyce was the last man in British history to be hanged as a traitor.

Without two of my most important supporters – Les and Derek – I felt alone and lost on Saturday afternoons. Since Max and Alexander entered my world, I felt awkward standing on a platform talking to elderly supporters, a man with a dog and people going in and out of the nearby Scotch Ale House. Good-looking girls with bee-hive hairstyles and short skirts stopped, looked at one another, laughed and walked on.

At the end of my 138th meeting, Ron Clucas said to me, 'You're losing interest, aren't you? So many people said that would happen. Now it has.'

His mouth stayed open and with his white shirt, black tie and flash-and-circle belt buckle, he looked like a man selling washing powder on television. Perhaps he'll fly away with a packet of Mosley Washes Whiter soap-flakes in his hand to sanitise dirtier parts of Britain. Parts no other washing powder could reach. I downed a pint of beer, alarmed that I'd even thought of a cartoon character that involved anyone in Union Movement.

I said, 'Of course, I haven't lost interest. How could I? Mosley and the Movement mean everything to me. It's just, well, we can't carry on like this if the only people we attract are people like Derek. I mean, we're not in the 1930s, are we? Young people don't want to spend hours talking about Hitler and Rudolf Hess. Those days are gone. We've got to have a new message, a new way of attracting the right people, a new way of seeing Britain and Europe and well . . . everything really.'

I must have looked at my watch because Ron said it was time to go to the pub. But in there, with us toasting our last meeting in Praed Street, I had only one thought in my mind.

Would Sonia turn up to the party?

Disappointment registered on Max's face.

By eleven fifteen there were only a handful of people in a very large, unfurnished but potentially luxurious flat not far from Buckingham Palace. It was November, and there was no electricity or heating and the motley collection of party-goers included Max Mosley; his new girlfriend, Jean Taylor; a film-star-looking girl called Joyce, who kept saying she was waiting for someone special to arrive; a few middle-aged stragglers from a local pub and six cold and hungry make-belief musicians, The Harlequins.

To my surprise, at eleven thirty Alexander Mosley arrived with Timothy. Max and Alex met Tim through me during a skiffle practice session. My mother said that if the Leader's sons liked that kind of music, we could use the front room for as long as my father was out riding his Velocette Mac 350 motorbike round London doing The Knowledge. Tim and Alex lit some candles and sat talking to one another. Later, Max and Jean, in skin-tight blue jeans, joined them and Joyce came across, swivelled her hips and squeezed up next to Alexander.

I'd put a half bottle of Scotch in my guitar case. We sang songs, the usual skiffle stuff, and when it was time for a break, I opened the bottle and swallowed several large tots in one go. I had only been drunk once before. After an evening speech at Praed Street, I'd gone to a pub in Dorset Square, the Dorset Arms, with Les, Ron and the vegetarian and non-alcohol-drinking Derek. I consumed several pints of beer, tripped over outside, was sick in the gutter and fell flat on my face. Derek helped me to my feet and said in his Welsh sing-song voice, 'Trevor, you're drunk. What would the *Fuhrer* say?'

The London jazz clubs closed around eleven. In they came, so thanks to some sort of signal or drum-beat that only the young can hear, Max's prediction that this would be the rock n' roll party of the year was coming true.

By two o'clock, there must have been close to a hundred young people scattered around the flat, some outside in cobble-stoned mews, some drunk, some singing, some laughing, all making one hell of a noise. It was the largest gathering of girls I'd ever seen. Until then, the only time I'd seen a large group of girls was at fifth-form and sixth-form school dances. Tenison's hosted a Christmas dance every year and invited girls from a neighbouring grammar school. They were told to wear flat shoes, wear dresses that fell below their knees and have sensible hairstyles, preferably pony-tails. We danced about two feet apart, watched by schoolmasters and schoolmistresses whose own youths were spent in khaki, dark and light blue uniforms fighting Hitler and Mussolini. It was then that I realised where I'd seen Max's girlfriend, Jean, and her close friend, Joyce, before. They were both Brixton girls who'd looked so out of place at a school dance the year before, mainly because they spent the evening dancing with each other and then disappeared with a couple of the best-looking boys from the Upper Sixth. Our English teacher Miss Fry said they were the new type of girl who were shameless and who couldn't be trusted when men were around.

After a while, Max stood up with his girl. He talked and whispered in her ear, and I had a distinct impression he wasn't trying to get her to join Union Movement.

By three o'clock, the noise was almost unbearable, and one of the Harlequins told me there were policemen at the front door.

'Who's in charge here?' one of them asked.

'I am,' said Max. 'And who are you, may I ask?'

'Well, you're making too much noise. We've had complaints. Loads of them. And who owns this place?'

Max said, 'Who owns this place is none of your concern.'

I remembered the night we'd painted a flash and circle on the wall near Edgware Road and the way Max had talked to the young policeman as if they were in a restaurant and the waiter had brought the wrong bottle of wine.

He said that the music was not at all loud and that young people had every right to have a party on a Saturday night. That earned him a loud cheer from the party-goers. 'That's right, Max, mate! You tell 'em. It's the law again stopping us doing what we want to. Same as usual.'

But Max agreed that the gramophone would be turned down.

But as soon as the policemen left, he signalled for the noise to begin again and pointed at Frostie and told him to play something by Elvis or his new friend Marty Wilde from 2Is, which was pronounced as Two Eyes.

Someone said, 'Good bloke, Max. We need more people to tell the police to piss off. Who is he, anyway?'

An hour or so later, the same policemen returned. About twenty-five people came downstairs to see how Max would handle things this time round. He was the essence of charm and said the party would end at six o'clock on the dot. The police left. More cheers for Max.

The noise subsided. The drinks were finished. The party was over. A cold Sunday morning walk home awaited us. And not a sign of Sonia.

Outside, one of the Harlequins took me to one side.

'There's some poor old sod upstairs with his wife. He's just come down in his pyjamas and told me that the people own this place are trying to get rid of them because they're on a fixed low rent and the owner wants them out so he can sell. Said he didn't know the owner's name but thought he lived abroad somewhere. Strikes me the noise we're making will drive them out alright. Is that why we're here, Trev? Is that what this is all about really? And Max is the son of Mosley. Where does he live? Someone told me France somewhere.'

How could I explain that the real reason was to recruit young people into Union Movement? And anyhow I was half drunk and tired, and I felt a couple of painful spots coming up at the back of my neck, spots and boils that were turning my teenage years into a living hell.

Max organised another party for the following week. This time on a Sunday, Britain's day of rest and quiet.

More came than before, young painters and designers from the Central St Martin's School of Art, the Royal Academy of Dramatic Art and the Central School of Speech and Drama at Swiss Cottage, which was close to where I'd gone to primary school. The Harlequins were given the slow hand-clap and asked not to play. Instead, skilled fingers on acoustic guitars were heard. Trained voices rang out. A young man with the looks of James Dean danced with a girl from Sweden, who resembled Brigitte Bardot, a girl Miss Fry would have dismissed as a person not to be trusted when men were around.

Again, the police turned up but went away after being told that the flat was no longer empty, that it was now a refuge for young painters and musicians, several of them trumpet and trombone players, with nowhere else to stay.

At six the following morning, Timothy told me that Max and Alexander had asked him not only to join Union Movement but also to lead the youth wing. He looked down at me and asked if I wanted to stay in a group led by him.

Timothy with the ever-blinking eyelids, the nervous child held by his father in his bedroom overlooking an LNER station in London, Little John to my Robin Hood when we played as children in Regent's Park. How dare he? Where was my bow? Where were my arrows?

'Max has convinced me about the need for European Unity. My parents are wrong about Mosley being anti-Jewish. Max says that he wants to see it announced in *Action* that the new youth leader is Jewish. And if my father objects, I'll show him what to do. He lost his hearing in the Tank Corps and now I think he's lost his brains listening to Harold Macmillan. Max says his father will be over the moon when he hears Jews are joining Union Movement. All Alexander can do is screw his face up and make sarcastic remarks but it's Max who has it up here.'

He tapped his forehead. 'He'll take-over when Sir Oswald retires. Who knows where I'll be then?'

Bewildered and lost, I took my guitar, as I had once taken my violin, and walked from that now silent mews flat towards the bus stop and my journey back to the safe but increasingly claustrophobic 40 Blandford Square.

But as I approached the bus stop, tears in my eyes, I heard the hoot of a car and tried to see who was trying to run me down so early in the morning. My first thought was someone from the 43 Group.

'Don't look so tragic,' said Sonia Marchand. 'You can't have played that badly.'

She opened the car door and I sat beside her, admiring her olive skin, black eyebrows and well-shaped nose and mouth and jawline. I thought of a girl I'd seen in a Renaissance painting. A curtain of dark brown hair fell like a waterfall on to her shoulders, and she wore a sky-blue sweater underneath a black leather jacket.

'Coffee at my flat and some breakfast and considering the way you look – and smell – a shower wouldn't be lost on you.'

As we turned right into Buckingham Palace Road, I saw five figures walking arm-in-arm towards St James's Park and Buckingham Palace – Max, Alexander, Jean, Joyce and Timothy. Sonia stopped at the lights. They stopped and looked in at Sonia, then at me and walked on without as much as a smile or a wave goodbye.

I left Sonia's flat at around eight fifteen the following day and closed the door softly. As I was tiptoeing down the flight of stairs, I bumped into Ronnie Fisher. He looked eager and alert and ready for Tenison's in his well-brushed black sixth-form blazer. Fisher knew what he wanted and that was to become a cartographer like his father after his 'A' levels in June 1958.

'What on earth are you doing here?' he asked. 'What are you dressed like that for? Where've you been all night?'

I asked him in a man-to-man voice not to tell anyone at school because I'd get my mother to write a note.

I noticed his pace increase as we approached the bus stop he turned and said, 'Lucky sod.'

I returned home but had forgotten my front-door key. My mother opened the door with a semi-tragic look on her face. She wore a cotton headscarf around her head when she did the housework and the image of a painting that I'd seen in the National Gallery of the woman at the well talking to Jesus came to mind.

'Where have you been?' she asked. 'I've been sick to death with worry.'

I said, 'Look, Mum. It's too complicated to explain and I want to have a bath and a sleep. I'm not feeling well. Will you ring the school secretary and say I've had another bilious attack? That always works.'

In the afternoon, she came to my room with a cup of tea, two boiled eggs and butter and toast cut up as soldiers.

'Alexander, The Leader's son, rung but I didn't want to disturb you. Some silly lass asked to speak to Anthony Perkins. Is that supposed to be you?'

She stroked my face.

'I've got some make-up that will hide that spot. They'll go away one day. It's all part of growing up.'

Alexander came round that evening. He lolled back in a chair with an amused look on his face. A picture of Sir Oswald in a black fencing jacket looked down on us.

'Well,' he said like a French father wondering how his troubled son had got on in the brothel, 'the deed is done?'

In those days, I believed if you told a friend something in confidence it was as safe as a deposit in a Post Office account. But it was always best to check.

'Of course, I won't tell anyone,' he said. 'Who is there to tell? You said she suddenly appeared in a car. You went back to her flat, had a shower and something to eat, lay down because you were tired . . . *tired*, with a girl like that around next to you? Go on. What happened next?'

'It was a nightmare,' I said. 'A nightmare.'

He sat up. 'A nightmare? What do you mean? How a nightmare? One of the best-looking girls in London picks you up in a car about seven on a Monday morning and you describe it all as a nightmare?'

Sonia had taken me back to her flat and explained that she didn't want to go to any of the parties because she felt she had nothing in common with anyone there, apart from me. She had telephoned to say she wouldn't be there but the phone was always answered by an aggressive man who said, 'You've got the wrong number. Nobody here with that name.' Fisher told her she should come to the second party and that it would go on all night, until dawn broke around six in the morning.

'When we got to her flat,' I said, 'Sonia told me that her husband had left for Canada and that they agreed on a trial separation. His mother had gone with him so we were quite alone and could talk about or do anything we fancied.'

'She told me that she left school when she was seventeen to live with Yvan but life with him was flat and boring. Recently, she'd met a crowd of under-graduates from the London School of Economics, including an aspiring playwright who wanted to write a BBC drama about modern alienation based on the 1942 book The Outsider by Albert Camus. She told him about her brief meeting with The Harlequins and how this, she referred to me as this strange boy, was a follower of Oswald Mosley and that although he played the guitar and used to sing in church choirs, he'd spoken at Trafalgar Square and had actually met Mosley, the most unpopular man in Britain. So, if that wasn't alienation, what was? She said the aspiring playwright wanted to meet me and that's why she'd contacted me. But then she said, there were other reasons, too.'

Alexander looked up at his father's picture and said, 'I do wish you'd take that down. But anyhow, what happened then?'

'I went to sleep and the next thing I knew it was seven in the evening. She told me to put on one of her husband's shirts, some socks and trousers because we were going for a meal. The playwright had fallen off his scooter and hurt his knee and wouldn't be joining us but would arrange something the following week.'

'There was no playwright,' said Alexander.

'No,' I said. 'I distinctly remember she said there was a playwright.'

I babbled on – 'After the meal and a bottle of wine in a French restaurant in Dulwich Village, we went back to Sonia's flat. It was still quite drunk from the party and doing my best to deal with a fresh intake of alcohol. Then she poured me a giant – sized Cognac and one, a bit smaller, for herself.'

'She put on some Italian music, took hold of my hand and asked me to dance. She moved in that sort of silky, sultry, cat-like way girls do now. When the record ended, she led me to her bedroom and we lay next to one another. Both of us were smoking cigarettes. Then she stood up, left the room and came back in a pair of shorts and a shirt. She looked at me for some time and then took the shirt off. That's when it happened, Alexander. That's when it happened. It was absolutely awful. But I think you being The Leader's son, will understand.'

He shot up, knocking over the cup of tea my mother made for him. 'What was awful? What could have been awful about that? You are joking, of course. Aren't you?'

'Around her neck,' I said. 'Around her neck she was wearing a gold chain and hanging from it, you're not going to believe this . . . a Star of David. Can you imagine? She's Jewish. I was in bed with a married Jewish woman who had the Star of David round her neck! Naturally, I pushed her away from me and went back to the room with the sofa in it where I'd been sleeping, locked the door and the next thing I knew, thank God, it was morning. Monday morning. This very day but earlier.'

I told him that I had a horrendous headache but when I felt better, knocked on her door. 'I wanted to say "thanks" for the supper but that I had to get to school.'

'And then, well, then I left.'

Alexander stared at me in blank disbelief. 'You mean to say that you pushed away a semi-naked Sonia Marchand, one of the most beautiful girls in London because she had a Star of David round her neck. Oh God, I'm in pain. Deep, deep pain.' I watched him roll around in the chair as if he really was in agony. He started to speak in Spanish or Italian or whatever it was, I couldn't say. It sounded like a prayer for help.

My mother opened the door. 'Would you two boys like another cup of tea and a cheese and onion sandwich?'

After a long silence, I said, 'Alexander, I couldn't have. I mean, think how I'd be letting down The Leader. And can you imagine the look on my mother's face if I'd got a Jewish woman pregnant?'

He looked at me with bemused contempt. 'My father would have ravished her. I would have ravished her. Everyone on in this damned crazy planet would have ravished her, apart from you. You're insane. Hopelessly and utterly insane.'

He stood up, half-snarled at the picture of his father above my mantelpiece full of books about Fascists and Nazis, and left.

'Please God,' I muttered to myself when I heard the front door close. 'Please God he doesn't tell Max.'

9

ON THE MOVE AT LONG LAST

March 15 was my eighteenth birthday. And on that bright Saturday morning in 1958, a telephone call to my mother changed my life.

She knocked on the door and came into my room carrying a tray with toasted soldiers on a plate and a cup of tea and a single birthday card.

'Wake up,' she said with a smile but commanding voice. 'Do you think Mosley will come to power if everyone's fast asleep? Do you know who I've just been talking to? Sid Proud. The man who runs Spanish Travel who gave Alf Flockhart a job when he came out of prison and the father of that blousy blonde girl who was with Alexander at Trafalgar Square. Wake up or I won't tell you.'

She sat at the end of my bed and I thought how beautiful and alive she looked.

'Mrs Grundy,' she said imitating his Irish/Cockney voice, 'Mrs Grundy, an opportunity for the right person has arisen at Spanish Travel. I need someone with his wits about him to take people from Victoria Station to Port Bou and Barcelona in Catalonia. I need a young, intelligent young man, ideally with a UM background and thought of Trevor. Alexander Mosley tells me that he needs a break after all the work he has done for OM. I'll base him in Barcelona for six months. He'll be there from the end of April until the first or second week in October. He can learn Spanish, take his school books with him and sit his whatever they are exams at Christmas. All he'll have to do is see people on and off trains and make sure they're comfortable in their hotels. It's a doddle. But someone with his background would help dealing with the Spanish authorities. I'll start him on ten pounds a week, all expenses, plenty of tips if the punters like him.'

I sat up straight. 'But school. What about school? I'm supposed to be sitting my A levels in three months. And the youth group. Who will run that if I'm in Spain?' Only then did I realise that I was no longer in charge and had stopped speaking at street corners at weekends. My mother looked up at Mosley on the wall and gave

DOI: 10.4324/9781003375722-10

one of her 'God, give me strength looks.' I thought she might make the sign of the Cross. She picked up the card and showed me that my father and Bonnie the dog had also signed it. I saw so little of him. He was either on night duty at Paddington Telephone Exchange or out on his bicycle learning the whereabouts of every public building and back street in London.

'You can take them at Christmas and in Spain, you'll have time to study and bring in some badly needed money. What's a few months here or there when you can learn Spanish and French?' She took my hand and held it tightly. 'I've only ever wanted to go to two places in my life, Spain and Egypt. I feel that deep down inside I'm from there not Seaton Sluice or Whitley Bay or here. Certainly not with your father.'

She stood up, a striking figure in her headscarf and working clothes. She dusted the picture of Mosley. 'One day, when you've got some money, you can take me to Egypt. That will make up for everything.'

I waited downstairs by the school gate opposite the Oval Cricket Ground to say goodbye to The Harlequins. Only Ronnie Fisher came down with a cheery grin on his face. He opened his schoolbag and gave me an envelope which contained a book. He said, 'I thought you'd chicken out. No surprise there. Now we'll have to get another guitarist but it shouldn't be difficult to find someone better than you. That's from Mrs Marchand who gave it to me last week before she left for Canada. She says to send you her best wishes on your birthday.'

On the tube back to Baker Street I opened the envelope. Inside was a copy of J.D. Salinger's *The Catcher in the Rye*. I spotted the word 'phoney' several times between The Oval and Waterloo, where I changed onto the Bakerloo line to get back to Marylebone. Inside was a letter. She wrote, 'He was always on the lookout for phoneys. Hope you don't become one. When you read this, I'll be somewhere else. Your mother will be pleased. If you'd let yourself go a bit you might start enjoying life more. But then you wouldn't have time to sell your newspapers or speak on platforms. Silly, lovely boy.'

At Marylebone Station, I sat on a passenger seat and started reading the book about a confused and complicated teenager and then returned to Sonia's letter. She wrote, 'You will be like one of those young men who believe in things so strongly up to about the age of twenty-five, maybe even thirty and then for the rest of their lives, never believe in anything again.'

She'd underlined the words *never believe in anything again*.

I walked slowly up Harewood Avenue, past St Edward's Convent and in to Blandford Square where so many great writers and artists lived in the mid-nineteenth century before moving to the Vale of Health in Hampstead in the late nineteenth century and said to myself, 'But why should I be concerned about her gloomy forecast? A new life awaits me in General Franco's Spain, not in boring Canada with someone I don't like, yet alone love.'

I asked Jeffrey Hamm about Salinger. He told me that books like that were designed to muddle the minds of young people so they believe in nothing at all, like John Osborne, who said there were no great causes left.

'Keep your powder dry for when it's needed and don't be taken in by Jewish propaganda.' He patted me on the shoulder. 'And before I forget, I haven't had your sales figures in for the last three weeks. Not slacking, I hope.'

Union Movement members didn't have to keep their powder dry for long.

In April 1958 the Campaign for Nuclear Disarmament held a large rally in Trafalgar Square. Bob Row said to me, 'Nelson will be looking down on that trail of human trash asking what was the point of protecting England from foreign invaders.' The rally was followed by a march from London to Aldermaston and about twelve thousand people ended up protesting outside the Weapons Research Establishment. Bob Row said it was the same crowd who were demanding sanctions against South Africa. Both were financed by the Soviets who wanted to end white rule in Africa and hand over Europe to the Red Army.

'Jews and Commies again,' said Ron Clucas.

One of the CND marchers was Mosley's novelist son, Nicholas, who was Sir Oswald's son by his first wife Cynthia Curzon, the daughter of the legendary Lord Curzon.

My brother-in-law John Wood said we must do something to show our disgust and anger and win support from those who were nervous about a Russian take-over of Europe. So, before we left Blandford Square, we packed cardboard cartons full of eggs discarded by the local grocer Mr Griffin of Bell Street, which would be smelly when they landed on the heads and faces of Christian and Marxist protestors.

Mr Griffin gave them to us for free saying that he didn't fight the war to hand over his grocery shop to the Russians.

Alexander was passionate about the protest and said we should hurl verbal abuse as well as rotten eggs at the marchers. We planned to ambush them at Hammersmith Bridge.

I had returned as part-time youth leader because Timothy had already quarrelled with Max, who he labelled a bully and an inverted class snob with his acquired cockney voice and Teddy Boy clothes. Tim had now fallen under the influence of a group that circled around Sid Proud, my future boss. They were what Jeffrey Hamm and Bob Row called the 'lunatic fringe,' and they were scorned by Mosley who called them 'dwarfs posing in the jackboots of dead giants.' They retaliated by calling Mosley a 'kosher Fascist' and asserting that his first wife, Cynthia, was a Jewess and with a nose like his, Mosley might be one, too.

Before we left, Alexander urged us to adopt the Spanish Civil War slogan, They shall not pass.

They did but not before we splattered a few faces with Mr Griffin's rotten eggs. They passed alright, some of the sandal-wearing clerics making the sign of the Cross as they ducked in-coming eggshells.

Then, as they walked by in their hundreds, Alexander suddenly left us and joined them.

'Is he insane,' said John Wood. 'God only knows,' I snapped back. I felt confused and betrayed and threw what was left of the eggs into the gutter.

On the way back, we managed to steal a few Hammersmith Communist Party banners, which we carried back to Blandford Square and on the wall of Lovene and John's basement flat. We took photographs of us posing alongside them, me next to one which had on it, 'Workers of the world unite – you have nothing to lose but your chains.'

'Nothing to lose but your brains,' said Ron Clucas.

About a week later, Alexander rang the bell and came and sat miserably in my room. He explained that the man he'd joined on the march was his step-brother.

'Nicholas is helping me to see the world differently. And he's helping me with my father. Dad insists I become a chartered accountant but I want to go to university, maybe in America or South America. Not here.'

He said his father was also putting pressure on him to drop his relationship with Sid Proud's daughter. 'Perhaps he can't bear the idea of me marrying her and her being greeted as Cynthia Mosley.' Then he said that Nicholas had spoken about religion and introduced him to senior Anglican Church intellectuals. 'They are,' he said, 'amazing people.'

He wished me luck in Spain and said that he was going away for a little while to think about the past, present and future at a place called Mirfield in Yorkshire. Later, I found Mirfield was the headquarters of the Community of the Resurrection and one of the Community's best-known members was Father Trevor Huddleston, who wanted to end white rule in South Africa, and I was worried that Alexander and he would exchange fiery words. I wondered if I could join considering I also believed in the Risen Lord. But then I also believed in apartheid because OM said it was right. Then, I too would clash with the man who shared my first name.

But his newfound hunt for God didn't make him any happier, and he became even more miserable when I told him I'd found God at Christ Church when I sang in the choir years ago. I told him that God would change his life, and he gave me one of his I'm going to be sick looks. He rose and said he had to go and have supper with his parents at their Cheyne Walk home. 'No one will be talking about God there,' he said.

'Has he gone?' asked my mother. 'Without saying hello? You know, Alexander looks more and more like The Leader when I first saw him in Brighton before you were born. Have I ever told you about that night? 'Perhaps Alexander will take-over from The Leader when he dies.'

It was the first time I'd heard my mother admit that Oswald Mosley was mortal.

But a few minutes later, Alexander returned. He'd forgotten his expensive leather gloves. He was so serious. First, he looked at his father on the wall. Then at me.

He put out his right hand and said softly. 'Goodbye and thanks.'

The front door closed and a wave of sadness swept over me because I knew how badly Alexander wanted to get away from a family that was destroying him.

The following week, we heard that the Communists and left-wing Labourites who were in charge of King's Cross and St Pancras Council planned to fly the Red Flag over the Town Hall.

I received a telephone call from 302 asking me to turn up with a group of Union Movement members and speak against the Communists at the flag-raising ceremony. It was a week before my scheduled departure for Spain.

I turned up opposite St Pancras Town Hall wearing the uniform white shirt, black tie and sixth form blazer minus the school badge and mounted a wooden platform. A picture was published in *The Times* showing me ranting, raving and pointing my hand at a Communist speaker, who was ranting, raving and pointing his finger at me.

It was the last time I ever spoke for Union Movement, and I'd just celebrated my eighteenth birthday.

I heard that a copy of the picture was put up in the small study room for sixth formers at Archbishop Tenison's.

One of the boys in the lower sixth invented a new political party in memory of Hereward the Wake and sent a letter to a local paper under my name urging young people in South London to join and save Britain from the Reds, Jews, West Indians and anyone else who might offend, or try and destroy, the England we all loved so much.

After finding out who was responsible, I cycled to the home of the boy responsible in Streatham and then wrote to the same newspaper disclaiming any association with the organisation and denying I had ever written to the paper.

A week later, the *Sunday Dispatch* carried a front-page story on the sixth formers at a prominent local school, Archbishop Tenison's, who had caused so much confusion in the press by claiming that a new right-wing party had been founded at that school and that the organisation wanted to send all West Indians back to where they came from immediately.

I phoned Fisher about all of this, and he told me he never wanted to see or talk to me again. Neither did any of the other members of The Harlequins. He said that Dr Robinson had suffered a mild heart attack soon after the report was published.

Fisher said that the prefects had been told to remove and destroy the *Times* picture and under no circumstances mention my name to reporters. Parents of juniors concerned about the bad publicity were told that I had been expelled for un-becoming conduct.

It was a sadly fitting end to my inglorious time at Archbishop Tenison's Grammar School, where my mother believed I would be first-groomed to one day become the Mosley of the Anglican Church.

FIGURE 1 Trevor Grundy on his bicycle at Blandford Square.

Source: Courtesy of Trevor Grundy.

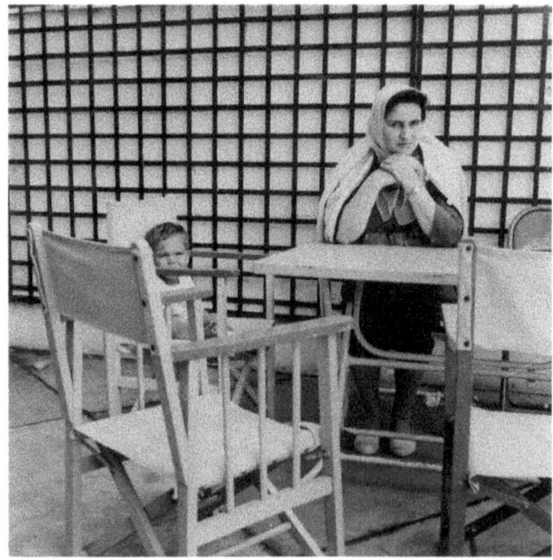

FIGURE 2 Edna Grundy in pensive mood (her grandson Nick is in the baby chair) soon after Trevor's departure for Africa (April 1966).

Source: Courtesy of Trevor Grundy.

FIGURE 3 Edna Grundy at the age of sixteen in Whitley Bay, Northumberland.

Source: Courtesy of Trevor Grundy.

FIGURE 4 Edna (Morris) as a child with a crucifix round her neck.

Source: Courtesy of Trevor Grundy.

FIGURE 5 Trevor Grundy (far left with guitar) with school friends who formed a skiffle group called The Harlequins in 1957.

Source: Courtesy of Trevor Grundy.

FIGURE 6 Edna, Trevor and Lovene at London Airport before his flight to Zambia on April 28, 1966.

Source: Courtesy of Trevor Grundy.

FIGURE 7 Trevor Grundy with his mother at St Albans in 1962.

Source: Courtesy of Trevor Grundy.

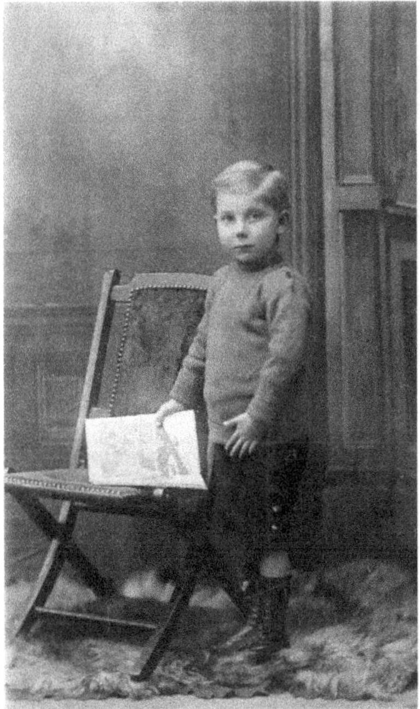

FIGURE 8 Sidney Grundy at the age of three or four.

Source: Courtesy of Trevor Grundy.

FIGURE 9 Lovene in her late teens at an English seaside resort.

Source: Courtesy of Trevor Grundy.

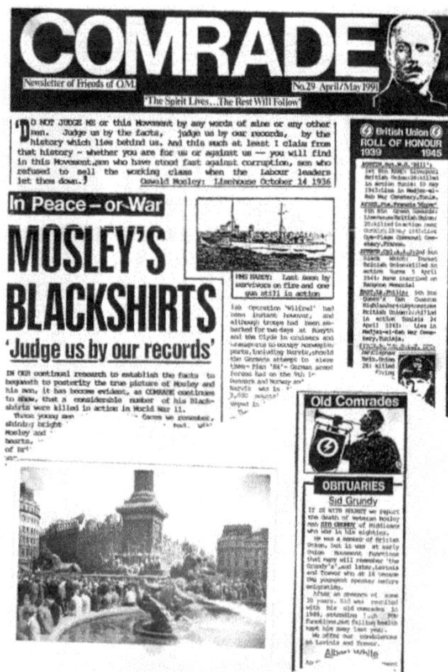

COMRADE

Newsletter of Friends of O.M.

No.29 April/May 1991

'The Spirit Lives…The Rest Will Follow'

'DO NOT JUDGE ME or this Movement by any words of mine or any other men. Judge us by the facts, judge us by our records, by the history which lies behind us. And this much at least I claim from that history – whether you are for us or against us — you will find in this Movement men who have stood fast against corruption, men who refused to sell the working class when the Labour leaders let them down.'

Oswald Mosley: Limehouse October 14 1936

In Peace – or War

MOSLEY'S BLACKSHIRTS

'Judge us by our records'

IN OUR continual research to establish the facts to bequeath to posterity the true picture of Mosley and his men, it has become evident, as COMRADE continues to show, that a considerable number of his Blackshirts were killed in action in World War 11.

HMS HARDY: Last seen by survivors on fire and one gun still in action

British Union
ROLL OF HONOUR
1939 1945

Old Comrades

OBITUARIES

Sid Grundy

FIGURE 10 Front page of *Comrade* with an obituary to Sid Grundy and mention of Trevor and 'Lavinia.'

Source: Courtesy of Trevor Grundy.

FIGURE 11 Oswald Mosley greets fans in Trafalgar Square shortly before the 1959 General Election.

Source: Courtesy of Trevor Grundy.

FIGURE 12 Poet and author Alan Neame who rescued Trevor from the clutches of Union Movement.

Source: Courtesy of Trevor Grundy.

FIGURE 13 Sidney Grundy in black shirt poses for a picture in the early 1950s.

Source: Courtesy of Trevor Grundy.

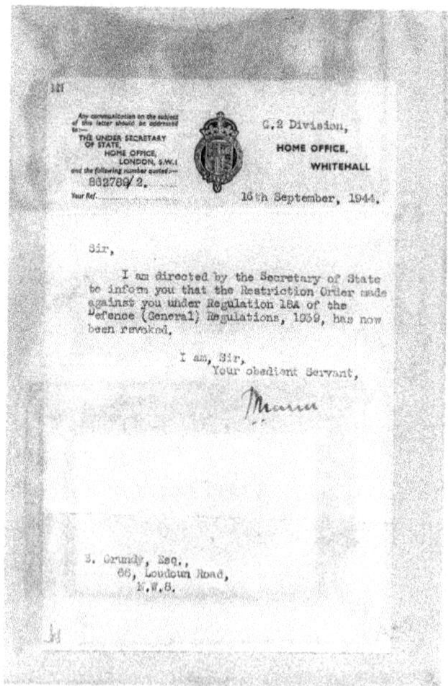

Any communication on the subject of this letter should be addressed to:—
THE UNDER SECRETARY OF STATE,
HOME OFFICE,
LONDON, S.W.1
and the following number quoted:—
862789/2.
Your Ref.

G.2 Division,
HOME OFFICE,
WHITEHALL

16th September, 1944.

Sir,

I am directed by the Secretary of State to inform you that the Restriction Order made against you under Regulation 18A of the Defence (General) Regulations, 1939, has now been revoked.

I am, Sir,
Your obedient Servant,

S. Grundy, Esq.,
66, Loudoun Road,
N.W.8.

FIGURE 14 Letter telling Sidney Grundy that the 18A restriction order against him had been lifted in September 1944.

Source: Courtesy of Trevor Grundy.

FIGURE 15 Trevor Grundy in the newsroom of *The Standard* newspaper in Dar es Salaam, Tanzania in 1969.

Source: Courtesy of Trevor Grundy.

FIGURE 16 Trevor, Lovene and their father shortly before his death in 1991.

Source: Courtesy of Trevor Grundy.

10

PORT BOU AND BARCELONA, 1958

I left England with a suitcase crammed full of 'A' level textbooks. I also had a *Teach Yourself Spanish* book, which I bought at Foyles, a Spanish-English dictionary and a steel-stringed guitar.

At Victoria Station, I looked around for tourists carrying Spanish Travel SS shopping bags. 'SS' meant something like 'limited company' in Spain. Proud thought it amusing that his couriers and representatives wore red armbands with the letters 'SS' on them. Most of the travellers were in their early to late thirties, factory and office workers from Manchester, Leeds and Liverpool, going abroad for the first time after spending a lot of their growing-up days in air-raid shelters, damaged houses in bombed streets.

Someone said in Proud's office next to Piccadilly Circus while making a booking for himself, his wife and three-year-old son, 'Never 'eard of Port Bou till I got 'yer brochure. £18.10 for ten days, nosh chucked in and rail fares. Can't be all bad, can it?'

As a reward for hard work, Proud took me and Johnny for lunch at the Trocadero Restaurant. He laughed and said I'd make so much money I'd be footing the bill next time.

He said Port Bou was the place where Jews tried to get to after Hitler took over France in 1940. He said some Jewish writer fellow called Walter Benjamin committed suicide there while trying to escape from the Nazis and that he was buried at a cemetery in the hills overlooking what wasn't much more than a long-neglected village next to the Pyrenees.

But waiting on their own for me to lead them to the train that would start the journey at Newhaven was a group of four with 'middle-class' stamped all over them.

I introduced myself and learned that the father was the harbour master at Ramsgate and his 17-year-old daughter was a schoolgirl at that seaside town. Her brother was

DOI: 10.4324/9781003375722-11

a studious-looking 14-year-old. Her name was Avril. She was tall, fresh-faced and well-built. She asked me if I could help her with her Spanish. I laughed and said I couldn't speak a word of it. Her father said, 'But you're supposed to be our courier.'

Travelling to Spain with us was a woman called Vivienne, an experienced courier who spoke several languages. She tolerated me but only just and didn't hand out tips about how to make money on the side by buying up *couchettes* on the train and then selling them at double the price to holidaymakers anxious for rest and sleep during an overnight journey from Paris to Port Bou.

Apart from a suitcase full of books, I carried a Gladstone bag full of pesetas bought by one of Sid Proud's many ex-Mosleyite hangers-on at a bank in London. My job was to take them to Port Bou and hand them in at a local bank so that hotels could be paid in local currency. I stuffed extra wads of money into two breast pockets so must have confused people about my sexuality during the twenty-four-hour trip to a tiny part of a country close to the rest of the world since the end of the Spanish Civil War in 1939.

In Paris, I met Spanish Travel's French representative, Andre Nagar, during the change from one station to the next. He was in his mid-forties and told me that when he was young he fought with the Free French against the Germans. I told him that I loved history books and had just read one about Marshal Petain and his great courage during the occupation. Later on when I spent more time in Paris, he took me to a bistro for a meal and then to a tourist nightclub in Montmartre listening to someone play Edith Piaf songs on an accordion and thinking I was Ernest Hemingway or Scott Fitzgerald or both together. After a bottle of wine and a spirit so strong I nearly fell off my chair, he said, 'You're an ignorant but likeable fool. What can one book tell you about the Germans in France?'

Avril Hardy was no Sonia Marchand but in her blue and white dress, her youth, her boyish haircut, fresh, smooth skin and large round brown eyes, she looked a lot more manageable.

On the second night of her ten-day holiday, I took Avril to an open-air café that reminded me of Van Gogh's *Terrasse de café la nuit*, which he painted in 1888. Lovene had a copy of that on the wall of her flat. We sat and watched local girls go by with elderly women walking alongside them, teenage boys looking and half-bowing as they passed, their virgin Roman Catholic wives of the future.

I said, 'Someone should have a banner reading "Not to be touched before marriage."' She said, 'Isn't that how things should be if you love someone?'

I drank three or four small glasses of brandy and smoked cheap Spanish cigarettes. The brandy tasted like cough mixture, but it took away the fear I had of being next to a girl I liked. We listened to a man playing the guitar. He was the local butcher who hung red and yellow carcasses from a hook and offered customers little glasses of local wine if they bought any of his meats or home-made sausages. Next to him was a large woman from the grocer's shop who sold fresh vegetables, the greenest beans in Catalonia (said a notice on her shop window), strings of garlic as long as your arm and cucumbers the size of truncheons. She stamped her feet, and it was hard to say if she was singing or shouting but electricity was in the air that night. We laughed a lot and watched some of our tourists, drunk on cheap red wine, dancing, a man from Birmingham pretending to be a matador and flashing his new British Home Stores sports jacket at his wife who was bending down low and charging like a bull. We left and I took Avril up to the hills that overlooked Port Bou, and looked down at its tiny bay and smooth sea dotted with fishing boats, a sea with just enough energy to send small and gentle waves towards a curved shoreline and stony beach. I told her we might find a cemetery where a famous man was buried but I couldn't remember his name. We didn't search for long and lay down in the grass and looked up at the trillion stars above us, not moving, not touching but then a kiss, her first. We walked back to the rundown Miramar Hotel hand-in-hand, not knowing we'd just walked through a door that led to first-time teenage love.

At the end of her short holiday, Avril leaned out of the window and held both her arms out to me. Captain Hardy frowned and looked at his watch. The train was late leaving, and he was used to things running on time. When it pulled away, I promised to write and said that I would see her in September before I went to university. I told her I'd already passed my 'A' levels and was waiting to hear whether I was going to Oxford or Cambridge. Then I laughed and said, 'Some hope. One of the lesser red bricks, more likely. But I promise. Ramsgate., September. I'll be there . . . I love you.'

A few days after Avril's departure, I was told by one of the Spanish guides about a brothel in nearby Figueras.

Manola told me that in Spring and Summer, Spanish men went with English, Swedish and German girls because they were so easy. But in winter they weren't around, so young men like him visited whores who were skilled and clean and some of them quite pretty. But a couple of years before, the Church had stepped in and tried to force the Fascist authorities to ban brothels. But that didn't stop young and quite old priests from changing their ways. They were just a bit more discreet. He said priests were familiar sights entering and leaving the Figueras pleasure dome, and you'd meet the same people on the other side of the confession box before mass on Sundays.

But God help you if you tried those tricks on with a Spanish girl. Their brothers or fathers would think nothing of sticking a knife into you and leaving you in the street like a dying dog.

I said I'd join him on a trip to Figueras when the season ended but deep down knew that would never happen. Perhaps I was destined to be a virgin forever.

Anyhow, after a few weeks in Port Bou, I received a telegram from Proud telling me to move to Barcelona and stay there until he contacted me again. So, I left the Miramar Hotel and the damp and claustrophobic room I'd been allocated with my suitcase again full of unopened books and a steel-stringed guitar I still didn't know how to play. One of the waiters who spoke a smattering of English said he was sorry to see me go but everyone said I should be careful, I drank too much and local brandy was a gut rot and stopped (he patted his crotch) 'this thing from going up.'

But if I could get him a job as a waiter, then I would have a friend for life. I was so lucky because now that no-one cared about Franco or Spanish Fascism, English girls were flooding into Barcelona, all of them anxious to learn Spanish and meet off-duty bullfighters, who all of a sudden were everywhere.

I took a train to Barcelona, checked in at the designated hotel a few yards from the main station, and before lunch arranged a guided tour of the Ramblas and a visit to the local Black Madonna at Monserrat. When I sat down in the dining room, I was handed a telegram by the *concierge*. It was from England and said, 'Crisis in office, Return immediately. Bring bank deposit receipt. Proud, Spanish Travel SS.'

The hotel manager saw my face drop and asked if someone in my family had died. I told him I'd brought everything with me from England and had been told I'd be in Spain for six months so I could make money and study and go to university. That was what I'd been promised by the head of Spanish Travel in London.

He said, 'You were promised that by Mr Proud himself. Well then, now I understand. But the room is for one night and was booked only last week. I fear there has been some misunderstanding. Perhaps you have been misled?'

He gave me a bottle of red wine on the house and I ate my salad, beef steak and chips sadly on my own, a dream of freedom fading fast. While wondering if anyone anywhere was worse off than me, I looked down and saw a human face close to the floor, moving quickly but grimacing both at the same time. The man must have been in his fifties or even sixties, and he had leather pads on his elbows and knees. The manager told me that he was a sort of hotel mascot and allowed in at mealtimes. He said the man had been blown-up in the war. I asked, 'The war against the Germans?' He said, 'No. Our war. The Spanish war.' I said, 'Blown up by the communists,' remembering all the books I'd seen at home in my father's draw next to the gun I'd taken to school and the knuckle-duster he carried with him when he went to Speakers' Corner at Hyde Park. He said, 'No. Not the communists. The Fascists. Mercenaries from Morocco. Some say it was a landmine. Others say he was tortured and the Moors removed his arms and legs. He won't speak. He has to live. Eat your lunch. Drink your wine. Try not to think when you're eating.'

The following day, I took a train back to Port Bou and from there to Paris, where I managed to telephone Andre and meet him at the Gare du Nord.

'Beware, my young friend,' he said over a coffee and cognac. 'You are in bed with a monster. Swimming with a shark. You should still be at school. How old are you? Seventeen, eighteen? Why are you working for a man like Proud?

He saw my questioning look.

'Me? That doesn't matter. I work for six other people, that's who I am and that's what I do to make a living. I have a wife and three children. But you. You can't speak French or Spanish and spend time asking me if I admire Napoleon and Marshal Petain.'

Then he smiled and ordered two more cognacs. 'It's well known in travel circles that Proud is a crook, some say a Fascist crook, that he was a communist during the Spanish Civil War and will never be allowed to return but he has connections with that Oswald Mosley man who now lives in Paris at a palace built by Napoleon for one of his marshals, a place called Le Temple de la Gloire, the Temple of Glory.'

He coughed, lit a cigarette and swore in French.

'Proud uses people to smuggle money into Spain to pay all his bills and gets pesetas from a fellow crook in London at dirt cheap rates. Then he puts the money into Spanish banks and that's illegal, a punishable offence. Money laundering. If he asks you to carry money for him say No and leave immediately, otherwise, my friend, you are going to end up in a deep, a very, very deep, puddle. You will be skating on very thin steam.'

He went away and came back with a baguette filled with cheese and tomato and handed it to me.

'We have time to talk. Your train is delayed. So, shall I tell you what your life will turn into if you stay with Proud? He will use you as a dogsbody, a mule. He will wear you out running between London and Barcelona and when he's finished with you, he will toss you aside like an old pair of socks. Don't carry money for him. People know him and what he is like. He pretends to be a big fan of Franco and says he knows that man who rescued Mussolini during the war, Otto Skorzeny who lives in Madrid with a crowd of Nazis. They are trying to revive the Nazi Party. Mosley is one of them. But ask Proud why he never crosses into Spain. Ask him why he never goes to Port Bou. He is a crook and his people bribe crooked Fascists in the government. But he never takes a risk himself. He gets other people to do his dirty work for him.'

He touched my arm and we stood up. 'Proud says he is a British Fascist but he's really a Pope and Jew hating anarchist. He is one of those men who walk the earth blowing up everything and everyone he touches. The Fascists and the Nazis are dogs and you are too young to know anything about them. But beware of sleeping with monsters and swimming with sharks.'

I returned to Blandford Square with the regulation allowances of wine and spirits and cigarettes which I gave to my mother. She saw I was unhappy about being brought back so early. She said that Mr Proud rang that morning and told her it was a temporary crisis and that he needed me with my various capabilities and charm to cope. 'Those were the very words he used,' said my mother. '*Capability and charm*.' He said that I should get to the office first thing the following day and bring with me a receipt from the bank in Port Bou confirming that all the money I carried out of the country had been safely deposited.

The following morning, I was in Proud's Coventry Street Office at nine o'clock. He was waiting for me with an East End bruiser known in Union Movement circles as 'Punch,' a former light heavyweight who'd taken too many beatings and who was three-quarters brain dead.

'Where's the receipt for that money you were supposed to have deposited?' he snapped without saying 'hello' or 'how was the trip?'

I felt as if I'd flown to another planet occupied by fire-spitting robots. Timothy appeared from nowhere with a hideous-looking boy-man called Spike.

I fumbled nervously in my wallet and produced the receipt from the Bank of Spain in Port Bou. A look of great relief and then of total calm registered across Proud's cracked and ravaged face.

'Oh, so there it is! Now, that's well done, Trev. That's good. So, you managed all right then, did you? Wonderful. Time for a spot of lunch later, new place *The Creole* or do you prefer the *Trocadero*? Too early yet for you to pick-up the bill, Trev. My treat. So well done. Off you go for a coffee somewhere with Tim and Spike and a bit of a rest and I'll tell you what I've got planned for you over a spot of lunch. Off you go and well done.'

Timothy alone came with me for coffee, and I asked him how he came to be working for Spanish Travel.

'I'm working for him personally,' said Tim, who ordered a large whisky with his expresso. 'Twenty- five quid a week for starters and expenses. That's more than my old man earns and he's been at it since the war.'

As he was speaking, drinking, smoking and boasting I realised what harm I'd done by introducing him to Oswald Mosley's part-time backstreet world.

'And the Movement, Tim. Do you still do things for the Movement?'

Tim spat it out. 'Fuck the movement and fuck your Oswald Mosley and his fucking sons Alexander and Max. If you see Alexander Mosley tell him Mr Proud would like a word with him about what he's been saying about his daughter. And you can tell him that if Mohammad won't go to the Mountain, the Mountain, me and Spike and Punchie will be going along to see him wherever the fucker's hiding.'

'Tim,' I said, still unconvinced that our Robin Hood/Little John relationship had irrevocably ended, 'you sound like some hoodlum in a "B" movie we used to watch at the Odeon in Edgware Road. What on earth is wrong with you and what has Alexander done to you? He's a great guy. You used to like him so much.'

Tim finished his second large whisky.

'I'd stay well away from Mr Alexander Mosley if I were you,' he said standing up and leaving me to pay a quite large bill.

At eleven o'clock I went to see Sid Proud in his office. He told me that because of staff shortages and a cash flow problem, he'd need me in the office every Thursday and Friday but only half-days on Saturdays. That meant me leaving London with tourists on Sundays, travelling to Paris and after changing trains, going overnight to Port Bou. After I'd banked the money, I would have the whole day to myself, completely free to do what I wanted to do as if I was on holiday. 'Have a few drinks, chase a few of those frisky-looking Spanish girls. You're on the pig's back and you can even learn a bit of French and Spanish while you're about it.' I'd stay at the Miramar overnight and return to Britain via Paris on Tuesday well in time for work in the office on Thursday morning. And if I was quick and smart I could sell couchettes before I got to Paris cutting out that 'greedy' Frenchman, Andre, who he was getting rid of because he'd told someone in the new de Gaulle set up that Spanish Travel SS was taking business away from French firms sending tourists to the new open doors Spain.

'From next weekend, Trev, you'll have two Gladstone bags to take with you to Port Bou. And never ever lose or replace receipts. We won't want to waste time and money sending Tim or Spike down to Spain to help you look for them, now do we?' And he added, 'You might have to do all your school-studying-stuff when the season's over and there's plenty of time for study and things like that. But by then, you'll have made so much money you won't want to be reading all that stuff about lakes and daffodils. The world's your oyster with all the experience you'll be getting. You happy about all that?'

For some reason I said 'Yes,' and we walked to the Trocadero as if we had the relationship of two men in the same boat rowing towards the future.

While I was in Spain, my mother had taken a call for me from a Welsh woman who sounded hysterical. The woman said, 'Derek's been taken ill. I told her you'd gone to live in Spain and she said she wouldn't tell her son that in case it made him even worse.'

On my work-free Saturday afternoon, I went to Derek's house, which was close to the Tate Gallery and received the same treatment that I'd received from Leslie's mother.

'I blame you. Not completely because he's always had this thing about Hitler. He had it even before he got involved with you and that Mosley man. Library books, I suppose. But you people made it worse. You made it so much worse because you made it acceptable. That's what you did, you made it as if it was normal to be that way. His father hasn't spoken to him for years and why should he? My husband lost his eyesight and leg in the war. It's just as well he can't see what's stuck on the walls of Derek's bedroom.'

Derek was in the basement in bed. 'You've come at last, Trevor.' He had a disturbing half smile on his face.

I sat on the edge of his bed and looked at the pictures of Hitler on the wall.

He told me how Jeffrey Hamm had expelled him from Union Movement. 'He doesn't understand the Fuhrer as I do. The Fuhrer was God's messenger. He will come again. Hamm is a Roman Catholic and believes Jesus was God. How can a Jew be God? Who circumcised God?'

I told Derek I was working in Spain and I would see him again when I'd finished and that he should look after himself. He had no job, no friends, no girl in his life, no political organisation or community that wanted or needed his support. I remembered what his mother said, that I had made it all acceptable and normal. I remembered Leslie Rochdale beaten to pulp. Who was responsible for that? Me, I suppose. I wondered if Mosley ever blamed himself when things became so violent at his meetings. It was as if Mosley was enjoying himself, sending his warriors into battle, encouraging them, nodding his approval and giving them a half-Nazi post-war salute that was like a blessing by a high priest. He called us the flower of the English working class. In private, Hamm told us that Mosley promised that one day his followers would again wear the blackshirt, which was, he said, the outward and visible symbol of an inward and spiritual grace. The rector told my mother that was a quote from St Augustine and she replied, 'Rubbish, rector! Mosley said it first.'

Derek stared at me with his strange, dangerous smile, his fine brown hair combed across one side of his forehead. 'Trevor! They've got you. The Jews have got you. Franco is a Jew. He refused to support the Fuhrer who asked him to close the Straits of Gibraltar so Mussolini could have the Mediterranean as an Italian lake. Franco let the Jews out of Spain and the Fuhrer said he'd sooner have all his teeth pulled out than meet the Jew-loving el Caudillo Franco again. And now, you're working for him. The Jews have got you.' He raised his right arm and saluted the wall. I stood up and left without saying goodbye to his mother, who was making tea for us, and listening to the BBC radio saying that left-wingers in St Pancras planned to raise the red flag over the town hall and give all Council workers the day off on Monday, May 5.

Every Sunday between May and September 1958, I travelled to Spain, banked Sid Proud's *pesetas*, went to the Miramar Hotel and fell onto the bed like a dead man.

Monday night was special and precious. Most of the time, I sat on my own in one of Port Bou's small, warm and welcoming Van Gogh look-alike cafes drinking copious quantities of cheap Spanish brandy, listening to well-stacked girls from Birmingham and Manchester talking about film stars and a new wave of British pop singers influenced by Elvis Presley, while dreading the long journey back to London the following day.

The highlight of the week was stopping for a few hours in Paris where I'd meet-up with Andre Nagar, the man who'd warned me never to carry money for Sid Proud.

One night walking to the train that would take me to Dieppe, I shook his hand and told him he was the wisest and best man I'd ever met. He laughed and said that I couldn't have met many people in my short life but that he liked the 'wise man' bit because 'Nagar' was a Hebrew word that means either carpenter or scholar.

He said that early Christian documents described Jesus as son of a nagar. 'So Joseph might have been a carpenter or a rabbi. Who knows? Who cares?'

I said, 'I do. I care.'

'So serious in one so young,' he laughed. 'Well, in the case of Jesus, I'd go for the latter rather than the former. How could a boy of twelve argue with rabbis in a temple in Jerusalem if he was just the son of a man making dovetail joints all day long?'

He handed me a French loaf and an envelope that contained a book about a Greek writer I'd never heard of. Nikos Kazantzakis.

The train pulled away and I tucked in to the bacon and egg baguette.

'So, my new and most valued friend is a Jew.' I thought of Derek lying in bed looking at the pictures on the wall.

My valuable friendship with Andre was tested by Proud encouraging me to take over the sale of *couchettes* on trains from Paris to Port Bou. That was Andre's territory and part of his summer income that fed mouths and paid school fees. I told him about Proud's suggestion and he said, 'Go ahead. But you won't ever be my friend again.' So, I stayed with ten pounds a week which seemed a lot for a schoolboy but which was a pittance compared with what others in the travel business were making.

One night, I told Andre about my strange beginnings and the influence Oswald Mosley had on my life. I told him about my mother's hope that one day I'd be ordained a vicar in the Church of England and expose the Jews who killed Jesus two thousand years ago. He said I was the first English person he'd met who supported Fascists. 'How we ever let that miserable man live in France is beyond me. Why France? Mosley would be more at home in Madrid with his Nazi friends.'

He said, 'End your contact with Proud. Save as much as you can. You can live with us here while you get on your feet. Learn French. Teach English. Learn to write for newspapers. Don't go back. Break from them. Break from your family. Do something but get away from those people who will destroy you. And stop drinking. Stop running. Stop thinking and start looking. Better still, keep those damned Gladstone bags full of pesetas and do a run to Morocco and then go south. If a man with money sets his mind on disappearing in Africa, no one will find him again. Africa is full of on-the-run people pretending to be missionaries. That way you might even become the Mosley of the African Church.'

The idea of stealing Proud's money appealed to me but not for long because I knew he would put Punchie and Spike on to me without a second thought. But with money, I could hire my own bodyguards so the idea of doing a bunk with the bags was not over yet.

I asked Andre about the Germans and why, if they were such barbarians, they didn't destroy one of Europe's loveliest cities, Paris. He said Hitler wanted to show English aristocrats, who he so admired, that he wasn't a monster. He said, 'They watched what he would do in Paris but later on when he turned East, they couldn't give a damn what he did.'

On the train to Dieppe and then the Channel crossing to Newhaven, I realised for the first time that I wasn't blocking my ears or closing my eyes when I heard someone say bad things about Hitler and Mosley.

I wrote in my diary the last thing Andre Nagar ever said to me. 'You need madness to enter your life. Not the madness you have known when you were a child. But the madness that cuts the ropes that bind you to the past, the joyful madness that sets men free.'

On May 13, 1958, there was a military *coup* by soldiers representing the *pieds-noirs*, the French settlers, in Algeria. The following weekend, there were huge traffic jams in Paris and it took several hours to move tourists from the Gare du Nord to Gare Austerlitz and onto trains leaving for Spain.

At the station, a large man from Lancaster with ham-sized fists landed me one on the shoulder. 'This is all your bloody fault. You should have told us this was going on before we left England and we'd have turned round and gone home rather than stand here without anything to eat or drink. This is all your bloody fault,' he shouted as I stood back beyond hitting range. 'Fucking foreigners. Look at them. The police are a bunch of Nazis with their batons and guns. We fought on the wrong side in the war. Hitler would have dealt with this before it started.'

On June 1, the war hero General Charles de Gaulle took over as premier of France. At first, he sided with the white settlers but later praised Algerian freedom fighters.

What's going to happen next? I asked my brother-in-law John Wood, who had been made office manager at Spanish Travel SS.

Bob Row told me during one of my less frequent visits to 302, that not even Winston Churchill could tolerate de Gaulle and that if he betrayed the French settlers then someone would kill him. He said the *pieds-noirs* had built Algeria out of nothing, just as whites had built South Africa, Southern Rhodesia, Kenya and Uganda out of nothing.

He said he was overjoyed that the French people were making their anger seen and heard on the streets of Algiers and Paris. That would encourage the British to do the same.

He said that Britain had its own settler problem.

'In Algeria, the settlers are white. Here, they're black from the Caribbean, West Indians getting free housing and money from a crazy government that should be giving it to hard-working white working-class families not to immigrants from the other end of the world.'

After scribbling on a pad, thinking, pausing, standing up and sitting down and looking around him as if someone was about to pounce, he came up with the week's front-page headline which read, as it had so many times before, '*Mosley warned the West.*'

The Leader's secretary Ann Good wobbled in with a cup of tea and a single biscuit on a tray. Bob Row stood up and smiled as if someone had brought him a three-course meal and a bottle of wine.

'They'll turn to OM in their millions,' he said. 'Then we'll hear those church bells ring. And they'll all be ringing for Mosley.'

I returned to London one Wednesday in July that year exhausted. I opened the kitchen door and put on the wooden table covered in oil-cloth an assortment of gifts, wine and chocolate bought in Paris for my mother, a Spanish 45-rpm record for Lovene and loads of cigarettes and cans of French beer for myself. But there was no excited greeting. Standing squarely in front of me was a woman besieged in a headscarf and a pinafore without the Cream Puff Tempting Touch cosmetics that turned her Italian Renaissance face and Roman nose into a mask.

'There you are, Mum,' I said. 'One for you, two for me. One for you, six for me,' but there was no smile, no reaction.

She looked at me with her large brown eyes full of tears.

God, I thought, what now? What new drama? Couldn't we, just for one split-second, be normal?

She put her arms around me and whispered, 'You're not to be upset because it's not your fault but Derek is dead.'

The night before, Jeffrey Hamm telephoned her after Derek's mother rang him and said her son's body had been found in the River Rhine but where he couldn't remember. He said she was in control of herself and apparently without bitterness or rancour. But before putting down the phone shouted – '*Damn you. Damn you all, you Fascist bastards.*'

Hamm said he was used to language like that from Jews but not from decent Welsh people. After all, he was one of them.

Derek's mother said that her son seemed a lot better after I'd gone to see him and last week had taken down all the pictures of Hitler and put them in a file in his father's desk, which he used before the war when he lost his sight and left leg.

She told Jeffrey Hamm that Derek left London with a bag with nothing in it but his passport and a copy of *Mein Kampf* and his brown shirt with a Swastika armband sewn on it.

When the German police found his body, they contacted officials at the British Embassy in Bonn, who contacted the police in London who went to Derek's house in Pimlico.

I turned the screw-top on a sherry bottle and handed a glass to my mother. I knocked back the sweet, sickly drink and then another, and another and remembered how Derek told me that one day we should visit the place where the ashes of ten hanged Nazi leaders had been scattered after the trial at Nuremberg which Derek, like his mentor Julius Streicher, called 'Purim 1946.'

My mother opened a packet of cigarettes and lit one and blew the smoke towards an open window and wafted her hands up and down to get rid of the smell.

'If your father saw me doing this, he'd have a fit.'

She said, 'Derek was a strange fish. You're not to feel responsible. If we all threw ourselves into a river when we felt like it, who'd be left to fight for Mosley?'

But for days, I couldn't get the picture of Derek in a brown shirt with a Swastika on it floating on the surface of one of Germany's great rivers or erase what his mother said, those chilling words that wouldn't go away.

'You people made it worse. You made it worse because you made it acceptable.'

Perhaps Jeffrey Hamm or Bob Row told The Leader about Derek and the effect his death had on me. But soon afterwards, I received a telephone call from Ann Good. She said that Sir Oswald and Lady Mosley often spoke about the way my brave and loyal Union Movement parents had hosted their two sons so often. How, too, they had looked after young Germans at a time when girls with long blonde hair and boys in leather shorts were looked upon as dangerous intruders. In short, would I join the family for drinks and a light supper at their home at Orsay, a few miles from Paris, next time I was passing through?

My heart leapt. A meeting with The Leader and Lady Mosley at their home in Paris.

I rang Ann Good and a date was fixed. I begged my mother to help me say the right thing when I met Sir Oswald and Lady D. She said it was simple. All I needed to say was 'Hail Mosley.'

In August, most of France shuts down because of the heat. The 1958 travel season was drawing to a close, and Sid Proud told me I could have a few days off as unpaid leave and start looking for work somewhere else because there were only a few more Gladstone bags destined for Port Bou and he had nothing to offer someone who wasn't fluent in French or Spanish with only four 'O' levels and no prospects.

'But,' he said 'I won't be paying for any hotels or fancy restaurants as you get ready to bow and scrape before Mr Bloody Oswald Mosley.'

I said – 'Sir Oswald Mosley.'

He said Alexander had abused and betrayed his daughter Cynthia and that Spike and Tim were looking for him. To get her away from things, he'd paid for her to enrol as a student at the Sorbonne studying French literature.

'Student of French literature?' said my disbelieving mother. 'Student of picking up men in Bayswater, more like it.'

I was horrified. I told Lovene who said she'd heard things much worse than that when my parents had had a few drinks.

'How,' I asked my beautiful, clever sister, 'how could a woman who is so kind and considerate to cripples at Christ Church make such an unkind, cruel remark about a girl she'd only seen once and never spoken to? And anyhow, what on earth would Mum know about picking up men in Bayswater?'

I took a train from central Paris to Orsay, a journey that took three-quarters of an hour to cover about fifteen miles. I cannot remember a time in my life when I was more nervous.

At Orsay station, Sir Oswald's Irish chauffeur and house servant, Jerry Lehane, drove me to where they lived, *Le Temple de la Gloire*, which Bob Row told me had been built on the orders of Napoleon for his military hero, Jean Victor Moreau. He told me that at weekends, the man who should have been king, the Duke of Windsor, and the man who should have been Britain's leader, Oswald Mosley, met there at least once a month for lengthy discussions about how to save Britain from the Jews. He said, 'All will be told when the Leader comes to power.' He said with an almost self-mocking smile, 'When the bells ring.'

He said what an honour it was that a working-class boy like me should be invited to the home of The Leader.

I should keep my wits about me and not touch the furniture or take in mud on my shoes because a large black and white chequered carpet had been bought at great expense, along with Lady Mosley's Louis XIV tables and chairs, survivors of the fire in Ireland.

Jerry's wife, Emily, brought in drinks on a silver tray and gave me a re-assuring smile as if to say, 'I know what it's like. It's how I felt when we were being interviewed for the job.'

Sir Oswald sat next to me and asked if the Youth Wing of the Movement was doing well.

I told him that teenagers in England were more interested in Elvis Presley than in politics. That made Max laugh. He stood up and walked towards a large record player called a Black Box in a room where the Sun King would have been at home.

Before putting on 'Jailhouse Rock' he said – 'If Elvis was prime minister of Britain, the world would be a groovier place.'

The remark, delivered in Max's recently acquired mockney voice, delighted his mother who watched her favourite son – *the determined one* – perform an almost perfect imitation of Presley in action.

At the end, he threw out both hands towards his father and said – 'And now your favourite, dad.'

Into a room filled with the music of Wagner and Beethoven, Debussy, Chopin and Brahms came the voice of Presley and the song that made even The Leader tap his feet and smile, 'I don't care if the sun don't shine/I get my lovin' in the evening time.'

He waved at Max. 'Enough of that, Max. Quite enough. See where Alexander is. Why isn't he here to say hello to Grundy?'

Max said, 'He at The Lido with his new bird.'

I said, 'The Lido. The one in Venice?'

Max looked at his mother as if to say, 'What is this cretin doing in our house?'

Mosley tried to put me at ease and said there was a club in Paris also called The Lido. He said, 'Young men like you fighting for change in Britain and my own son spending time chasing after Salvador Dali, Jean Cocteau and a collection of third-rate film stars.'

He said that one day soon the long-predicted economic crisis would come and overwhelm the British people, who would then call on the man with six arms and six legs and the body of a giant to come and save them, to hold up the roof in a house about to collapse. He said it would be like a plane about to crash. Passengers would demand a skilled pilot to take over in the cockpit and land the plane safely. Only then should there be criticism about the way he handled the controls. 'Not while you're up in the air but when the plane lands and lives are safe. I've always said, allow the technicians to clean the plane and oil the works and let the pilot get on with the job of flying it.'

I thought, 'But he's talking to me as if I'm a ten-year-old.'

Lady Mosley rolled her china doll blue eyes and looked at me for the first time as if to say, 'Oh god, how many times have we heard this?'

Sir Oswald went to another part of the house and to my surprise Lady Mosley sat on the sofa next to me.

I didn't know what to say but then for some idiotic reason told her that everyone was looking forward to the Leader's Autumn speaking campaign and how it had been so cold in London the previous winter but that members had rallied and had all gone to meetings, even the outdoor ones.

I said that it had been so cold that big companies that would be owned by the workers and not by foreign exploiters in the Middle East had put up the price of paraffin and so it was much more expensive for my mother to run the oil heater.

She looked at me with her large, beautiful, almost cow-like eyes and asked, 'What is an oil heater?'

Before I could reply, Sir Oswald returned holding what looked like a piece of paper or a pamphlet. He beckoned me to stand next to him on a balcony overlooking a garden, a small lake and two swans gliding like white ghosts across it with the sun starting to fade telling me it was over, time to go.

Sir Oswald looked at me and flashed his eyes and asked me what I would do when I stopped taking people to Spain.

I told him I had to get three 'A' levels and go to university.

He said Jeffrey Hamm told him I was destined for the Church. He said, 'Max and Alex tell me you are close to your mother. I was very close to my mother. That's something I understand.'

Then he asked me if I still felt destined to become a vicar.

I told him I was no longer sure and anyhow, I would postpone any decision about that until after he came to power.

I told him that in Spain, I'd met a reporter from the *Newcastle Journal* and I'd told him how I'd started writing book reviews and short reports. And the journalist told me to apply for a job in Newcastle and that I might do that because then I would be able to write about Union Movement and encourage people to join if they lived in north-east England, where my parents came from, so that would be a good connection.

He reached out and put his right hand on my right shoulder and then handed me a booklet he'd written called Wagner and Shaw.

He put on a pair of glasses, leaned forward and patted the side of his brown corduroy trousers and then took a red biro pen out of the top pocket of his heavy tweed jacket and wrote on it, For Trevor Grundy who has done so much for our movement. Oswald Mosley.

On the train back to Paris, I read the opening paragraph twenty or thirty times. 'The man of action in the realm of art is a helpless being.'

I would always remember that, along with Lady Mosley's inquiries about oil heaters and her scanty knowledge about how ordinary people lived in a Britain that her husband hoped to lead when he received The Call to form a government from Queen Elizabeth II and when the bells throughout the land began to ring.

11

NORTH KENSINGTON, LONDON, 1958/1959

As I walked towards Port Bou Station for the last time, an American newspaper caught my eye. 'Race riots break out in Notting Hill,' screamed the front-page headline. My heart thumped. I bought the paper, turned towards the nearest bar and ordered a large cognac and lit a cigarette. Full of dread, I read the article.

London, September 9 – Race riots flared in Britain last night. Petrol bombs and thousands of milk bottles were thrown at police in West London after white youths taunted black immigrants with racist slogans. Rioting continued throughout much of the night, and this morning the streets of Notting Hill Gate are strewn with broken glass and debris.

Several people were badly injured when a group of white youths began demonstrating outside a house occupied by black people in Blenheim Crescent. They were met by a hail of milk bottles and a petrol bomb, which exploded on the pavement.

Within minutes, black men had begun a counter-attack with iron bars. Although police broke this incident up and dispersed both mobs, sporadic fighting continued, with police advising black people to stay home.

A black man and his girlfriend were chased down Lancaster Road by a white mob shouting, 'Let's get the blacks' and in Bayswater black men were ambushed as they left a club in Ledbury Road. Three petrol bombs were thrown.

Special Branch is investigating the possibility of extreme right-wing movements behind the rioting.

I felt sick. I returned to the Miramar Hotel just half an hour before the departure of a train to Paris. I asked for a typewriter and, as fast as I could, wrote an airmail letter to the news editor of the *Newcastle Journal*.

I told him that I'd received his kind letter offering to interview me in Newcastle at the expense of his newspaper. He'd written and told me there was an opening for a trainee reporter with 'O' level certificates including, of course, English, Pitman's

DOI: 10.4324/9781003375722-12

Shorthand, and a good knowledge of north-east England. If I was suitable I could start in mid-October working under his supervision.

I wrote and said I'd telephone him the moment I got back to London. I stuck a stamp on the envelope and slipped it into the hotel mail delivery tray, wondering how long it would take me to learn shorthand.

I said goodbye to the hotel manager who told me in broken English that I should rest, put on weight and not drink so much. He slapped his fat face and then pointed his finger at mine and said something in Spanish. The Spanish Travel SS resident guide said, 'He wishes you good luck because you will need it. It's our way of saying goodbye.'

I packed my few belongings and a guitar and looked at myself in a cracked mirror. Sad brown eyes stared back. I examined my face for fresh spots.

In Paris, I stayed the night with Andre and his wife. He told me that French radio reporters said Oswald Mosley was behind the Notting Hill race riots. Interviewed people said Mosley should never have been allowed to live in France. But a Union Movement spokesman told AFP that Mosley had nothing to do with race riots and was nowhere near London when they broke out.

Andre asked, 'What will you do now? You must stay away from those people.'

I told him about the possibility of a job as a trainee reporter in Newcastle, almost as far as you could get from Notting Hill Gate.

In his life, Andre had seen a lot of young men confused and on the run. For a moment, I thought of Walter Benjamin. But he was old when he killed himself and I was young. Anyhow, who wanted to die a virgin?

'Be careful,' said Andre. 'You are vulnerable. The hardest thing in the world is to move away finally from what has been pumped into you when you were a child. Remember what Ignatius Loyola said, *"Give me the child of seven and I'll give you the man."*'

The train from the English coast arrived at Victoria Station shortly after six in the evening. I was tired with a weariness I'd never known before.

It was all over. Almost six full months of moving up and down the line of rail with Gladstone bags in either hand, shepherding tourists onto trains, receiving abuse when things went wrong, often sleeping at night in rumbling train corridors, drinking like a fish, smoking and hankering after girls in love with rock n'roll singers in Soho.

All I wanted to do was sink into bed at Blandford Square and hear my mother knocking on the door and coming in with tea on a tray and toast cut up as soldiers. And to be with my sister Lovene, now pregnant for the first time in her small basement flat which she'd turned into an arty den, a beautiful but tormented woman of twenty-three who was married to a man who, like all the rest of us, lived in fantasy land, running around night and day for either Sid Proud or Oswald Mosley.

The more I knew them, the more I asked-

'Did Oswald Mosley break their wings or were they broken long before they met him?'

'Hello, old man.'

John Wood was waiting at the ticket collection gate with three or four Union Movement members, including Jimmy Elves and Barry Aitken, who I'd known since I was eight years of age.

'Welcome home,' said James. 'We're going to need your dulcet tones. Have you heard the news? The whole of Notting Hill is up in arms? I tell you, Trev. It's going to be as big and if not a whole lot bigger than the East End before the war.'

I wanted to run but it was like one of those dreams where your legs won't move. They jostled around me, helping me with my suitcase, one offering to carry my guitar.

A voice said, 'Jeffrey has called a meeting of all London branch leaders at 302 tonight. He wants you to be there. That's why we're here. We're going to need you up there on The Elephant putting OM's policies across to the Teds and angry people seeing blacks on the dole moving into their homes, wrecking the place, playing bloody jukeboxes all night and driving out old sitting tenants from where they were born. And the place is full of Irish who remember it was OM who first denounced the Black and Tans.'

Another chipped in and said, 'Sometimes you've got to laugh. Some Ted I know asks some Irish woman we met if the Black and Tans was either a pint of beer or a West Indian pop group.'

302 Vauxhall Bridge Road was close to Victoria Station. So instead of going home for tea and toasted soldiers with my mother, I went with them to a nearby pub, The Shakespeare, where I fell into a corner chair surrounded by still young Mosleyites waiting for the Old Trevor Grundy to be with them again.

'I'm really, really tired,' I said to John. 'Honestly, I think I'm going to skip this meeting and go home.'

He ignored me, bought another pint and said that this is what we'd been waiting for all our lives. 'What would our oaths of loyalty mean if we ran away now? As OM says, it would be like the Salvation Army running away on the Day of Judgment.'

As the beer went down, I left them to it and went across the road to a telephone kiosk.

My mother said, 'Well, so you've heard the news from Johnnie. What will you do? You'll go, of course.'

'Should I?' I asked.

'Should I? Did I hear right? Should I? This is Mosley's greatest opportunity since the war and a son of mine says 'Should I?' Did St Paul say Should I? when he fell off the donkey?'

I returned to the crowded table near the bar.

'Wow!' said Johnny in his best public schoolboy voice. 'You certainly know how to knock them back. Spain must have put some hair on your chest.'

After a couple more brandies and Coke, I trundled across the road to 302 and joined the rest of the people who'd been summoned to the upper room of 302 to hear what Jeffrey Hamm had to tell us.

A transformation had taken place in Jeffrey Hamm's appearance. He wore a double-breasted grey suit, a white shirt and a silver-coloured tie, his hair neatly cut and shaped, which revealed a prominent widow's peak. A few days before, a reporter from the *Evening News* interviewed him and commented on his dirty shirt and grubby appearance. Now, he looked like a buyer at D.H. Evans or John Lewis in Oxford Street.

We sat down; about forty people crammed into the room that served as Bob Row's editorial office. Soon, the atmosphere was filled with cigarette and cigar smoke.

Jeffrey Hamm delivered the official line. Everyone would follow it, and none of us should talk to journalists. And not a word was to be said about Jews. The days when Union Movement people hated Jews were over and anyone who couldn't adjust to the new policy should find a home in Colin Jordan's National Socialist gang. He said that Mosley described Jordan and his followers as *dwarfs posing in the jackboots of dead giants.*

'Racial problems have been building up in Britain for the last few years. All of you know that. But how did the situation come about? Why did impoverished black people leave their islands in the sun to make a new life in cold and foggy London, Manchester, Birmingham, Leeds and other parts of England?'

It was a Movement speaker's usual trick – ask a question and then answer it.

'Soon after the war, when Britain was bankrupt and living on American charity, like a whore lives off a client, the Clement Atlee Labour government made a deal with the Americans.' Atlee's men said, 'If you let our cars into America so we can earn dollars and pay back all the millions we borrowed from you so we could beat Hitler, we'll stop buying sugar from the West Indies and get it instead from Cuba, which is run by you people, even though a Cuban crook is in charge of the place.'

John nudged me. 'You should be making notes.'

'So, what happened next? What happened next was this.'

'The British government gave black immigrants enough money – our money – to eat three times a day and put a roof over their heads. And the crooks, our old friends from the past, packed them into rooms, twenty at a time. They call it hot-sleeping. A better name is day-light robbery. Multiply one by twenty and you'll see the sort of money they're making. There they are, the same old people singing the same old song – *Money, money, money*. The practice of foreigners driving decent white working people out of their homes to make way for foreigners and crooks. Can't you see them with their same old tricks pretending to help people in need? And so we ask, "Just when will our brave but over-patient people wake up? The few who are wide-awake (and he circled his right arm to include all of us) are in a tiny minority. But not for much longer. As that great G.K. Chesterton said – *We are the people of Britain and we haven't spoken yet*. But, we will, my friends. We will. And that time is now. Rise to it. Seize the moment."'

There was applause as Hamm stood up and gave us the officially banned Fascist salute.

It was as if he was back again at Ridley Road after the war when he attracted thousands of East Enders to his meetings, as well as large contingents of Communists and Jews who wanted to get hold of Mosley and his Hitler-loving wife, who'd both been let out of prison two years before the end of the war on the orders of Winston Churchill, and hang them from the nearest lamp-post.

Hamm's words rolled on, 'The smoked salmon socialists and the champagne swilling revolutionaries are at it again, telling working-class people what to do and how to behave while they get into their boats and planes and make off to the Mediterranean. Take a look at them. They've all got sun tans in the middle of winter.'

He drew in a deep breath, looked round the room and put his hands on his hips like Mosley.

'So, what's the answer, what's the alternative? The answer is to start buying West Indian sugar again and say to the people who want to come here, 'Look my friends, you have long, warm, lovely sandy beaches in Jamaica. Go home and dance on them and not on our streets and staircases.'

There were roars of laughter and I smiled and laughed along with these men, the courageous few who were ready to give their all that Britain might live again.

He brought us into his confidence with a priest-like gesture of comradely trust and told us that The Leader had been attending an important, highly secret, meeting of powerful friends in Europe and that he was now even more determined to return home and get rid of the crooks in Westminster who were destroying our country. 'But,' said Hamm, 'this will be bigger than the East End before the war, bigger than anything we've seen yet. And if we fight as we've never fought before for Mosley, we will win and with that mighty victory, win back the very heart and soul of Britain.'

His words were followed by tumultuous applause.

Baskets of fire came down from above and rested on our heads.

One old East-Ender slapped me on the back and said he hadn't seen me all year. Was I ill because I looked it?

Downstairs, Jeffrey Hamm took me to one side of the room and said that Mosley would publish a new paper called the *North Kensington Leader* and I should write for it and explain policies in simple English, nothing clever, just plain words and no sentences longer than twelve words. He said Mosley had been most impressed when I visited him in Paris and knew that the Grundy Family would do everything to support him.

Before I left, he almost whispered, 'And you'll be pleased to hear that Max has just got a place at Oxford University.'

I got to my room and lay on the bed and tears came into my eyes. Max at Oxford and me with four 'O' levels.

In a dream, I took down all the pictures of Mosley, Hitler and Mussolini and gave them to Derek. But then a voice said 'Derek isn't here. He's gone to live in Germany with Rudolf Hess.' So, I put them all up again next to black and white pictures of Antony Perkins and a large colour picture of Brigitte Bardot. I was with Avril sitting in a Van Gogh café in Port Bou and then with Andre in a nightclub in Paris listening to a man playing the 'Horst Wessel' on an accordion and then the voice of a man so tall his head clipped the clouds saying to me – 'Don't get involved. Get involved. Keep away from them. They will destroy you. Join in the fight. Did St Paul ask *Should I?*'

I got out of bed and dressed and spoke to my mother and then rang the editor at the *Newcastle Journal* and told him I had renewed my contract with Spanish Trave SS so I didn't want to train as a reporter after all.

How could I leave Mosley at the moment of his return to England? It would be impossible. I would not be able to live with myself writing about football matches at St James's Park and understanding geordie, which would be like learning a foreign language. What a betrayal at a time of The Leader's greatest challenge.

I was now wide awake and dressed and I straightened up and saluted Mosley on the wall and said to myself, 'You were and you always will be a member of a hand-picked elite ready to give your all so that a great land might live again.'

And then, a knock on the door and my mother's voice asking me if I wanted a boiled egg or a kipper.

12

NORTH KENSINGTON, 1959

Notting Hill Gate gave the sixty-three-year-old Oswald Mosley his final chance to shine. Like Don Quixote, an earlier legend who also found it hard to live in his own century, Mosley turned up in the race-torn London borough of North Kensington on a clapped-out horse with a collection of Sancho Panzas, who were prepared to walk, ride, jog or slide with him to the edge of British Fascism's last cliff.

Union Movement set up a second headquarters in North Kensington, and members were asked to spend time handing out leaflets, selling *Action* on street corners and circulating the free broadsheet, the *North Kensington Leader*. In its first issue, I wrote an article which repeated almost word for word what Jeffrey Hamm told us the night of my return from Spain. It ended with words that were sometimes quoted by visiting journalists, 'Most coloured immigrants are decent folk. They are victims of a vicious system which they cannot understand.'

Peter Shaw, who said he'd lay on the floor and let Oswald Mosley walk over him if that meant there'd be one less Jew or black in England, didn't agree. 'Instead of writing your fairy-tale fuckin' articles in a paper that nobody reads, we should get hold of an immigrant and hang him upside-down from Blackfriars Bridge with a notice round his neck saying, 'Coloureds go home!'

What he said went straight to Jeffrey Hamm, who'd told people not to mention the word 'Jew.' Shaw was called in and reprimanded by Mosley but later in the pub he told us, 'OK, the Old Man gave me a good telling-off. Some bloke from an American paper was in the corridor waiting for an interview. OM shouted at me and said, "Shaw! Never say anything like that again. This movement attacks some Jews for what they do but we never attack Jews for what they are. This is my final warning." Then, and this is god's own truth, he winked.'

DOI: 10.4324/9781003375722-13

Several well-known Teds joined the North Kensington Branch. My brother-in-law, John Wood, was branch leader, but he was angling for a full-time job with Oswald Mosley now that the tourist season was over.

Hundreds of Irish people promised to join Union Movement, and hundreds more attended open-air meetings during which Jeffrey Hamm was at great pains to stay on the right side of the law. He called for an end to riots but demanded firm action by the government to end what the Movement called 'the coloured invasion.'

There were thousands of Irish people living in North Kensington, immigrants to Britain from an earlier time. But even in 1958, there were notices on doors and windows, 'No Irish, dogs, coloureds.'

Mosley walked to meetings, followed by East End supporters and a growing number of Teds who thought it was great that a man with Sir Oswald's background and class thought the same way as they did about immigrants. In dark and crumbling doorways, West Indians stood and stared as a man they knew little about walked by.

I'd grown my hair quite long and started wearing a duffel coat. One night, one of the Teds guarding Mosley's truck, looked at me and said something about 'fuckin lefties.'

'He's one of us.' said Ron Clucas

'Don't look it,' said the Ted.

I told Jeffrey Hamm that I would never speak during this campaign because the people we were attracting were not interested in parliamentary reforms or Europe a Nation, just in wading into coloured immigrants who Jeffrey told reporters had been given just as raw a deal as the people whose homes they were now occupying.

Hamm said, 'You're letting the Movement down. It will be remembered when Sir Oswald wins a seat in Parliament and there's money to spare for the right people to tour with him throughout the country.'

I often saw Max Mosley and his girlfriend, Jean Taylor, canvassing alongside Lady Mosley.

Max no longer looked my way, yet alone spoke.

They knocked on doors and told Irish housewives how 'pleased' Sir Oswald would be if they voted for him and how he would continue his fight for Irish unity when he returned to Parliament.

Max was about to study physics at Oxford, and Bob Row told me in strict confidence that Lady D used her influence to get him a place at Christ Church College. He said, 'She knows the right people and that's how the system works. But that will all change when OM comes to power.'

Soon after that, a leading British tabloid published a picture of Max and his older brother Alexander dressed like Teds saying they were in North Kensington to support their father. 'We've come down here to help,' Max told a reporter. He looked almost pretty in his riches-to-rags get-up. Alexander, with fists clenched, looked more like his father when he was twenty-one.

Soon after that photograph appeared, Alexander came to the house.

'I want to get away from this god-forsaken island. I want to go and live in South America where people are alive and issues are real. God, this anti-immigrant campaign sickens me. We lived in Ireland and now in France and my father condemns immigrants. I need to get away from him. Trouble is, I look so much like him and you probably didn't know but my first name is Oswald.'

He looked at his short and stumpy hands.

'Peasant's hands just like my Aunt Unity, the one who shot herself when war was declared.'

He put them around his ears as if to shut out a noise only he could hear. 'He laughs because I do weight-lifting and tells everyone in Paris that it's the only sport where you compete against yourself.' He turned and looked at the photograph on the wall and then at another which showed his father in a white fencing outfit smiling and patting a Swedish champion on the shoulder.

He said, 'My mother's no help. She sympathises with me but gives in the moment my father says anything. You know she couldn't be in the same room as Cynthia Proud. And she thinks that you're a bad influence, too.'

I felt like he'd stuck a knife into me. 'Me? Or my family?'

'You.'

'Did she say why, give a reason?'

'Why would she? When she doesn't like someone she never mentions them again. You go onto her non-speakers list. It's some code used by those Mitford girls everyone thinks are so wonderful. My father calls them The Sillies.'

My mother knocked on the door, came in and placed a tray with coffee and two chocolate biscuits on a plate.

She said, 'I've got something special to show you, Alexander.' It was the Christmas card she'd bought to send to The Leader in France. It cost seven and sixpence but that includes postage.

I thought Alexander would do his charming act. Instead, he drew a stiletto and plunged it into her.

'Mrs Grundy. I am tired of Old Members treating my father as if he was some sort of Jesus Christ or St Paul. He's just a rather ordinary man, an ordinary human being with many failings as a person and as a father. Do you know what happens every year when you send your precious Christmas cards that cost seven and sixpence including postage to France? Every year, our house-keeper and her husband gather them up, put them in a large brown cardboard box, light a fire and burn them. Strangely enough, the flames don't seem to bother the swans one little bit.'

She left the room and I heard the kitchen door close.

'Christ, Al,' I said. 'Why did you say that?'

I went along the corridor that was still covered with cheap lino bought when we first moved to Blandford Square after the war.

She was smoking and staring into space. I didn't know what to do or say to comfort her.

'The Leader's Christmas card. So that's what happens.'

I put my arm around her. 'No, of course not, Mum. Alexander's just fed up. He's had some row with his father and is lashing out. He didn't mean it.'

My mother straightened up. 'Of course not.' She smiled. 'And if your father could see me smoking, he'd have a fit.'

When I went back to my room Alexander had gone. I never saw him again.

Though I was no longer comfortable at the heart of Union Movement, I didn't know where else to go. I had no friends other than the young Fascists I'd been with since I was a child. There was no place to go apart from Blandford Square, and I lacked the courage to go and live with Andre and his wife in Paris. I became a sort of fellow traveller canvassing for Mosley but no longer completely believing in him or his message.

On April 6, 1959, at Argyl Hall, North Kensington, Mosley out-did Laurence Olivier as an actor when he modestly and with surprise written all over his still handsome face accepted an offer by the local branch of Union Movement to stand as its candidate at the general election scheduled for October that year. That was only a couple of years after Harold Macmillan told the British people that they'd never had it so good.

At that meeting, about six hundred people heard Mosley explain the intricacies of the wage-price mechanism which would control the economies of a Federal Europe. He repeated highlights from his pre-war speeches, which opposed war against Germany and which warned that if Britain went to war it would lose its Empire and end up on the scrap heap. He hardly mentioned immigration or the coloured invasion, which left his followers loyal but confused.

My father said in a pub after that meeting, 'He's lost it. Something happened when he was in prison. He talks about the wage-price mechanism to an audience of Irish women singing songs about the wearing of the green. He should pack it in. Mosley's finished. When he stopped attacking the Yids, that's when I asked myself, "Is this the Oswald Mosley you went to prison for during the war?"'

But Mosley gave the appearance of enjoying himself immensely at street meetings. After his main speech, which would leave the Teds shouting for more, he'd offer the platform which was on the back of a hired van, to anyone who cared to speak about life in North Kensington and Notting Hill.

Mosley stood down and became a member of the audience, towering like a high-rise building over everyone else as Irish housewives told how immigrants had taken over their streets, flats and houses and installed jukeboxes which were played all night, forcing elderly sitting tenants to leave and look for accommodation somewhere else in London.

Mosley shook his head in disgust and then applauded.

Then he'd get back up and let rip about corruption and betrayal, using all the verbal tricks he'd picked up in the 1930s from various Fascists and Nazi leaders in Italy and Germany.

'You, the hard-working people of Britain have been betrayed by the old gang and their old and rotten political parties. Put 'em all in a box. Shake it up and down, roll out the dice and look at what you've got. You can't tell the difference between one and the other. They all look the same. They all act the same. They all betray the same. *Tweedledum and Tweedledee.* Vote for me at this election and together we will change, not only North Kensington but the whole country and show the world that Britain can be great again!'

On the way to the Warwick Arms, a Mosley-friendly pub, one of the Teds shook his head and said to Clucas, 'Where's this Tweedle bloke 'ang out? Sounds like he's up for a good kicking.'

One night I spotted the writer Colin Wilson in the crowd. Wilson, author of the 1957 best-seller *The Outsider.* He wrote regularly for a Carmelite magazine called the *Aylesford Review* whose editor, Father Brocard Sewell, was a friend of Henry Williamson and a man who often stuck his editorial neck out on behalf of the pre-war Fascist leader. The novelist Nicholas Mosley was also there, along with several members of the Roman Catholic Church, who'd been invited to attend by Jeffrey Hamm.

Mosley started calmly and spoke about Europe a Nation and how the collective genius of the European would give birth to the greatest civilisation the world had ever seen once he came to power and encouraged a new kind of politician to work hand-in-hand with the great scientists of our age. I saw Roman Catholic heads turn and look at one another.

But the audience showed signs of boredom. This was not what they'd missed an episode of 'Coronation Street' to hear.

Like Archie Rice in John Osborne's play *The Entertainer*, Mosley sniffed the air, sensed the mood and changed position.

He crouched and threw both fists forward like a boxer in the ring. He started raving about West Indian men capturing English girls and keeping them locked in flats, where they were beaten and raped.

When he saw how this engaged and enthralled the non-clerical section of his large audience was, he stood up tall and straight and directed his gaze at some almost Presley-looking Teds in the audience. He spoke calmly and told them that after the election, he'd tell his sleeping colleagues in the House of Commons to wake up, visit North Ken and learn at last to call a spade a spade.

The audience roared with laughter, and a high-pitched voice rang like a bell in the cold night air – 'Fuckin' Spades.'

Mosley, once again calm and almost statesman-like, said that all coloured immigrants should be sent back where they came from where they could eat their bananas in the sunshine and not live off the hard-working British taxpayer.

This giant of a man from one of England's great families, which once owned large parts of Manchester, said something that registered shock on the faces of even the most hardened, roller-pin-holding Irish housewives that night.

He said they could all return home and eat their own fresh fruits and vegetables and erase the North Kensington slogan – 'Lassie for dogs. Kitty Kat for Wogs.'

It was a reference to the rumour going round that West Indians ate cat food so they'd have more money to spend on drugs.

I looked up to see how these startling words had affected Colin Wilson and the Roman Catholics from Brompton Oratory but they had already left.

As the election grew closer, Mosley's confidence grew stronger. Jeffrey Hamm said the vast majority of residents were now behind the Leader and the question was no longer if he'd win. The question was how large his majority would be.

At a tactics meeting at the Union Movement headquarters at 47 Princedale Road, Jeffrey Hamm said that although the police confirmed that no one in Union Movement had been involved in the murder of an Antiguan carpenter called Kelso Cochrane on May 16 at the corner of Southall Street and Goldborne Road, it did go to show how explosive the race problem was throughout North Kensington.

Left unchecked, said Hamm, race hate would spread through London and other parts of Britain.

'So, you should feel proud you're doing something meaningful to end that problem. The people who are guilty, are the liberal do-gooders and champagne socialists in St John's Wood and Swiss Cottage who bury their heads like ostriches in the sand hoping the problem will go away without doing the first thing to solve it.'

'So, when people say "You're the racists" turn round and fight back and say, "No. *You're* the racists because you're doing nothing to solve the problem. Just looking away and making it worse. You're the ostriches. We're the people who are facing up to the problem and trying to solve it."'

'By drawing attention to the slum conditions in North Kensington you should say that we're the people looking after blacks just as much as we're looking after whites. All we are saying is that they should have their home and we should have our home – Britain. And Lady Mosley has stepped in and given good advice. She says we should stop referring to immigrants as *fuzzy-wuzzies* because that might give some people the wrong impression about us. So, watch what you say when you're canvassing, selling *Action* or having a drink when there's people around you don't know. As to the thousands of whites who attended Cochrane's funeral. They're outsiders from different parts of well-off London, people looking for something to make their lives interesting – communists, anti-apartheid people. By this time next year, no-one will remember the name of Kelso Cochrane.'

My brother-in-law John Wood was Mosley's election agent. He worked round the clock for Union Movement and spent little time with Lovene and their new baby, a boy named Vincent after Lovene's favourite painter, Vincent van Gogh.

On the underground going home to Blandford Square, he said, 'Max and his mother seem to be running the show. But it's good what she says about not talking to journalists. The Leader says the only people who should talk to reporters are Jeffrey and Max. Reporters from the "News of the World" have started snooping around the Earl of Warwick and after a few pints, tongues loosen and blathermouths like Ron Clucas don't know when to stop. If our people spent less time in the pub and more time on the streets canvassing, we might get somewhere at long last. The Old Man's not getting any younger and I don't know what he's up to but when Lady D is back in Paris, we can't find him for days on end. And that lunatic

Peter Shaw is doing a lot of damage, telling people he knows who killed Kelso Cochrane. If the "News or the World" or "The People" get hold of that it could cost OM the election. Mosley has already told him to wind his neck in. But does he? It's as if he doesn't take what the Leader says at all seriously.'

But it was impossible to separate the death of Kelso Cochrane from Mosley's decision at Argyll Hall to stand as the Union Movement candidate on the immigration issue. Labour Party supporters told voters that Mosley accepted on April 6, and Cochrane was murdered a month later on May 16. Mosley told his followers to ignore claims that there was any link between the two events and that the police said Cochrane's death had nothing to do with racism. Mosley said that he was ready to speak at the site where Cochrane was killed and that when difficulties arose his advice to his followers would always be the same, 'Don't look back. Never regret the past. Say it again but be ruder the second time and above all – Move on!'

One night at Princedale Road, Mosley examined a number of black and white photographs taken by the Movement's official photographer, John Warburton. He held them up to a light bulb without a shade, smiled and then looked at me and said, 'Nice pair of eyebrows, Grundy.' It was a picture of Mosley at Trafalgar Square and in the background a headshot of me looking at him. After a while he chose one of him walking towards the camera, looking like an elderly Clark Cable in *Gone with the Wind*. He said that was the one he wanted and that underneath a life-sized poster would be the slogan, He is Coming.

I caught the eye of my brother-in-law. Was it possible? Didn't he understand what a joke that would be, especially with his reputation as a womaniser?

Mosley said, 'I hope it doesn't sound too Biblical.'

A week or so later, every Mosley poster in North Kensington was defaced. Between his legs, a massive, upright penis. Underneath in paint or crayon. the words 'whoopee' and 'lucky sod.'

Several times, I went canvassing with my mother who was suffering from severe depressions, mood swings and headaches. A semi-paralysing form of arthritis went into both her hands, which she'd put into a large bowl full of hot wax hour after hour but with little relief from agonising pain.

She often said, 'What is to become of me, Trevor?'

When I was a child and she said something like that, I'd put my arms round her waist and say, 'Mummy. It will be alright when The Leader comes to power.'

But now I had nothing to say, no help to give. I watched, without knowing what to do, the decline and fall of a once beautiful and fully alive woman who removed all my own doubts when she told me to be like St Paul, stand tall, walk forward and preach about a new world within the grasp of all who believed in Oswald Mosley. But now, she was staring into an abyss no one else could see. And the abyss was staring back.

Climbing up several flights of stairs at a council flat in North Kensington one night, I asked her what was really wrong and she said she didn't believe in Mosley as she had in the past. 'I still admire his courage,' she said, 'but he's not the man I thought he was when he came in from the rain that night in Brighton before you were born.'

I wanted to say, 'But Mum. You're not that same woman.'

But it was cold and raining and I was tired and there were several more flights to climb, several more doors to knock on, doors that would open and then shut again the moment the name of Sir Oswald Mosley was mentioned.

Afterwards in the kitchen, she said, 'I'll never be able to see him the same way again, not now that I know all the Christmas cards are put into a box and burnt.'

'Huh,' snorted my father. 'If Mosley was in power, the first people he'd get rid of would be us lot, his old members. Mosley would be more *national* than *socialist*, wining and dining with his upper-class mates at Whites Club or wherever he goes for lunch in London. When they're in power, they're all the same.'

Late September along the Portobello Road, my mother said, as if she was quoting lines from a play, 'I think I made a mistake muddling Mosley up with Jesus.'

I felt a wave of anger overcome me.

I wanted to grab her and shake her and yell at her and say, 'Yes, and what do you think you've done to Lovene and me over the years growing up with your obsessions?'

It started to rain and she put up an umbrella and gave me her Mosley look.

'I think he's more like John the Baptist, paving the way for someone else. Until now, I hoped that someone would be you. But maybe it'll be Max or Alexander. How are they? They haven't been round to the house for ages. You haven't quarrelled, have you? Is Ali still with that Proud lass? She had trouble written all over her face. And Max with a policeman's daughter from Brixton. Can't they find girls like their mother?'

As gently as possible and fearful that tears would swell in my eyes as I spoke, I told her that I regretted the way I'd been brought up because it had distanced me from everyone I knew outside Union Movement, from boys at school, girls of my age, in fact everything that was normal.

'*Normal*! Are you trying to tell me that you're not normal?'

I said that someone I'd been very fond of told me that I'd never believe in anything after the age of thirty.

'If the blacks take over, you won't reach thirty,' she snapped back.

And so, on and upward we went in an uncomfortable silence, knocking on doors which were shut seconds after they were opened.

One night when she was in a happier mood, I pulled her leg and said that if the Jews really did run the world, she should cash in her chips and join the winning side.

'There are times, Mum, when you'd have no trouble passing as a four by two.'

She looked pleased.

'Do you think so, or is that your father talking? I've got my mother's nose and eyes and when we were little, she told us we had Spanish blood. No one said anything about being Jewish. Anyway, they were all kicked out of Spain in 1492 by the

Catholic royal family. You can thank your lucky stars that I'm not Jewish because if I was, you'd be one, too, because our line is matriarchal.'

I stopped dead in the street. '*Our line*? What on earth do you mean? *Our* line!' She was quick to change the subject and never replied.

It was too bizarre to even think about and anyhow, her moods were up and down like the Tower Bridge so she probably didn't know what she was saying.

But soon afterwards, during a final canvassing session before election day, something happened that began to turn my world upside-down.

My mother knocked on a door of a rather expensive-looking block of flats where people paid key-money before moving in. After she rang the bell, she looked for the name of the occupant on a piece of paper supplied by my brother-in-law. 'Oh, goodness,' she said. 'I've made a mistake. Too late now.'

The door opened and my mother said, 'Mr Lewin. Mr *Harold* Lewin?'

He smiled, perhaps wondering where they'd met before. 'That's right,' he said. 'Harold is my name. Insurance is my game.' What can I do for you, good lady, on this rainy but far from unpleasant September evening?

She returned his smile. 'Mr Lewin. We're representing Sir Oswald Mosley's Union Movement and we'd like to talk to you about next week's election. We believe that a vote for Oswald Mosley will be a vote for the British people in Parliament and even though you might have heard a lot of nonsense about him before the war, we'd like to invite you to his final meeting which will be at . . .'

'*Hold on, hold on, hold on*,' he said dogging half his lit cigarette with his foot.

'I get the joke. But where've we met before. Your face is familiar but I just can't think where or when we met.'

She carried on with the Movement election waffle.

He said, 'Come on now, who are you kidding?' I know who put you up to this. It was Larry, wasn't it? Larry. If he spent more time flogging cars and less time playing silly sods, he might get somewhere. We were only talking about Mosley the other night and he said North Ken is in need of more jokes, so I suppose this is what it's all about. Some sort of birthday joke? That was last week. I mean, you couldn't possibly be serious.'

A long pause and then, 'Right! Now, I've got it! You're his relatives, the ones moving from Bristol to Netanya who were going to call in when you got to London. Come in. Come in. You're welcome. You look as if you're in need of a stiff one. Bring the boy, too. And what's your name, son?'

He waved us towards his lounge but instead we turned and fled.

'Don't go,' he said. '*No offence. What I meant when I said a stiff one was . . . don't go! I didn't mean anything untoward.*'

His pleading voice faded away, and we went down flight after flight of stairs. My mother was breathless with laughter as we half-walked and half-ran back towards Mosley's temporary headquarters not far from the area's synagogue.

'He thinks I'm a Jewess,' she said. 'He really thinks I'm a Jew. Wait until I tell your father. He was certain, wasn't he? Tell me I'm right, Trevor. Tell me. He really thought I was a Jew? Wait until I tell your father when he gets home. Thank goodness you were there otherwise he'd say I was making it up.'

But when we got home that night, my now taxi-driver father was tired and hungry but pleasantly surprised that he'd made over twenty pounds that day.

My mother made no mention of her experiences at the doorstep of Harold Lewin.

My father was in a light-hearted mood and told us that the whole black cab sector was run by 'Jewboys.'

She said, 'If only they knew.'

'Perhaps they do,' he replied. 'You don't get one of these (he touched his driver's badge) without the cops knowing about who you are and where you come from?'

He said, 'They surely knew about Naumann's son staying with us, and Skorzeny's daughter, Hans Ulrich Rudel, Ribbentrop's and Himmler's daughter and all those kids of Nazi leaders strutting round Regent's Park with Trevor and Lovene, the boys in their *lederhosen* pants and the girls looking like waitresses at an Oktoberfest in Munich, all here for their summer holidays paid for by Oswald Mosley.'

Again, he looked at his silver cabdriver's badge and kissed it. 'I won't be handing this in for anyone. Better than some silly war medal in exchange for your arms and legs.'

He laughed again.

'I'm taking some Jewish kids down to Brighton next week. Some charity that the Yids organise once a year. I'm not sticking my neck out anymore for anyone ever again. Not even Mosley. Never again. Never.'

She kept quiet and fingered the pound notes in the hat as if they were candles around a birthday cake.

At the height of the North Kensington campaign, Oswald Mosley telephoned the house and asked to speak to me. My mother told me when I returned from work as a clerk at the nearby National Cash Register Company. It was an easy job and one that fitted my academic qualifications, or lack of them. I looked at my mother and thought she had St Virus's Dance. Despite her recent doubts about Mosley, she still clearly adored the man. I rang him back at his home in Cheyne Walk.

It was like a general speaking to a private. 'Grundy. Good of you to call. If you have time, it would be appreciated. It's personal, not political.'

I went by tube to Sloane Square and walked the rest of the way. I looked around and wondered if Cheyne Walk and North Kensington were on the same planet. I passed large, expensive cars parked outside rows of magnificent homes whose walls were decorated with blue plaques commemorating the lives of famous people who'd lived in one of London's most picturesque and expensive areas alongside the River Thames.

Jerry, Sir Oswald's manservant, let me in with a look of slight amusement on his face, the sort of look you get from door-men outside the Dorchester Hotel once they've sussed-out that you're from the lower down end of the class thermometer.

'Sir Oswald is expecting you upstairs,' he said in his Irish lilt.

Mosley wore a herringbone jacket and an open-necked shirt. He told me he'd been writing and was tired and thanked me for coming at a moment's notice. He came quickly to the point. He knew that I was a friend of Alexander and that I'd worked for Sid Proud. He was concerned that Proud would publish and circulate a pamphlet accusing him of encouraging Alexander not to do his National Service. It had ended for those born after 1940. But Alexander was born in 1938. He had been brought up in Ireland but an accusation that his son refused to do his patriotic duty would do enormous damage to his campaign to get back to Parliament. By the time the case went to court, the election would have been ancient history. Mosley asked me to go and see Sid Proud and find out what needed to be done to stop a further flow of bad blood between two men who had been comrades in the struggle.

For me, this was a massive honour. I was to be a discreet ambassador acting for Sir Oswald Mosley. I promised to do my best and report back the moment I'd seen Sid Proud at his large rented flat close to Earl's Court tube station.

The following day was a Saturday. I telephoned Proud and asked if I could meet him at his Coventry Street office. When I got there, Proud was with Joe Warren and a tall, mean-looking man with a moustache and an elderly man called George Sutton, who had once been Mosley's private secretary. I passed on Mosley's message and stood nervously waiting for Proud's reaction.

'So, now you're a Mosley nark,' Proud snarled. 'First a Jesus nark. Now a Mosley nark. Tell your Bleeder that his son has treated my daughter like *trash*. Like *scum*. Tell him that from me. Like *dirt*. Tell him that pamphlet will go under every door and into every letter box in North Kensington. Tell him that from me and bugger off and don't let me see your face again. Mosley nark.'

I went back to Cheyne Walk and told Mosley what Proud had said. I dared to add that Proud was a disgusting little man, and it was terrible for me to see a man like Sir Oswald asking such a person for a favour.

Mosley looked at me and waved his hand towards the open door.

As I left the room, I heard him say to his servant, 'Get me Lane.' Lane was his solicitor. But I knew he was also Proud's, so perhaps a clever lawyer could sort things out and end a war between two litigious-minded men he jointly served.

The following week I heard that Alexander Mosley had left England for somewhere in Europe or was it Latin America?

My father spent most of his life picking up fares and so the money rolled in. When his father died, he inherited a bungalow in Northumberland but soon sold it to pay off all his old debts acquired after the 43 Group told him his days as a street photographer at Hampton Court were over and done with.

He bought his first car, the latest version of the family saloon designed by Frederick Porsche in 1935 and made financially available to German families by Adolf Hitler, a VW Beetle.

One night he came to North Kensington. He skipped Mosley's speech but when it was over joined supporters in the Earl of Warwick, not far from where Kelso Cochrane had been beaten and stabbed to death.

'Haven't seen you in a while, Sid,' said one of the old members he knew from his days as a Jew-basher in Hye Park after the war.

In a loud, provocative voice, he said that Mosley was trying to repeat his days of glory in the East End of London but that he didn't stand a chance in North Kensington.

'People are too comfortable. It's what Macmillan said – You've never had it so good. Ordinary people don't want Mosley telling them about problems because there aren't any problems for them to see. All he ever does is work people up, stand back and enjoy the cheering. What do they all do then? They go home to a warm house or flat, have a beer, see what on their television sets, go to sleep and wake up and wonder what all the noise was about the night before. He's wasting his time and should pack it in, call it a day. He was never a real Fascist, anyhow. Not like Benito Mussolini.'

I thought there'd be a fight, so I left my father to it.

It was then that I noticed a man standing on his own in a corner taking notes. He wore a long brown leather coat and had an interesting aristocratic face, thinning hair and a large nose. Possibly a Jew. He stood up when the pub door opened and Jeffrey Hamm came in. Then a voice that was calm and clear and which came from another world.

'Jeffrey! My *dear* Jeffrey! What *would* you like to drink? *Blissful* beer or *dreamy* gin? You must be quite *exhausted* coming so *heroically* out of the trenches.'

For a moment, silence reigned. But Union Movement heads soon returned to the night's true business – ordering more pints to toast The Leader and victory on October 8.

Jeffrey Hamm and the man in the leather coat sat and talked for about ten minutes.

'Who on earth is that?' I asked Bob Row. He said, 'That's Alan Neame, a friend of Lady D. Writes poetry for The European. Some world expert on Ezra Pound. Family owns a brewery in Kent. Great friend of Desmond Stewart and, of course, OM.'

The poet must have had his antenna in our direction because he looked up and gave a half-smile. Minutes later, he was at the bar talking to my father. I bought myself a drink and heard him talking about his days in prison and how the Jews were running Britain, Europe, America and the world.

Bob Row said it was okay to talk to him because he was UM friendly and was doing an article for the Roman Catholic weekly magazine *The Tablet* about what was going on in North Kensington and the impending election.

My father went to the lavatory and Alan Neame turned to me and said, 'Your father is quite wonderful. He seems to think that your Leader is copping out, taking on the blacks instead of the Jews. I rather agree. My goodness, at least the Jews were a reputable enemy. I can't say that for most of the poor dears walking around this part of the world with their banjos and bananas. I feel rather sorry for them. I mean, moving from their lovely islands to Latimer Road. What next, may I ask?'

I called him Mr Neame. He said, 'It's Alan. You are Trevor. You spoke at Trafalgar Square when you were just seventeen and you went to a Church of England grammar school but left to go and live in Franco's Spain. How dreamy. Such bliss. Your dear father has told me all.'

He said he had to go and write in his tiny room in Paddington, but would I like to join him for supper the following week at a *divine* and totally *dreamy* and *Il Duce-friendly* Italian restaurant in the Edgware Road. He said, 'Sidney is quite wonderful but I don't think we need to invite him, do you?'

He tightened his belt round a coat that made him look quite a lot like the famous SS number two to Himmler, Reinhard Heydrich.

He left and a group of Freddie Shepherd's boys from North Islington came across. One said, 'Watch out, Trev. Did I 'ear 'im ask you out?'

'Why not?' I said. 'He's a friend of Lady Mosley and writes for The European. We did poetry at school and I'm interested because he's a published poet writing a novel about black people in Africa.'

'Poet, my arse,' said Shepherd. 'One of *them*, more like it.'

Bill Dodds took me to one side. He had been a part of the Grundy family for years, a man to look up to because he'd been imprisoned on the Isle of Mann during the war. But like so many who'd passed through the ranks of the British Union of Fascists before the war and Union Movement after it, he'd lost faith in Mosley but couldn't quite let go. North Kensington drew him back, a honey pot for a bee.

That night in the pub he was young again but wary because in the past he had rubbed shoulders with so many of the fanatical Fascists who hated Jews too much but who had been placed inside the BUF and Union Movement by M15 and Special Branch.

'Be careful,' he said. 'People like him are from another world. He's one of Lady Mosley's entertainers. She has a thing about homosexuals. They go across to Paris to have meetings about what's to go in or take out of The European and everything turns into a party. Alan Neame and Desmond Stewart are part of that set, along with some of their intellectual friends who went to Oxford with them after the war. They all have homes in Italy, Portugal, Spain, the Middle East. All of them have private incomes, remittance men. When they were young they found England intolerant. Now they're older, they find it incomprehensible. But they do make Lady D laugh. It's how she judges people. Do you or do you not make her roar with laughter? So, what does someone like that want with you?'

13

LONDON, OCTOBER 1959

Alan Neame didn't ring but that was just as well. I'd received so many warnings to steer clear.

Jeffrey Hamm told me a little about him, how he was the *scion* of a family who ran Shepherd Neame in Faversham in Kent, which was said to be Britain's oldest brewery, how he went to Cheltenham College and then to Oxford University. His degree course was cut short because of the war.

'He was an officer somewhere in the Far East but he never spoke about what he'd seen and done there.'

When the war was over, he went back to Oxford and studied languages, the classics and literature at Wadham College, where he met and teamed-up with a formidable and brilliant same-age Scot from Norfolk, Desmond Stewart, an Oswald Mosley fanatic who'd fled to Ireland in 1940, was never caught or imprisoned for refusing to serve but who went back to Oxford and openly campaigned for Mosley to address the Oxford Union.

In the mid-1950s, Stewart and Neame whizzed off to the Middle East, where they taught English and good manners to the children of upper-crust Arabs at Baghdad University.

To earn extra money, they edited a fiercely anti-Israel English monthly magazine the *Arab Observer*, which was based in Cairo where they met ex-Nazis and German scientists.

They made their names in Arab circles as two polished, well-educated and upper-class Englishmen who opposed Zionism and supported Arab Nationalism and its leading representative, President Nasser.

Hamm looked at his watch and said the morning UM election briefing was soon to begin.

DOI: 10.4324/9781003375722-14

'So, your Mr Alan Neame is also a respected translator, a friend of Jean Cocteau and Ezra Pound and a regular contributor to The European. He mainly writes about Pound's cantos which no one is able to read without an interpreter. Lady D adores him because he makes her laugh. She also likes his brand of Catholic Fascism which so helped Mussolini during the Abyssinian Campaign in 1935. Of course, Alan Neame and a lot of people like him who are thinking of crossing over, have problems with some of the Vatican's teachings on certain subjects. He was brought up a strict Anglican but appears, at long last, to be batting for the other side, in more ways than one. So be careful.'

But he did ring and said the delay in getting in touch had been caused by his mother's sudden flight of fancy to do all her Christmas shopping in Rome that year. And then a laugh which became so familiar over the coming years, a laugh he called the 'Mitford Roar.'

He said Italy was the best country in the world for leather shoes and that I should drop everything and go there before meeting him for supper at the Il Duce-friendly restaurant he'd mentioned at eight o'clock on Saturday, October 3.

I told him that was not possible because October 3 was my mother's fifty-second birthday and that my father had booked tickets for a Frankie Vaughan Show at the Metropolitan Music Hall that evening, followed by a fish and chip supper in Bell Street.

He said, 'What bliss,' adding that the following evening would do just as well and that I needn't bother with a tie and should not be late.

That Sunday, I popped into St Mark's Church as the evensong worshippers were coming out. I sat in a pew at the back of the church and looked up at the pulpit where Father Crisp had spoken so loudly and so well against nuclear weapons and *apartheid* and said a prayer to make my meeting with Mr Neame a success so that it would lead to something other than a clerking job at the National Cash Register Company.

When I reached the restaurant, Alan was there, tanned and smiling. He poured oil and vinegar into a large spoon to prepare a salad dressing, something that seemed so clever and different.

I told him about how Jeffrey Hamm chose me to speak at Trafalgar Square and how Max and Ali Mosley came to the house and how Bob Row told me when Mosley came to power boys from working-class families would get into the same schools as the children of the rich and that's why it was essential Mosley won the election but there'd been a problem with Sid Proud and . . .

He held up his hand to divert a river of words.

'My dear boy,' he said, 'surely it's time you started thinking of yourself and stopped whizzing around London on schoolboy errands on behalf of Sir Oswald and his rather annoying family. After all, he has a legion of lawyers to call on if he wishes to do battle with the demonic Mr Proud.'

I watched the way he ate his food and sipped his wine and imitated him.

'When all this Notting Hill business is over, your precious Leader will take off for Venice and you'll be left wondering what to do next with your life and your four "O" levels, slaving away for a cash machine company with people who wouldn't be able to spell the name "Mosley" yet alone understand his wage-price mechanism or how he will re-build Jamaica and send thousands of black people home with pounds in their pockets and smiles on their faces. Surely, that's not what a good National Socialist young man such as yourself wants out of life?'

It was hard to understand if Alan was joking or serious. He made me laugh so much that I could hardly eat. Most of his jokes involved Mosley and the Mitford gals. But where did that leave him? Was he, or was he not, one of us? Did people like Alan spend their lives turning gossip into art while writing amusingly but cruel poems and letters about their friends?

At the end of the meal, he called the manager and said something in Italian. Someone put on a record. Mario Lanza singing 'Be My Love,' which made me remember Loven's sad wedding day two years before. The manager said, 'My friend Mister Alan likes this one because Mario Lanza sang 'Giovinezza' for 'Il Duce' in Rome.'

The manager, a man in his late fifties or early sixties, stood to attention and his tenor voice rang out in an empty restaurant.

Giovinezza. Giovinezza
Primavera di bellezza.
Nel fascismo ela Salvezza
Della nostra civilia.

I told Alan that I often sang the English version.

Brother Blackshirts, form your legions
Keep the flag forever high
For the Fascist Greater Britain
Stand we fast to fight or die

'My word,' said Alan. 'Ignatius Loyola was right. Give me the child of seven and I will give you the man.'

On the way out, I was both confused and excited. The Milan-born manager gave us a full Fascist salute. Alan and I shook hands and he patted me on the shoulder and said that he would call and say hello to Sidney and meet my mother, perhaps on the day before the election. He said I would get nowhere without 'A' levels but if I sold more Unions and knocked on more doors, I might find someone to help me get them.

'How odd it all is,' he said as if talking to himself, 'Your great leader insists that he has gone beyond Fascism and National Socialism. Yet, the only songs his young supporters know are the English versions of the Horst Wessel and the Giovinezza.'

On the way home, a song that my father and his friends sang before they drifted to Hyde Park on Sunday nights went round and round in my head and I couldn't get rid of it.

Mosley leads on
In Britain's name.
Our revolution
Sets men's hearts aflame.
Fearless, faithful unto death
All to dare and give.
For the land that we love and the People's Right,
For Britain yet shall live.

I put the key into the front door lock and remembered to write down the name 'Ignatius Loyola' and find out if he was a UM member. Then, I saw John Wood's head pop up from nowhere. He was standing on the rickety wooden stairs that led from the pavement to the basement where he and Lovene and baby Vincent lived.

He had a look of anger, even disgust, on his face and said, 'I hope your new homosexual friend Mr Neame wasn't quizzing you about Kelso Cochrane.'

Alan Neame appeared on the doorstep at six o'clock on October 6, two days before the general election, with a large bunch of flowers. 'Are these for me?' asked my father.

Alan laughed and said that was rather up to my mother because they'd been especially picked for her on her birthday and were as fresh as they could be from his garden at Fisher Street, near the village of Selling in Kent. My father ushered him into the front room, which my mother always called 'the best room' even though it had a double bed in the corner for all to see.

'My dear, Sidney,' said Alan. 'Tell all. Will the divine Sir Oswald be returned to Parliament on Thursday?'

'Mosley's had it,' said my father. 'The other night, I saw it with my own two eyes, half a dozen or so blacks turned up, some with bricks and knives and off scarpered our lot, running into that office place, locked the door and called the police. I ask you. And my so-called son-in-law organising the whole bloody show. Mosley's lost it and should call it a day. The Russians are landing Sputniks on the Moon. Krushchev is about to fly to America and Mosley is telling people who live in slums that unless they vote for him the communists will take over the world. He should have packed it in long ago. Something happened when he was in prison. He's a different man. I think the Yids got him. I'm not even sure it is Mosley. You know, there's a story going round that the Jews killed the real Mosley. This one looks like him but isn't him. Whether that's true, I don't know.'

He said, 'So, I don't know but I do know that there are more things in heaven and earth, Horatio, than are dreamt of in your philosophy.'

Alan said, 'Sidney you are quite wonderful. You quote the Bard. May I quote you?' 'Wartime Fascist detainee says – "This is not the real Oswald Mosley."'

My father said he could but not to use his name.

He thought for a while, shook hands with Mr Neame and then pinned his driver's badge onto the part of his tweed jacket coat that once held a large silver flash and circle badge and said he had to go because he had a fare from the Dorchester to Heathrow.

'Had him before, Some Jewboy off to Israel. But he's a good tipper.'

The front door closed and there was a knock on my door and the sound of a tray with cups on it. My mother had just had her hair permed by her Jewish hairdresser, Mr Dollop. She looked wonderful and said, 'I am Trevor's mother and I'm delighted to meet you. Trevor has told me such a lot about you. Do you have sugar in your tea? Or perhaps something stronger. I still have a half bottle of whisky that my son brought back with him from Spain. Did Trevor tell you he went to a Church of England grammar school?'

She was at her fascinating best but how many more times in my life would I have to hear how she first saw Mosley in Brighton and how he came in from the rain, his hair wet and shining and how she knew there and then that Oswald Mosley would always be at the centre of her life?

But after an hour or so I noticed her speech started to slur, just a little. Then, I saw how much of the whisky Alan had poured into her glass.

'Mrs Grundy,' he said. 'With your permission, you shall be the *heroine* of my next book. Only female fanatics can change the world. We need them more than ever. We must be led by people who feel and not those who think. This wretched Traitor Island is led by intellectuals paralysed by thought and insufficient contact with those with deep roots in the soil. Rootless cosmopolitans can be in Rome one day, Paris, Brussels, Vienna or London the next. At home wherever they are. But the people, the sons and daughters of the soil, they are rooted and cannot pack their suitcases and follow the you-know-whos who rule our lives.'

'Thank you Alan.' she said. 'And it's Edna. But I really shouldn't have more to drink. If Mr Grundy saw the amount I'd had.'

'My dear . . . Edna,' said Alan, 'your heroic husband might well be planning to have a tipple of two himself once he parks his cab after taking the gentleman from Tel Aviv to the airport.'

'He's not heroic. The only brave thing he did in the war was give up smoking.'

And then –

'You know, Alan. There's one place I must see before I die and that's Egypt. Trevor says you've been there. Trevor has promised to take me there, haven't you Trevor?'

He said, 'Well Edna, a trip to Egypt is not beyond the realms of possibility. Because I speak more than passable Arabic, French and a smattering of Hebrew and write books about desert saints and religious oddballs – or should I say "fanatics" – I spend most of the summer taking well-off Catholics to the Real Holy Land where

Our Lord was brought up between the ages of twelve and thirty. I shall ask the Monsignor at Brompton Oratory, who is an old Oxford pal, what chance there is for one free ticket to Cairo. Often there are empty seats on planes. The Suez Invasion was hardly a blessing for the Middle East pilgrimage industry.'

'But for now, one more question.'

'Sidney believes the man who is standing as Union Movement's candidate on Thursday is not the real Oswald Mosley and that the real one was replaced somehow by Jews in 1943 when Winston Churchill ordered his release. Have you noticed anything odd about the Leader during this campaign?'

Another tot. Another cigarette.

'Trevor wasn't well. He has a bad chest, like his Uncle Rolly. So, I went to one of OM's house meetings on my own. The Leader said it was important to see how people live. It was a technique he'd picked up when he was the star speaker at Labour Party rallies before he left Parliament. Alan, I couldn't believe my eyes or my ears. There were about thirty people in the room, most of them Irish women who ran a bagwash centre. He spoke for over an hour, mostly about the First World War, Lloyd George and his friendship with Harold Macmillan, John Strachey, Aneurin Bevan, Lord Keynes and Edward V111.'

'Then, he started talking about why he opposed the Second World War and how he liked Mussolini but not Hitler. He said he kept quiet about his marriage to Diana Mitford because if his opponents had found out, they might have attacked her or her children by her first marriage.'

'It was boiling in the room and the window wouldn't open. I thought some of the women were falling asleep with boredom.

'*Then,*' – my mother's eyes flashed and Alan looked up fascinated, no doubt slotting her into his next novel about female fanatics – '*then* all of a sudden he stood up and started waving his hands and telling them that while in prison he read all the Greek dramatists and philosophers and that made him realise the bonds we British shared with our brothers and sisters in Europe. He mentioned names no-one had heard of. Two beginning with an "S." I told Trevor their names but I've forgotten.'

'Socrates and Sophocles,' I said.

My mother continued and told the fascinated Biblical scholar, poet and translator – 'Suddenly the woman with her back to the wall stood up and said *I don't know about your Greeks, Sir Oswald but I've got niggers in my basement.'*

For a while there was silence in the Grundy *lebensraum*, but it was broken by the sound of Alan's helpless laughter. His breath came in short gasps as he repeated what my mother said, *I don't know about your Greeks, Sir Oswald, but I've got niggers in my basement.* Soon they would be words bounced like balls around London drawing rooms and literary gatherings in London or Paris and settle on the notebook of Nancy Mitford who so enjoyed lampooning her brother-in-law.

Later that night Alan and I sat in the 'Portman Arms,' a pub round the corner from Dorset Square.

He said, 'My dear boy, there must be some method in Mosley's madness. At a gathering of Irish bagwash ladies he talks about Socrates and Sophocles and in front of an audience that included Colin Wilson, a reporter from The Times and half the Roman Catholic Church in London, he tells people about *Lassie for Dogs and Kitty Kat for Wogs*.'

That night, after several pints and a great deal of laughter, I fell off my donkey and lost my faith.

Alan had said that when he had time, he'd coach me so I passed at least two 'A' levels – English and History and if I got one more on my own, I would be able to enter a halfway to decent red brick university.

He said, 'Sadly, I don't have the connections Lady D has which got Max into Christ Church College at Oxford University but surely anything would be better than working as a clerk at National Cash.'

But the offer came with a condition. I had been told he was *one of them*, so I braced myself.

'You will get rid of all those books and pamphlets about skull shapes and nose sizes in Nazi Germany. How can you begin to understand Shakespeare, Chaucer, Wordsworth, Keats, Byron and all the rest if you are limited by religious prejudice, class hang ups, and nose lengths?'

And then the inevitable joke that I didn't understand.

'And with all respect to you dear mama. I very much doubt she would have passed one of the Fuhrer's comb tests.'

Before I went to sleep, I did what I had not done for a long time. I kneeled by my bed and tried to pray but my brain was on hold and I couldn't remember any of the words.

I switched off the light, closed my eyes and wished I could turn back time and stand, once again, next to a group of boys turning into men singing about being glad, the *Midnight Special* and those old cotton fields back home.

14

NORTH KENSINGTON AND A NEW BEGINNING, 1960

The last night of Mosley's 1959 campaign ended with him making a magnificent speech in Ladbroke Grove, which revealed, once again, his amazing power as an orator of the grand style. He spoke about Europe, the need for unity and for a massive display of national will to save Britain from becoming a third-rate country, an appendage of America and little more than that. His speech was reasoned and reasonable. In it, no reference to cat or dog foods or derogatory remarks about non-white immigrants. When he came down from his platform, Mosley was shining again and all my old feelings for him returned. Fanatical supporters raised their right arms to salute him. Mosley smiled and laughed, making them, daring them to love him even more. When he started his march back to the local headquarters, men on either side of him linked arms, all comrades together. I saw the face of Bob Row and knew that for him, the bells were ringing at long last.

I did not join the march but walked alongside it clicking, a camera recording a great event, taking shots of something I would one day go into a darkroom and develop.

I saw Jeffrey Hamm, the Bailey Brothers, Freddie Shepherd and Ron Clucas, all smiling and laughing with Mosley and in that happy crowd saw so many of the faces I'd known since I was a child, men and women who Mosley called the cream of the English working class. They never seemed to change. But that night in my donkey jacket and long hair and a copy of Shakespeare's sonnets in my pocket next to the last edition of the *North Kensington Leader*, I believed I had.

A Ted in the crowd shouted at me. 'Fuckin' journalists. What you gonna say about this, prick head?'

As the crowd progressed, it grew until there were thousands of cheering, excited Mosley supporters and Mosley onlookers. There was a joyful, party atmosphere in the air. Mosley was ten feet tall and shining. I was transported back to 1948, when I

DOI: 10.4324/9781003375722-15

first heard the 'Horst Wessel' song, my mother wanting to touch him as he went by like the woman touching Jesus in the Bible, my father with his hand over his heart, Lovene restless and wanting to go home and me saying to her, 'But Beamie, mummy says this is the greatest night in the whole of history.'

A small group of us crammed our way in to the small headquarters, while outside hundreds of people chanted Mosley slogans in the dark street so close to where Cochrane was killed. The Leader looked at us with such pride on his face. He stood tall and smiling, showing his small, sharp teeth, eyes flashing as he heard for the hundredth time

Two, four, six eight
Who do we appreciate?

And then people in that room and in that street chanting back

M-o-s-l-e-y
MOSLEY!

'We've won,' he said. 'We've won.'

But the following night it was all so different. I was not an official so could not get into Kensington Town Hall, where votes were counted and where candidates gathered to hear the result.

Labour won and Mosley came bottom with eight per cent of the vote, just 2,811 votes. For the first time, he lost his deposit.

I watched a blonde woman with a group of West Indians jumping up and down. 'He's come bottom. Mosley's come bottom.'

When he appeared from inside the hall, Mosley walked to the car, turned and gave us a half salute. He got in and Jerry drove him into the night.

Like the disciples, we stood and watched, knowing we could not go where he was going.

I waited for John Wood and thought he was lucky because he had Lovene and Vincent in his life. Most of the others had nothing apart from memories, dreams and reflections about the handsome prince across the water. John said – 'Before he got into the car, he turned and said to me that we must get over this small set-back and move on.'

We walked home in silence. When we reached Baker Street I said to John, 'It's all over. I'm not going to waste any more time. I need to get some qualifications and I'm not spending any more time selling "Action" at street corners on Saturday nights or screaming my lungs out in Praed Street with no one listening apart from old age pensioners, a half-a-dozen or so UM people waiting to get to the pub and talking shit about beating up Jews.'

Before he disappeared down the stairs to his basement flat, he looked up and said, 'I suppose you know what everyone's saying about you and that Alan Neame man.'

A month later, Jeffrey Hamm telephoned the house. John Wood was allowed to talk to him in our front room with my father listening-in.

That evening, a distraught Lovene told me that the multi-millionaire Oswald Mosley, who had returned to France and his palace of a home at Orsay outside Paris with Diana who still adored Hitler, refused to pick up the bills that had mounted-up for renting a house used as Union Movement headquarters during the election campaign.

Hamm told John that the local branch of Union Movement asked Sir Oswald to stand as its candidate. Therefore, rent and everything else was the responsibility of the local branch leader, John Wood, who throughout 1959 earned £9 a week to keep himself, a wife and a baby son.

Only after weeks of wrangling, and a threat by my father to write to the editor of the *Kensington News* and tell him what was going on did Mosley shut up and pay up.

Soon afterwards, Lovene told me she wanted to end a marriage that involved three people – herself, John Wood and Oswald Mosley.

With the help of Alan Neame, I went to work on my quest for 'A' levels. It was November 1959, and all the pictures of Mosley, Hitler and Mussolini had come down and were gathering dust in an alcove in the basement close to my father's old darkroom. Books and pamphlets about skin colour, nose sizes and skull shapes were all in the bin.

'And,' said Alan emphatically the night he became my tutor, 'let us be clear from the start, despite what those silly people in the Movement are saying about our new friendship. You have your way. I have mine. Perhaps the two shall never meet.

But that is of no importance. What is of great importance is that you never open a book by Franz Kafka until you are at least thirty, otherwise you might, as the saying goes, top yourself. Then Edna would be left to clear up the mess. And that simply wouldn't be good enough. Secondly, you must realise that the days of Jew-baiting are over and done with.'

He said our friendship might last forty days or forty years. If it was long, he would introduce me one day to the various books he had about *The Upanishads* at his home in Kent. He said they were for Hindus what the *New Testament* was for Christians.

I asked him to spell the word and wrote it in a notebook.

'They tell simple stories, just as Our Lord told simple stories that changed lives. One doesn't have to go round falling off donkeys to show change. But how do we begin to know we have? You must ask yourself that endlessly and take the advice of Goethe and conquer your freedom anew every day. We might never locate the exact moment of change.'

There was a knock on the door. It was my mother.

'Alan. I can never remember if you take sugar in your tea.'

Alan smiled and lit another cigarette because he was almost a chain smoker.

'We start off in a small boat with a guide who tells us where we must go and what we must see and do. After a while, we arrive at an island we don't much like. We look around for a different boat and a different guide. That happens time and time again. Boat after boat after boat, place after place after place, guide after guide. Then comes the moment when the water from a river turns into the salt of the sea and we can never be the same again. Then, at journey's end, we stand on a shore opposite where we started and that is when we thank our Creator for the leaky as well as the sound boats, the awful as well as the wonderful guides who brought us to our final resting place.'

'As the Spanish poet Garcia Lorca said, Life is not a straight road but that we live on a series of floating islands.'

'I will say no more but for your age, you have been through a lot that is unpleasant. If you'd given up you wouldn't be sitting here with me today to hear about Chaucer and T.S. Eliot and all the others I have in store for you in weeks to come, all of them men and women who travelled on small boats with guides of various moral persuasions. So, try and see Union Movement as the small boat in which you started your journey and Oswald Mosley as the guide who took you to a place you no longer want to be.'

Her voice came again.

'The cups are on a tray with biscuits. The plain one's for you, Trevor and the chocolate one with cream on it is for Alan. Trevor, try not to knock them over because I've just had the carpet cleaned.'

He slapped his leg, laughed and said, 'Sermon over. Now, we must think of real things and (he gave a look that said, here comes a quote worth remembering) "*beat on, boats against the current, borne back ceaselessly into the past.*"'

'So tell me, Trevor Grundy, why do you think Chaucer saw the month of April so optimistically at the start of the Canterbury Tales, while that dreary Anglican T.S. Eliot begins *The Wasteland* with those terrible words about April being the cruellest month?

In June 1960, I passed three 'A' levels, English Literature, History and Geography, and was called down to see the newly appointed Education Officer at National Cash Register Company.

He said it was quite unusual for an office clerk to gain 'A' level certificates, but the American head office agreed to put me on a three-year day release course with two evening classes a week, to earn a diploma in business studies, which would be followed by a more advanced sales management course in America.

That night, I told my parents and my mother said I'd be crazy to give up the chance of learning while earning.

I told them I dearly wished to go to university and leave NCR. My mother said I was dim-witted. 'What will those commies and lefties do to you when they find out you spoke for Mosley at Trafalgar Square? You'll be a dog's dinner and where will you be without my support?'

So, I walked the easy road and stayed on an island I knew I had to leave one day. Lord, give me courage. But not yet.

After all, I was in a new boat with a new guide, Alan Neame, who introduced me to people who lived in another world; his great friend Desmond Stewart, who whispered one evening that his book *The Memoirs of Alcibiades* was really about Oswald Mosley, not the Greek legend who sided with his country's enemies; Henry Williamson, who lost most of his fans in Britain after calling Hitler the great man across the Rhine, whose symbol is the happy child; Colin Wilson, who said Mosley was the most intelligent politician he'd ever met; the Beat poet Michael Horowitz and Father Brocard Sewell, who had several rows with the Pope on various theological issues and who edited a magazine for literary outsiders called *The Aylesford Review*; and at a dinner party held at Alan's Kent home, a place called Fisher Street near Selling, and close to the family's brewery, John Freeman the editor of the *News Statesman* and after that Britain's ambassador to Washington.

Alan said, 'But when I introduce you to these people you stare and say nothing. It is a great shame you never went to public school.'

At Foyles in Charing Cross Road at the launch of a book called *Blood Royal*, I met the author Gerald Hamilton and learned from Alan that he was the model for Mr Norris in Christopher Isherwood's novel *Mr Norris Changes Trains*. Hamilton and Alan were close friends. Alan told me in strict confidence that he'd written most of the book. At the launch, Hamilton, a dirty, scruffy man who smelt of whisky and garlic, tried to pick me up and said, 'Come with me, dear boy, to dark and dangerous places. Leave behind this England where they the serve soup cold and the beer warm.'

Later, quite drunk, Richard Aldington's first wife took me for a drink at the famous Salisbury pub and told me to admire the stained-glass windows while she powdered her nose and poured some powder into her gin and tonic. She told me to keep away from 'those people' the Alan Neames and Gerald Hamiltons of this world. She called them upper-class hooligans on the lookout for working-class bum boys. But if they ever got into trouble or faced blackmail, they ran helter-skelter to the family solicitor and paid fortunes to get them off the hook while they waited in line for their OBEs and MBEs and a pat on the head from someone in the royal family.

She told me to buy her more gin and then she would tell me what her late husband, who wrote the first literary attack on Lawrence of Arabia, was forced by M16 to remove from his book some of the things he knew about the legend's real feelings towards Hitler and who caused Lawrence's mysterious death in 1935 on the eve of his departure for Berlin. But when I returned from the bar, the lady had left.

At the City of London College, I met young men of my own age, some of them public schoolboys who worked for family businesses but who'd been turned down by main universities.

I formed a friendship with one of them, Christopher Andrews, who was the adopted son of the chairman of Mentmore Manufacturing which made the famous Platinum fountain pens. Chris drove a new MG sports car to Moorgate on Wednesday mornings and lived in one of the most luxurious houses in Marshall's Drive in St Alban's. He had his hair cut and shaped once a month by an Italian who charged more than I earned in a month. Chris spent his holidays in different parts of Europe, picking up language skills and preparing for the day he would become chairman of the family firm.

I made friends in St Albans and, for a while, went out with a tall, intelligent and very attractive student at St Alban's College of Art. I met her at Chris Andrews's twenty-first. Her name was Jose Allen, and I took her to Blandford Square to meet my mother. Afterwards, she said, 'Leave that place as soon as you can. Why are you still there? You're twenty – two years of age. In that kitchen, I felt as if a bomb was about to go off.'

I said, 'I will I will. As soon as this bloody course is over. I'll be off. America. I might stay there if I can get a Green Card and then become an American and if they won't have me, a Canadian.'

At the end of my three-year course in June 1963, the education officer at NCR had been replaced by a woman journalist on secondment from head office in America. She said she'd never heard of me and had no record of any kind of advanced training course in America, or anywhere else.

Max Mosley had a degree in physics and was training to be a barrister. His mother's contacts in the physics department at Oxford University were second to none.

It didn't take me long to find out that nepotism rules the world.

Through Alan Neame, I was introduced to some of the senior Arab journalists and diplomats based in London. One of them, a man called Mahmoud Amr. He was a scion of a wealthy Egyptian family which had been forced to slim down, thanks to Nasser's socialistic policies and land reform programmes. Alan Neame said that many of the top civil servants would love to see the back of Nasser and return to the old days. But none of them had the courage to speak out or question the colonel's commitment to the *fellahin* and his costly fight against Israel.

I'd written a review of *The Destruction of Dresden* by David Irving and Desmond Stewart, who lived and worked in Cairo, published over three pages in the *Arab Observer*, which, that month, had as its front-page cover a cartoon of Golda Myer wearing the tall coned hat of a witch sitting on a broomstick and flying over Palestine.

Mahmoud Amr's wife was a professor of Islamic Studies at Cairo University. They had three sons. Alan took me to lunch with Mr Amr and a week later I was offered a part-time job with MENA at 27 Chancery Lane, a few yards from Fleet Street, where real journalists worked.

And so, I left NCR and told friends I was going to re-train as a journalist specialising in the Middle East. I soon found out that Amr took me on so as he'd have a cheap English teacher for his children, someone to distribute the *Arab Observer* in left-wing bookshops, a telex operator at the weekends and a general dog's body to answer the phone and take down stories from ambitious press officers in the Syrian and Iraqi embassies, who spent most of their lives denouncing Israel and Zionism in press releases that never saw the light of day anywhere but the office of MENA.

John Wood, who served in the Canal Zone during his national service, said the Arabs were a bloody sight worse than the Jews and if it came to war between the two sides, he'd fight for the Jews any day of the week.

On Saturdays, I worked from four in the afternoon until the Sunday papers appeared between ten and eleven at night. I picked them up, took them back to the office and watched Mr Amr and an Armenian journalist summarise the main stories of the day. I read their words carefully and sat at the telex machine and made sure they were all well-received in Cairo before packing up and going home.

At around midnight, Mr Amr drove me home, rarely speaking, always smoking. The following day, I was back in the office at 9am, working until five or six in the evening when Mr Amr came in to the office after a day of entertaining Egyptian officials at his home in Willesden.

Over the coming months, I picked up the 'ABC' of journalism and after a year was allowed to attend Tuesday morning briefings at the Foreign Office and cover debates about the Middle East in the House of Commons. I was overjoyed when I was accepted as a member of the National Union of Journalists (NUJ) and was as proud of my press card as my father was of his taxi badge. After two years at MENA, Mr Amr raised my salary from £9.00 a week to £19.10 a week, the Fleet Street minimum.

I taught the sons of Mrs and Mr Amr three times a week and was paid extra for doing that. But I would have done it for nothing because at long last I was in a warm and welcoming family setting, hearing so many speeches in Arabic, a language that sounded like music when spoken softly.

Mrs Amr taught me a little Arabic and lent me books about Arab history. She said hating Jews was a sin against God, and there was a huge difference between Judaism and Zionism. She lent me an old and rather expensive first edition of T.E. Lawrence's *Seven Pillars of Wisdom* and *Trial and Error* by Chaim Weizmann and a book in German, *Der Judenstaat* by Theodor Herzl.

'But I can't read German,' I told her. She gave me a mock-stern look and told me to go to Foyles and buy an English-German dictionary.

So, it came as a shock one day in around April or May 1964 when a tall, good-looking man with golden hair came towards me in Chancery Lane, round the corner from Fleet Street and close to the Law Courts.

Max Mosley looked at me but didn't greet me. I imagined I had put on weight or had a different hairstyle and he didn't recognise me.

'Max,' I said and he stopped.

He had a cold, almost cruel look on his face, which reminded me of his mother, Lady D, when she wasn't pretending to be blissful and dreamy. He gave a scornful look as if I'd waylaid him, a street vendor trying to sell him something he didn't want.

He must have grown at least a foot since the night in October 1956 when the Russians invaded Hungary and two sixteen-year-olds painted a Flash and Circle on a wall near the Edgware Road.

I extended my hand which he ignored.

I told him I was now a journalist and a member of the NUJ and would soon go and work alongside Alan Neame and Desmond Stewart in Cairo. I told him I'd seen the *Pathe* newsreel, which showed him defending his father who'd been beaten to the floor by Jews and Communists at Ridley Road in June 1962. I asked him if Alexander was in England or South America and if he was still married to Jean Taylor, the policeman's daughter from Brixton.

I expected him to at the least ask about my mother and father and Lovene, but he said not a word. It was as if none of us had ever entered his life.

Without saying a word, he joined a group of other tall, good-looking young men with briefcases and ties showing which public school they'd attended, the schools that Bob Row said Mosley would abolish soon after the bells started ringing throughout the land.

15

LONDON, 1961–1965

Alan Neame changed everything, and for a while I thought it possible if I could put memory on hold I would be able to wipe away the past in the way teachers wiped away old lessons on blackboards.

Needless to say, Union Movement people told one another that I'd faded away because of Alan Neame's influence and that I was now 'one of them.'

In fact, Alan had his own homosexual friends, and I saw very little of that side of his life, although to celebrate my 'A' level success he invited me to have 'cocktails' at a place he called 'my slightly less than salubrious club,' a place called The Carousel in Soho.

It was there that I first heard the words 'camp' and 'straight' and 'gay' and 'queen' to describe men.

The music was loud and for a while Alan left me on my own.

He seemed to know everyone and introduced me to two or his best chums from his days at Wadham College at Oxford University, whose names it was easy to remember because one was the son of a prominent Conservative minister in the Macmillan government and the other was the heir to a huge dairy firm based somewhere in the Midlands.

I tapped my feet and probably shook my shoulders in time to the music and watched what appeared to be a 'straight' girl in a flowery dress and Mary-had-a-little-lamb bonnet try and plant a kiss on the cheek of a barman known as The Princess.

His mock-shock voice rang-round the room and then the whole place exploded with laughter when he held the girl at arm's length and said at the top of his voice-

'Some one tell her, *please*. We don't kiss girlie-whirlies.'

Several of my new friends at the City of London College said that The Carousel sounded like the sixth form at a public school.

DOI: 10.4324/9781003375722-16

But a nineteen-year-old friend of Chris Andrews, a good-looking loner called Nicholas Ashford who'd been to Haileybury College and for a short while to Sandhurst, said I should be careful. He said that M15 took pictures of people they didn't like, and my new friend Alan Neame might be one of them.

Alan said that one of his tasks was to provide me with something Germans took seriously, a *Weltanschaung*.

He took me to see the film 'Lawrence of Arabia' and told me how this 'chocolate box' hero was despised by most Arabs.

After watching Dirk Bogarde in 'The Servant' he said – 'Robin Maugham got it right. You see, so many of the English upper classes are quite helpless without the aid of their nannies or servants. Often, the lower classes provide the only real love they ever get. When Mrs Everest died, Winston Churchill couldn't cope for days, weeks, possibly years. Who else was there to love that vile brute?

And, years later, to celebrate my rise from tea-maker, telex operator and unqualified dog's body at MENA to a card-carrying journalist covering the Foreign Office and House of Commons, Alan paid for me to attend the Aylesford Review Weekend Conference at Spode House, Hawkesyard Priority in Staffordshire from Friday, June 5 to June 7, 1964.

He told me Colin Wilson would be there, plus the up-and-coming novelist Laura Del-Rivo. My literary hero Henry Williamson would talk about his huge admiration for Mosley and his post-First World War novels, and he would bring with him the young, attractive Anne Quinn who had written avant-garde novel called *Berg*.

A week or so later, I spent the weekend at Alan's home in Kent and met one of his new part-time lovers, a rough lad about my age called Johnnie from Glasgow who wanted to be a footballer but who was hardly able to kick a ball more than few yards without falling over, so drunk or so high on non-prescription drugs.

But Alan made sure that young Johnnie from the Gorbals wasn't anywhere near his house when he entertained his upper-class friends, one of them John Freeman and his new wife.

I sat silent like a mouse understanding next to nothing while they ate and drank and exchanged views about the world as it was and as it should be.

Before I went to bed, Alan said, 'If you intend staring like a scarecrow whenever the great and the good open their mouths, I suggest you give up the thought of being a journalist and enrol as a novice Trappist monk. Remind me to ask Father Brocard if he knows of vacancies. My dear boy, people like John Freeman aren't gods. They are human beings who find it just as hard to talk to people like you as you find it hard to talk to them.'

Alone in bed, I spent a restless night thinking about what he'd said.

But in the morning, when light poured through the window, singing birds told me to thank God I was into a new world at last.

On New Year's Day 1965, Alan made it clear that I was now on my own and should stop seeing him as either a saviour or lifebelt.

He twisted open a bottle of red wine, which shot up like a fountain defacing a freshly painted pure white ceiling at my upstairs flat in Blandford Square.

He told me to contact a lecturer friend of his at the School of African and Oriental Studies near Russel Square, who was an old pal from Cheltenham College. He would put me in touch with an Egyptian student who wanted to improve his spoken English and who would, in turn, teach me basic phrases in Egyptian Arabic.

Once able to communicate, I should keep asking Mr Amr to arrange a transfer to Cairo.

'He could if he wanted to. But will he? As far as I can see, you are now running the London office on your own, reading newspapers all day and night, writing reports until your fingers give way, sending messages off on the telex while he spends more and more time at home, or lunching with the information people at the embassy talking about holidays in America, salaries and car allowances.'

'It might happen if you devote yourself to Mr Amr's welfare and slavishly obey all the conflicting dictates that emanate from Cairo. Egyptians are charming but the ones here are not at all like the ones there. In Egypt simple souls – the *fellahin* – are kind and generous and the men so often bewitchingly attractive but one should never take seriously what any Arab says or promises. It's not so much that they lie. It's that they simply leave out the truth.'

And then a semi-Mitford Roar.

'Oh, do put on that *dreamy* Beatles song again. 'Such bliss,' he said, tilting an almost empty wine bottle towards my glass, looking up as a wet and blushing ceiling looked down.'

'So the old bastard's dead,' my father said on Sunday, January 24, 1965, after hearing the news about Sir Winston Churchill's death on the BBC. 'Good riddance to bad rubbish.'

My mother said, 'Without Churchill, Mosley might still be in prison,' a reference to the fact that the war-time prime minister ordered the release of Sir Oswald and his wife, who Churchill loved and called *Diana-mite*, in 1943 when it became clear that Hitler couldn't win the war and so Oswald Mosley was no threat to anyone but himself.

On Saturday, January 30, Mr Amr told me that I would be alone all day in the office and only to file to Cairo if something truly sensational happened. And if MENA carried exclusive stories from the Arab world, I should make sure they were sent immediately to Doon Campbell, editor-in-chief of Reuters over the road at 43 Fleet Street.

He told me he would be at home working on a lengthy feature about Churchill's role in the Middle East. It had been ordered by Mohamed Heikal, editor-in-chief of *Al-Ahram*, Egypt's most important newspaper.

He said thanks to Desmond Stewart, the man closest to Nasser had been reminded that Churchill wrote a long article in the *Illustrated Sunday Herald* on February 8, 1920, called 'Zionism versus Bolshevism.' It showed how the then secretary of state saw the need to wean secular Jews away from Bolshevism which they dominated in Russia towards Zionism and how, if there were three to four million Jews running a new state in that strategic part of the world, it would be, in Churchill's words, 'in harmony with the truest interests of the British Empire.'

I sat watching television all day, a one-bar electric fire providing a little warmth, some sandwiches and a flask of coffee, for company.

The only time the telephone rang was when Mr Amr wanted re-assurance that nothing in London had happened and on one occasion if I knew anyone in the trade union movement who could firm up a story that dockworkers had been paid large sums of money to lower the cranes as a salute to Churchill as a barge carrying his dead body under a Union Jack went by.

I telephoned a new acquaintance at the East End of London News Agency, an Irishman called Michael Finlayson, who said the story was a load of bollocks and did I want to meet for a few pints at the Red Lion. I feigned activity and told him I couldn't because I was so busy filing stories. He said some bloke from Africa called Ian Smith was in town, and there was a rumour he was going to break from Britain now he'd imprisoned most of his most serious African opponents.

At midnight, I left the office and walked home wondering why in a world of busy and bustling reporters who were bonding with one another, I was always on my own.

The following day, Mr Amr told me his three-thousand-word story about Churchill in 1920 had not been used on the orders of President Nasser and that my story about dockers wanting money to lower their cranes had been spiked because it had not been sourced.

Not a good time to suggest a transfer to Cairo, he said.

'Maybe in a year or two. Not now. You have so much to learn. It is a pity you never trained on a local paper. What were you doing between the ages of fifteen and seventeen? You should have been chasing ambulances and fire engines, not reading books about Oswald Spengler.'

16

THE BEATLES AND BEYOND

In September 1965, the Sonny and Cher song 'I've got you, babe' was everywhere. For me, it was a musical reminder that at the age of twenty-five no-one outside my immediate family cared if I was alive or dead.

Lovene had taken her two young sons, Vincent and Nicholas, and set up a shop in a small village in Catalonia, where she taught English and worked now and again for different British tourist companies now that hardly a soul in Britain knew anything about the Civil War or regarded Franco's Spain as a *pariah*.

Alan was constantly on the move, taking tourists to Egypt and Jordan and for extra sums of money, lecturing them after supper, about the world's three great inter-locked religions, Judaism, Christianity and Islam.

In his spare time, he did what he called 'research work' for his great friend Desmond Stewart, finding out what young male Egyptians under the age of thirty really thought about Israel, Arab nationalism and President Nasser.

During one of his monthly visits to London, he came into an empty, but for me, MENA office and opened a bottle of cheap Egyptian wine.

Then another cigarette, another glass of wine and another Mitford Roar.

When the bottle was empty, he stood up, walked to the door and from there blew a kiss in my direction after reminding me to have another 'go' at Mr Amr about a job in Cairo.

'Otherwise, my dear, I fear you will be in this rather dreary office for the rest of your life. But it's safe, you're earning and at long last understanding there is a world outside of 302 Vauxhall Bridge Road. Perhaps you will be a Trappist monk after all. Would that please Edna? One wonders. In the meantime, stay good and safe and remember what General Douglas MacArthur said so famously – A retreat is an advance in a different direction.'

DOI: 10.4324/9781003375722-17

'Write that down in your trusty notebook, the one you carry around with you all the time with my name on it.'

A day or so later, the boomerang I'd hurled towards the distant horizon circled the world and returned and hit me hard in the back of the head.

It came in the shape of the voice of Dan Crowhurst who had joined Union Movement after three years at Cambridge University. He said they were the worst three years of his life.

He graduated with a degree in English and became, first, a banker at Lloyds in Baker Street and then a reporter with the 'Marylebone Mercury.' After covering a Mosley meeting at Kensington Town Hall, he was swept away by Mosley's oratory and joined Union Movement, losing his job as soon as a local anti-fascist group revealed his new political affiliations.

He'd written articles for *Action* and Lady Mosley's magazine *The European*. Jeffrey Hamm was suspicious. He said Crowhurst was pretending to be a victim of the Jews to gain credibility within the Movement and that his true aim was to write a book making members look ridiculous and Mosley a crackpot.

Crowhurst became a friend of the family. My father said Hamm and Row detested intellectuals because they might draw close to Mosley who belonged to them, not fresh brains with new ideas.

He told me over a couple of beers in The George opposite the Law Courts that like me, he faded away after Mosley's election defeat in 1959. But that the Old Man was back again and was planning to fight a seat in the East End of London, probably Shoreditch his old stomping ground in the 1930s.

He said that Mosley at the age of sixty-nine was on fire after a few set-backs in Manchester and Ridley Road in 1962, when Jews and Communists knocked him to the floor and tried to kill him. Their fury had been caused by Mosley's decision to unite several nationalist parties in Europe and put them under his control – The National Party of Europe.

'I've seen all the speeches, Trev. He spoke so well about restoring the values and the genius of Hellas and how we, together and united, can triumph over alien values. He never once mentioned the Jews but we all know what he means when he talks about the rootless cosmopolitans who run international finance.'

I said, 'But the British people remember OM for only two things – Cable Street in 1936 and North Kensington in 1959. Racism and antisemitism.'

'Wrong,' said Crowley. 'Even Jews are criticising the Israelis for their treatment of Palestinians and look what's happening as we speak – twenty thousand steel-helmeted guardsmen patrolling the streets in Los Angeles with blacks on rooftops shooting at them with rifles. President Johnson has plenty on his plate without this. It will happen here one day. Mosley was right. Send the lot of them back to where they belong, the Caribbean. They can have their country back as long as the deal is reciprocal. We want our country back, too. And look at this pathetic government telling white Rhodesians to hand over to what, a bunch of Russian and Chinese-trained communist terrorists?'

I asked if our meeting was planned or had happened through chance.

He said my mother told him where I worked and how I might soon be posted to Egypt to work for President Nasser.

'We lost you some time ago, Trev. But if you can get the *gypos* to put their hands in their pockets and help the Old Man. After all, he's not made of money.'

I looked at my watch and told him I had to go, a press conference at the Egyptian Embassy.

Before I left, I asked him if he knew where Max was.

He sighed. 'Well, we all hoped he'd take over from OM. He's got a degree in physics from Oxford, was Secretary of the Oxford Union and he's a qualified barrister. And he's become a racing driver. The name "Mosley" is no drawback. So, that's a big step forward. Quite a character is young Max. Must be about your age. Still married to that Jean girl from Brixton. Did you ever meet her?'

'And Alexander, his brother?'

'That I do not know. Someone said he went off to America and was never seen again. Image of his father. You probably never met him.'

He handed me his business card.

'So, Comrade Grundy. Let's stay in touch. Your office is only just round the corner. Your mother proudly told me you got a press card from the NUJ. Bob Row has been trying for years. Sadly, mine was withdrawn.'

Before I stood up to leave, he said – 'If you don't call me, I'll call you or come in or better than that, pop and say hello and maybe meet some of your rich Arab embassy friends. After all, OM and President Nasser have a couple of things in common, don't they?'

It was Alan Neame who told me that when you are down and out, never to seek advice from a close friend or a relative.

And, he insisted, 'never reveal anything of any importance if you are sitting at a table near a band. By sitting in public, we show we have nothing to hide. That is taken. And a good National Socialist boy such as yourself surely has nothing to hide now you have got rid of all your badges and pictures. As for discreet alcoves, do not suppose me innocent of their pitfalls, their paper-thin partitions, their microphones and spyholes. Above all, make sure the music is classical, for with so much modern music you never know when it may stop and surprise you in a confidence, for the applause is often late and half-hearted. Many an eavesdropper, to my knowledge, has earned his fee between the last chord and the first clap of a Cole Porter song.'

Afterwards, I wondered where I'd heard or read it all this before and remembered the advice contained in chapter four of Alan's first novel, *The Adventures of Maud Noakes* published in 1962 by Chapman and Hall with its eye-grabbing cover by a New Directions artist, Andy Warhol.

The book was about a dotty upper-class woman determined to blow up Anglican missionaries in Africa.

In strict confidence, Alan told me that Diana Mosley passed his book to her sister Nancy Mitford for a review in one of the prestige Sundays.

That she did, with Mitford describing the new novel by her sister's literary friend as the funniest since Voltaire's *Candide*.

Alan said, 'She might have been even kinder had she read it.'

So, after seeing Crowhurst in Fleet Street, I spent the evening with Mike Finlayson who was four years younger than me with a couple of girlfriends who looked like teenage Beatle fans in Help! Could he, I asked, use his influence and get me a job with the 'East End of London News Agency' and help me find a room well away from Blandford Square?

He asked if I'd put some Swedish *au pair* in the family way.

I said it was more serious than that. He nodded and said, 'I'll do what I can to help but there could be problems. My editor Lenny Goodman is a Jew whose dad fought the Fascists at Cable Street in 1936. So, if he finds out I'm helping a mate who used to be a Fascist . . .'

What a fool my mother had been telling him I made a speech praising Mosley at Trafalgar Square when I was seventeen.

'You haven't been given the boot at the Egyptian place you work, have you?'

I said no but all the promises of being transferred to Cairo had come to nothing.

He said, 'I sometimes wonder if you should be a journalist. You're not really the type. I don't think you've got the rat-like cunning that's needed. I mean, the Middle East News Agency isn't exactly Reuters, is it?'

A week later, he slipped a copy of the *Press Gazette* under the door at 40 Blandford Square and circled in red an advert for a sub-editor to work on a two-year contract with a newspaper in Ndola called *Times of Zambia*.

In mid-October, a man with the Renaissance name of Arnold Raphael telephoned the office, probably to see if I really was an English journalist working for an Egyptian Government-owned news agency. He told me he had received my application and that it would be a pleasure to meet me at the headquarters of Lonrho which owned *The Times of Zambia*. He was its representative in London.

He told me that the editor of *The Times of Zambia*, Richard Hall would be in Britain for a short time at the end of the month, and we could meet and find out if I was the right man for the job.

He said he'd lived in Zambia when it was Northern Rhodesia. But since the British handed over to Dr Kenneth Kaunda in October 1964, the region was turning into a battleground between white Fascists and black nationalists.

He said, 'You don't need to be a rocket scientist to know who's supping with the devil and who's on the side of the angels.'

He asked me if I'd seen Ian Smith at Winston Churchill's funeral, or after any of the Rhodesian leader's meetings in London with Prime Minister Harold Wilson.

' From a distance,' I said.

' From a distance is the best place to see him. Fascist through and through. Disgraceful how the RAF people lay down the red carpet the moment he sets foot in England.'

He told me four other people had applied for the job but that I might have a slight edge, working for a foreign government alongside people who weren't white and who couldn't speak good English.

'So, that's that then. I'll write to confirm everything and enclose a street map so you know how to get to us. Saturday, October 30, ten o'clock. Jacket and tie and don't be late. Mr Hall has lunch with "The Observer" lot at the Waldorf and David Astor hates people turning up late, unless they're African presidents.'

17

FALSE START AND A NEW BEGINNING

A few days after the interview at Lonrho House in London, I received a letter telling me I hadn't got the job. It was polite enough. Richard Hall said that he was looking for someone who'd worked on a British or Commonwealth newspaper and who had experience as a sub-editor. But if the situation changed, he would let me know about a future vacancy and I screwed it up and tossed it in my waste-paper basket.

My brother-in-law John Wood, who was now an agent with the Prudential Assurance Company with ambition to start his own travel company in Spain, said I should thank my lucky star that I hadn't got the job.

'If Kaunda and that lot found out you're an ex-Mosley Man you'd be in the slammer before you could say Harold Wilson. And do you think anyone here would raise a finger in your defence? They'd say you were an agent planted in Zambia to find out what was going on and then sell information to whites in Rhodesia who look as if they're about to declare independence and break from Britain. At least you've got a job. I doubt there's a newspaper in Britain that would touch you with a barge pole. I suppose you could always tell some Jewish editor that the man who helped you get your precious "A" levels was an Oxford-educated queer who wrote articles for Diana Mosley's magazine and ran a campaign to release Ezra Pound who broadcast from Rome during the war on behalf of Mussolini's Fascist government. I'm sure that would impress him no end.'

I said, 'But I've never been arrested, never sent to prison. My track record is spotless.'

'That's more than can be said about your face,' he said.

The day after Ian Smith's illegal declaration of 'independence' on November 11, 1965, I saw Mr Amr and the Armenian who never smiled trying to make sense of what was going on in Central Africa.

DOI: 10.4324/9781003375722-18

Mr Amr spent that lunchtime with his Reuters friend Doon Campbell, who lent MENA one of his African trainees, a young Nigerian from the London School of Economics with a bright open face who detested white Africans.

Mr Amr said that Harold Wilson had told a group of Commonwealth reporters that Ian Smith's rebellion against the Crown would be over in a matter of weeks.

Mr Amr told the Nigerian to go to the Foreign Office briefing and say that Egypt was one of the leaders of the Non-Aligned Movement and would do everything in its power to see racist rule end in Rhodesia and eventually in South Africa with its policy of separate development which the rest of the world came to know and hate as *apartheid*.

I had nothing to say or contribute and kept quiet that I'd been reading up about Central and Southern Africa and had met Richard Hall, who was now such an important figure in the war that was bubbling up between the black and white races in Central and Southern Africa.

In the middle of February 1966, a letter landed on the mat by the front door of 40 Blandford Square. It was from Zambia. Richard Hall wrote that because of changed circumstances, he could offer me a two-year contract with *The Times of Zambia*. The final paragraph asked, 'How long will it take you to expedite yourself from your present position?'

'April 1. 1966 As good a day as any to sign up for Zambia for the next couple of years,' said the Lonrho manager in London, Arnold Raphael. 'Friday the 1st, Well, better than Friday 13th.'

He stared at a piece of paper on his oak desk as I entered his large office at precisely ten o'clock that morning.

Behind him, a large picture of Lonrho's great man, the six feet six inches 'Tiny' Rowland.

Placed around the walls were pictures of this German-born *entrepreneur* with various African presidents.

Full of light-hearted jokes about Africa and Africans and the people who'd gone out there and never been seen again, he handed me a single ticket to Ndola via short stop-overs in Rome and Entebbe in Uganda.

The Lonrho building was not far from the City of London College in Moorgate, where I had formed friendships with people of my age who'd never heard of Mosley. It was a Victorian structure, tall, imposing and here to stay.

He pointed to a photo on the wall and said, 'That's him, Richard Hall, with the man you'll be answering to over the next couple of years, President Kenneth Kaunda. He's a sort of Christian dictator, very popular with the Foreign Office people, so you only have to remember one thing to please the Africans and us. And it's this. What Kenneth Kaunda wants, Kenneth Kaunda gets. Fortunately for Lonrho, Richard Hall is a close personal friend of KK.'

He told me to take some British currency with me to tide me over until payday and to carry with me a certificate to show I didn't have pulmonary tuberculosis, a police certificate showing I'd never been in trouble with the law, a valid British driving licence, all school certificates and the also one showing I had a Higher National Certificate in Business Studies from a British college.

'Can you speak foreign languages, French, German?'

'Bits of both,' I said.

'You leave on April 27th sometime in the afternoon and with luck you'll be lunching with your new friends in Africa.'

He asked me if I'd read Mr Hall's book, 'Zambia.' I said I'd try and get a copy from Foyles on the way home. He said, 'And get Conrad's Heart of Darkness while you're there. Everything you need to know about Lonrho and Africa is in it.'

I asked, 'Why is it so special? So many people have told me to read it.'

He laughed. 'You'll find out.'

Before leaving, I asked what had happened to make Mr Hall change his mind and employ me.

Raphael said, 'He liked you well enough but was hesitant. He said you seemed in two minds, maybe three, when he asked you if you welcomed people of different skin colours, religions and cultures coming into Britain. He said you were ambivalent. But then you've never been a sub on a daily or a weekly. A reporter of sorts from a not exactly bona fide news agency owned by a government that is not exactly friendly towards this country. The man he chose, worked for a weekly in Wolverhampton. Full of charm. Hall thought he was just what he needed, non-racial, anti-*apartheid* movement, communist at some red-brick university but now a committed Third World activist and CND campaigner. Ticked everything in the box. When he got to Ndola, he persuaded our business manager there, a man called Hugh Leeds, to pay him his end of contract bonus of £500 two years in advance. Within a couple of months, he'd got some local woman in the ruling party's youth league up the spout, hi-jacked a company Mercedes, drove to Livingstone and crossed the border in to Rhodesia and that was that until this report in the "Rhodesia Herald."'

He pushed a news cutting across the table.

'He's writing a book to be published in South Africa called "Time to Fight – My life in Kaunda's hell hole" or something like that. He claims KK's political opponents live in a sort of Buchenwald prison camp. When he met Dick in London, he was left-wing of Lenin. Probably some bloody Nazi in disguise. If that story had got out it would have been God help Dick Hall and Lonrho for employing Fascists.'

I nervously replaced a teacup onto a saucer and asked, 'But why didn't Lonrho simply let the police in Rhodesia know and get the car back that way?'

It was then that I received a look that would become familiar in months to come, a look that asked, 'Which planet do you live on?'

He said, 'Hall needs a replacement immediately and thought of you. If he couldn't get a Commonwealth expatriate we would have been obliged to take on a local and that's the last thing anyone wants.'

He laughed. 'In Conrad's book, there's a young rather innocent man like you called Marlow who is also getting ready to go to Africa for the first time. Some harmless old fool who thought he was something of a scientist asked if he could measure Marlow's skull. He said, he always did that before white men left for Africa. Marlow agreed and asked if he measured skulls when they came back?'

Raphael looked at me, smiled and reached for a slim paperback on a nearby bookshelf and read.

'*Oh, I never see them,' he remarked, 'and more over the changes take place inside, you know. He smiled, as if at some quiet joke. 'So, you are going out there. Famous, interesting, too. He gave me a glance and made another note. 'Ever any madness in your family?' he asked in matter-of-fact tone.*'

He closed the book and grinned.

'Well, I'm sure there's no madness in your family. None in mine, despite what my wife says.'

He stood up and extended his hand.

'So adieu, adios, auf wiedersehen, kwaheri, farewell and go well. When you get there, try and stay calm. Sometimes the heat is over-powering. Some of the politicians are, too. Take my advice and get your hair cut. Dick Hall referred to you on the phone as the one who looks like Ringo Starr and can't sub. Don't forget to take salt tablets, never do money deals with Asians and if you're daft enough to get involved with any of the locals, always wear a condom. Two, if possible.'

The following day, I introduced Nicholas Ashford to Mr Amr. I told him that Nick was a great admirer of Nasser, that we'd travelled together in different parts of Europe and that he spoke fluent French and was anxious to get away from his part-time job on *Woman's Own* magazine and get into news agency journalism.

I told him that Nick had gone to a school I'd never heard of called Haileybury and it had been founded by the East India Company and then to Sandhurst but that something had happened and he left suddenly and worked as an English teacher in Greece and that later on I'd met him through friends who lived at St Alban's. I said, 'He's not your typical right-wing Englishman, even though his father and brother are stockbrokers. Far from it. His French wife is quite a prominent member of the anti-*apartheid* movement.'

I left them on their own in Mr Amr's office and heard the buzz of conversation which was punctuated by Nick's upper-class laugh and constant coughing by the chain-smoking Amr.

After about an hour, Nick appeared and said he would start at MENA on May 1. He patted my shoulder and said 'Thanks, Trev,' and we arranged a farewell dinner at his new house in Camden Town.

When he left, Mr Amr said, 'He is a remarkable young man. Of course, he won't stay long but that doesn't matter. I don't think the London office will last much longer, either. Mr. Nicholas Ashford. He comes from a quite different world from you, doesn't he? He will learn what he can from me, cover Parliament and the Foreign Office and people will ask him why he is working for an Egyptian news agency. But with his background, they might find that useful. No matter. He will be picked up by one of the quality papers. Young men who attend one of England's most prestigious military schools and then Sandhurst are at a premium in Socialist Britain. He tells me that he is a friend of David Lascelles. My goodness. You have never told me how you two became friends. People like Nicholas Ashford suddenly find they are writing for the Financial Times or The Times. My guess is that your Mr Ashford is destined to get to the top, perhaps the very top. I don't think he's a heavy drinker, either. Why do English journalists drink so much?'

He answered his own question.

'Perhaps it's because deep down they're ashamed about the trivia they write. Anyhow. We'll talk about that when you come to supper next week. Mrs Amr is expecting you and I have a bottle of whisky we will share.'

I said with a smile, 'I thought the Prophet said that his followers must never drink alcohol.'

He said, 'Not at all. The Prophet said one should not drink wine. He said nothing about whisky.'

At first, the bright and breezy voice of Alan Neame sounded little different from when I first met him at the 'Warwick Arms' at the end of Mosley's North Kensington election campaign in October 1959. He'd just read an article about the death of his generation's literary hero, Evelyn Waugh.

'What a time to go. Sunday April 10 and off he flew, barging his way through the Pearly Gates, knocking over Saint Peter and demanding an immediate interview with God for The Tablet.'

He said, 'Can you hear me? I'm ringing from a friend's house in Battersea and the line is far from clear.'

In the background, I heard a dog bark and the voice of a man singing along with Dusty Springfield, who had become an icon for men with what was then called 'a particular persuasion.'

'Dear Evelyn. You know they say he was in love with Diana? More likely with Oswald. Those two. They attracted people from their own world who loved dressing-up and pretending they were rebels until, of course, their sons and heirs went off to Eton and school fees had to be paid. And then there were people like Sidney and Edna from quite a different background, so one does wonder what it was about him that people loved so much.'

Alan could not stop talking. But when he did, I sensed sadness in the silence.

It was April 25, 1966, and he was ringing to say goodbye.

'Evelyn Waugh. Or should we give him his proper name, Gilbert Pinfold? How he so longed to be one of those upper-class hooligans he wrote about. How they made damned sure he wasn't.'

'But I didn't ring to talk about the departure of the Great Stylist, the Great Mocker. Perhaps he didn't want to live after the Archbishop of Canterbury kissed the Holy Father in Rome last month, ending four hundred years of mutual loathing. Poor Evelyn. His whole world shattered. Rather like how the Germans who stayed loyal felt after the death of the poor, misunderstood Fuhrer.'

I put my hand to my mouth and yawned.

'My dear, Trev. Time, like the ever-rolling stream. Your ole' friend, Al, will miss you but understands all. But let me give just the teeniest piece of unasked for advice.'

'Your own independence coincides with the independence of millions of people who have also been sat on for a very long time. Try not to over-identify. Above all, try not to find another Messiah. Try and remember leaders need you more than you need them.'

He said he would drop round a small gift and a letter which I must not open until I was at least one million thought miles away from the Traitor Island. If I was not in, then he would leave things with Edna.

'But for now, it's goodbye and I shall write and tell all. I see that after his last defeat in Shoreditch and Finsbury Sir Oswald has finally called it a day, leaving poor Jeffrey Hamm and Bob Row to carry the can on a pittance while he goes off to the Temple of Glory to write his memoirs. How one hopes he doesn't call them My Struggle.'

And then a few words that summed up so much. 'Oswald Mosley. Rather like Jose Antonio, the founder of Falange Espanol. A hero in an empty room.'

But then the phone went dead and for a moment I was glad.

My flat was empty apart from a couple of blankets and a pillow on the floor under a window through which I had viewed my small world for such a long time, a nineteenth-century railway station to my left, a much older Roman Catholic convent to my right and all around me a Victorian square ruined by German bombers so soon after my birth.

I sold most of my books to a man who ran a stall in the Church Street market on Saturdays, but the precious ones I stored in a cardboard box and asked Lovene to guard them with her life until I returned.

'This one, I'm taking with me,' I said to my sister who was moving in with her two small sons and John the following day.

She said I was crazy because it was the booklet by Oswald Mosley on Wagner and Shaw, the one Sir Oswald handed to me at The Temple of Glory during the summer of '58 and signed it, 'To Trevor Grundy, who has done so much for our Movement.'

She said, 'If they pick that one up at customs, you'll be back on the next plane home and you won't have anywhere to live or a job to go to.'

I wrapped the precious document in a plastic cover and placed it on top of books about Mosley, Hitler, Mussolini, and Franco, men whose names had been replaced those of Satan, Lucifer, Mara and Mephistopheles in a new world where The Beatles were more popular than Jesus.

That afternoon I got on a Green Line bus and said goodbye to Nick Ashford in Saint Albans.

After a quite boozy lunch at The Cricketers and a farewell pint at the Fighting Cocks, we walked around the Abbey together.

We examined the walls and statues desecrated by Protestant fanatics – Henry VIII or Oliver Cromwell, neither of us could recall and because it was a weekday, there was no-one around to ask.

Nick said, 'I'm not religious but when I'm in here, I feel this is all part of me. Do you feel that way?'

'No,' I said. 'I don't feel part of anything.'

That night I ate supper with Mr Amr, his wife and their three sons who I'd helped with their school English lessons. The meal seemed to go on forever, rich-stuffed vegetables, humus, falafel, shawarma, kebab and kofta, mashed fava beans, lentils and pasta and then a bush okra stew. I knew it was rude to show Arabs the sole of your feet, or to refuse their food, so I kept on swallowing, inwardly begging Allah to make Mrs Amr sit down and stop serving.

Afterwards, she and the boys left and Mr Amr spoke to me like a father saying goodbye to a son about to go off to war.

'Trevor, as much as I like you and enjoy your company, I am pleased you are leaving MENA and England.'

'You are now twenty-six years of age and your mother treats you as if you are still a little boy.'

'It's something I understand.'

'My own mother was like that. It is very common in Semitic families.'

The moment I finished one glass of whisky, he poured me another.

He said, 'The people who drink the most of this are the Saudi Royals. They drink it all day long but if a poor man even sniffs alcohol he loses his hand or his arm or his tongue is cut out. Thankfully there are no Iman's in Willesden.' He put his hand on my thigh, something I'd seen Arab men do when talking intimately.

'A few months ago, your mother telephone me and said that your new girlfriend had something to do with Christine Keeler and Mandy Rice Davies and would destroy your life. I said, "Mrs Grundy. I have met the girl and she is very nice, very beautiful and intelligent and I believe Trevor loves her" and she said, "Mr Amr. They all look nice where men are concerned, Will you tell Trevor you'll get rid of him if he doesn't get rid of her?"'

He looked at me with great affection.

'It is right that you're going away. Not just from MENA and England. You must become like a tree in Autumn and shed leaves. Cairo would have been good. But Africa is better. You told me something that warms my heart. You said, "No-one knows anything about me in Africa. I can start again." But the most important person to get to know you, is you. It was Socrates who said "Know Yourself." And it was the Prophet Jesu who said that before you could love your neighbour, you first had to love yourself.'

'Go away for a long time. For you, this land is cursed and has no meaning. When you do come back, everything will have changed because you will have changed. Maybe then you will find that you have more in common with your own people than ever you thought. But don't come back for many years and don't think about us and don't look back and don't give in to nostalgia. Forget about us and forget about the people who shaped your early years because sure enough, Mr Trevor Grundy, they will forget you.'

I said, 'Thank you for everything you have done for me. I don't know what I'd be or where I'd be now without your guidance.'

He said, 'Go to Africa and love it. And learn to be alone.'

On the way to the airport, sitting next to me in my father's recently purchased black cab, Lovene said, 'Vincent and Nicholas asked this morning why they couldn't go with you.' Then, 'I forgot to give you this.' She handed me a copy of a book called *The Lonely African* by Colin Turnbull. 'And like an idiot I've left the letter he sent with it on my dressing table. I'll send it on. Better still, I'll send it to Alan and he can send it to you when he writes.'

My mother said nothing during the journey from Blandford Square to the airport and when we got there my father shook my hand and moved forward as if he was going to kiss me. But he changed his mind and stood back and said, 'Be a man.' And then again, 'Try to be a man.'

I kissed Lovene and put my arms around my mother.

I never saw her again.

On the plane that night, I sat next to a large white man who told me he was an underground captain at one of Zambia's big copper mines. He looked at the book I was reading and said, 'Lonely African? They'll be lonely alright when we leave and they have to start doing things for themselves.'

He scowled and then laughed when I told him I was going to work for *The Times of Zambia* and said the paper was run by some 'commie' from England, a man called Hall, who was a sell-out, a cheat and a liar who spent his spare time chasing black girls.

He ordered a half bottle of whisky from the woman with the trolly, unscrewed the metal top, took a huge swig and handed the bottle to me.

'How long does it take for a young white liberal like you to become a hardened racist like me once you've seen what the blacks are really like?'

'I don't know,' I said.

'Three weeks. Sometimes less. You wait and see. *Lonely Africans* my arse.'

He went to the lavatory and while he was away, I gathered up my things, took another hefty swig from his now half-empty bottle and went to the back of the plane.

I closed my eyes, delighted that the sort of man who'd been in my life since the day I was born had damned me as a liberal.

I smiled and lay back in the chair. 'At long last, I'm on my way,' I said loudly as the woman on the other side of the aisle looked up and smiled because she thought I was talking to her.

18

NDOLA, LUSAKA, LIVINGSTONE IN ZAMBIA

In Africa, I felt free as never before. No one knew a thing about me apart from the fact that, as Richard Hall said to the chief sub-editor who was a Scot called Gordon Rollo, I looked a bit like Ringo Starr and couldn't sub.

So, he sent me down to Livingstone, the one-time capital of Northern Rhodesia, seven miles from the Victoria Falls.

Experienced subs laughed and said it was like being sent to the African Siberia.

My job there was to run the smallest newspaper in Africa, a publication called the *Livingstone Mail.*

I was there as a stand-in for the first black Zambian to be made an editor, Victor Zaza, who had been sent to Wales on a training course to knock the Marxism he'd picked up as a trainee in East Germany out of him and re-design him as a pro-British and pro-Commonwealth campaigner in the new Africa.

But I wrote book reviews for *The Times of Zambia*, first, *The Lonely African*, and then, *Neo-Colonialism: The Last Stage of Imperialism* by Kwame Nkrumah, who earlier that year had been toppled while on a Vietnam peace mission in China.

As soon as they appeared, I cut them out of the paper and posted them to my mother.

Inside a 1966 Christmas card, Dick Hall wrote that he was pleased to see that I had a spark of talent after all. He wrote, 'It's good to have a really left-wing viewpoint now and again. But not too often.'

At the end of my time in Livingstone, I returned to Ndola and was promoted as industrial correspondent in Kitwe, the very centre of the vital Zambian copper industry.

Months went by, and I thought I'd fallen in love, and in August 1967 married a pretty eighteen-year-old, who was born in England but brought up in Nigeria. I wrote and told my mother.

DOI: 10.4324/9781003375722-19

She replied saying I was making a terrible mistake marrying a black.

'Don't be daft, Mum,' I wrote. 'Lori has golden hair and was born in Liverpool.'

Her one-sentence reply read, 'Shirley Bassey wears a wig and was born in Cardiff.'

Towards the end of my two-year contract, I was offered a job as features editor of *The Standard*, a newspaper owned by the British conglomerate Lonrho in Julius Nyerere's Tanzania.

I wrote and told my mother that I wouldn't be home as planned because they needed someone on their features desk immediately, and it was an opportunity too good to miss.

She wrote back, a letter full of sadness and regret about her life. She said everyone had let her down, Mosley, my father, the rector and man she knew when she was a girl called Mr Lawes and now me.

I replied with all the sensitivity of an arrogant, little-caring and inexperienced young man who'd run away from everyone and everything he'd ever known to re-invent himself in a place where no-one knew a thing about him.

That is what I wanted. That was what I got.

I wrote back and said no one had let her down and she had let herself down by being such a fanatic, by hating Jews so much and making us believe in Mosley, who was an upper-class playboy who used people and then threw them away and into, I pompously used Lenin's famous words, 'the dustbin of history.'

I asked her if she'd ever thought what being brought up as Fascists had done to Lovene and myself, how it had alienated us from our peer group, our own generation.

I dared her to tell me about her own childhood and why she was so pleased when people mistook her for a Jew. I wrote about the night in North Kensington when we'd gone canvassing for Mosley and Mr Lewin had mistaken her for one and how pleased she was, rushing home to tell my father.

She wrote back.

She said I was right. She had let herself down and then blamed other people for everything that happened to her. 'I've been a clown all my life,' she wrote. 'Don't be like your silly mother.'

She said that when I returned to England, she would try and tell me about her strange beginnings and answer my questions.

But it was all too late.

In June 1970, three days before I was due to fly with Lori and our one-year-old son, Adam, to Egypt on a sponsored trip before returning to England for the first time in four years, I received a late-night call from Lovene in London.

She told me, between sobs, that our mother, gripped by yet another terrible depression, had committed suicide. She begged me to skip the trip to Egypt and fly straight back to London.

'Come now. Right now. Please, Trevor. Please come now.'

For a reason I will never be able to justify or explain, we flew to Cairo and stuck to an itinerary drawn up by the Egyptian Government.

We flew to Cairo and then to Alexandria and went down the Nile to Luxor, and visited so many of the places my mother had spent her life longing to see.

Within my heart, a pin-less hand-grenade.

'How dare she?' I asked myself sometimes speaking out in the middle of the night, awakening my confused wife.

'How dare she kill herself on the eve of my return? I had grown up at long last. I had a wife and a son to prove it. But where was she? Where was she to show this to?'

'Where is she?' Lori told me I'd cry out in my sleep. 'Where is she now?'

When we arrived in London, my father told me that the night before she killed herself, she said, 'Trevor will never see me like this, not like this with his wife and son.'

I felt as if I'd killed her; the mother I hated more than anyone on earth, the woman I loved more than anything on earth, killed herself because I was coming home.

In 1990, my father had a series of heart attacks, and I received a call from Lovene in California.

'I'm not doing it all on my own this time. You've got to do it this time. You weren't at Mum's funeral. It's your turn now.'

Lovene was living in the American state where dreams come true with her three sons. She worked at a Jesuit College. Like mine, her marriage had ended in divorce. She married again and that marriage also failed.

I married again in 1978 to a beautiful young English girl called Jane who I'd met at a party in Johannesburg the year before.

At the hospital near his small council flat at Rayner's Lane, my father looked frail and weak and helpless. But one of the nurses had been so kind to him, he said. 'And would you believe it,' he whispered. 'She was from Jamaica. And do you know what she did?'

I said 'No' as if I was listening to what a child did at school that day.

'She came in during the supper break with some *pasta* and sat right here by me on the bed.'

'Nurse, I said, what are you doing here, if I might ask? It's your supper break.'

He whispered as if he was in a confession box talking to a priest.

'She said to me, "Mr Grundy, I'd like to say some prayers by your bedside so that you'll get better." And I said, "Nurse. I've never been so touched in my life." And then she stood up and went away with the plate with the pasta on it, eating her supper.'

But a few days later, he was well enough to return to his flat with his wife, Peggy, my gentle Northumbrian stepmother. She was also my father's first cousin, and I'd met her when I was a child visiting my grandparents in Seaton Sluice. She and my father married shortly after my mother's suicide.

Back home, he sat looking at the television complaining about what was going on in Britain, that old aggressive 'I challenge the world to disagree with me' look back on his face.

When the football results came on, he turned to me and said, 'Do you know Sunderland's put a bloody nigger in the forward line?'

I looked at Lovene. I wanted to get hold of the nurse's pasta and stick it up his nose.

I said, 'Your nurse. Last week. The one you liked so much, she was a *bloody nigger*, or have you forgotten?'

He looked at Peggy who looked away.

'Africa's done you no good at all. You! You're like your sister. She's gone in with the Roman Catholics. Mosley would be turning in his grave. A couple of Lefties, both of you.'

The night before I left England to return to my home in Zimbabwe, where I worked as a freelance journalist, he poured himself a large Scotch. 'Hang about, dad,' I said. 'That could sink a battleship and you've just had a heart attack.'

Peggy was baking in the kitchen. He looked at the door to make sure it was shut and spoke softly.

'I always loved *yer mam*,' he said, returning to a long-forgotten Geordie way of saying things. 'She was wild but, my God, she was a fascinating woman.' He looked at the door again as if my mother's ghost would walk through it. 'After you left, she grew very old and tired and lost most of her glorious hair. Sometimes she went days without saying a word. It was driving me mad. It was no life. I'd come home after driving round London all day and ask why I was still alive. Then when we were told they were going to pull down Blandford Square, that was it. It was like living with a ghost. It was only going up North to see Peggy and, well I suppose touch base again, that kept me sane.'

He knocked back his drink savagely. 'I'm saying this because I know I could go at a moment's notice. I'm not stupid. I think Lovene knows about *yer mam* but I'm not sure. It's like everything else in this family. No one knows anything about anything. Everything a secret.'

I sat down and watched him twiddle with the top of the bottle. He then poured himself another drink, much smaller but still large. It was as if he had to half knock himself out before he could say what was coming.

'The day before she died, she took my best suit to the cleaner's and left the ticket to collect it on my desk over there. That night we had a terrible row about something or other and I said she'd spent her whole life pretending to be what she wasn't. Those damned Morris people. That mother of hers. Penniless and thought she was the Queen of England. Of course, I regret it now because of what happened but I said when you got back to England, I'd tell you what she was and what she'd hidden all her life.' And she looked at me with that look and said, 'Trevor will never know. He'll never know unless I tell him.'

Inside me came a voice that wasn't mine. 'Did she say that? Did she admit it and say finally, *I'm Jewish*?'

He stood up, poured himself yet another Scotch and put on a Wagner record which I immediately recognised, 'Siegfried's Idyll.'

He said, 'Yes. She was Jewish. Once when we were courting, I went round to see her at Whitley Bay. It was a Friday night and in their little house, all the lights were off and I thought they couldn't pay the bill because the old man had lost his money on the horses again. The only light came from candles. In those days I didn't know much so it didn't worry me. But some Spanish people from next door said they were devil worshippers and should be reported to the council and go and live in London where devil-worshipping didn't matter. One of them told me to keep away from the Morris's who signed their rent-book as Maurice. He called them "the *sheenies*," a word I'd never heard before.'

'When we were married, *yer mam* used to say they could trace their family back to the time of the Jews in Spain. She said they hid their origins because people in England hated Jews. Her bloody parents told her to wear a cross, hide her roots, go to church and get married to someone more English than the English, so I suppose that's where I came into the picture. Perhaps you don't know, but I was training for the church when I met your mother. After that. Well, that's another story. That bitch of a woman Lily Morris told Edna never ever to say where they went on Saturdays and told her to live in two worlds, the one at home where they lit candles and said their prayers in a language no-one but that lot could understand and the other world, the outside world, where the rest of us live. Judaism was their strength and their secret and I think when she met Mosley, she went from one secret world into another. She saw him as the Messiah that the Yids have been wanting all along. She never told a soul apart from me and that Mr Lawes man, ex-mayor of Whitley Bay and old enough to be her grandfather. One night when we were close if you know what I mean she called out his name. I could have killed her. Perhaps I should have.'

He took another long swig of his drink and I saw his hands shaking.

'Do you remember, she always wore a cross, that little gold one with a ruby in it. She told me once that the old lady – your grandma – used to tell her that as late as 1895 the Catholics in Spain were calling for a renewal of the Inquisition so they could persecute Jews. So, hiding is second nature to the lot of them and there are times when even I think who can blame them for that? *Yer mam* was brought up a Methodist. All that hymn singing, banging of drums and noise. She knew the lot of them, I think that's what she most loved about the BUF and UM, the drums and the sermons. And above all, the secrecy, the feeling you were one of them but you weren't at the same time. God, how I hated the Morris Yids. I think deep down she did too. But she loved them at the same time.'

'Dad,' I said, glad at long last to be getting some answers, 'why did you and Mummy get involved with Union Movement after the war? I mean, didn't you see that Mosley was playing some sort of game? First the Jews and when that was over and done with, the Jamaicans, the West Indians? Christ, at least Hitler believed in what he was doing, however terrible it was. Mosley wasn't really anti-Jewish. He simply used it as a ploy to get working class support in the East End, Manchester, Liverpool, anywhere where there were Jews. And you went to prison for that?'

It was as if a once tall and powerful building had been smashed by a huge steel ball.

He said, 'It was *yer mam*. I only got involved with Mosley because of her. I told you. Jews are fanatics. I became a Fascist because of the bloody Jews.'

And then in a whisper so soft he might only have been talking to himself, 'I think she was in love with him. He looked so Jewish himself.'

The door opened and it was Peggy with a frying pan. 'Sid, do you want honey with the pancake, or just on its own with lemon juice?'

He stood up and almost slammed the door in her face.

My father sat close to me for a while, and I thought he was going to take my hand but as always, he drew away.

'I knew she was foreign from the moment I met her. The way she was. That face, those eyes. The way she spoke about things. Those damned Jews and their secret ways. But how could I stop the love?'

Tears filled his watery blue eyes, and I touched his hands which my mother said were so strong and well-shaped.

'Dad.' It was all I could say. I knew I would never see him again.

He said, 'You've got *yer mam's* eyes. Same way of looking.'

We heard the kettle whistle and he sat up straight. I heard his knees creak. He smiled. 'Old age. You can keep it. Wait till it happens to you.'

He put the record back into its cover and replaced it with the 'Venusberg' from 'Tannhauser' and slid open the glass door of his bookshelf.

He said, 'Sit still. Just listen. That bloody woman and her pancakes.'

He handed me his signed copy of Mosley's post-war book *The Alternative*. Then, he gave me the German leather-bound picture book on Hitler and a copy of the *Protocols of the Elders of Zion*.

These were his most precious books, which he told me when I was a child would be mine one day if I grew up to be a good Jew-hating Fascist.

He looked sad like so many Union Movement people who could neither trust nor love again.

He said, 'When I'm dead, I don't want there to be any memories. I want there to be nothing which showed I ever walked the earth. Do you understand? No memories.'

19

LONDON, APRIL 1991

It was Friday and the following evening we would fly home to Zimbabwe. My father's funeral was over, and Jane had gone to stay with her mother in Kent and so I had a day to myself in London.

It was the night of the Bethnal Green party, and I imagined the drums with flash and circles on them being taken down from the attic, dusted and played.

I wondered how the new breed of middle-class yuppies who had flocked to the East End, sending house and flat prices soaring, would handle that.

I left Rayner's Lane and went by tube to Baker Street. From there, I walked past the imaginary home of Sherlock Holmes and the Volunteer pub into Regent's Park, where springtime's ice still rimmed the edge of the lake.

I walked around the Outer and then the Inner Circles and sat on the wall of the Triton Fountain in Queen Mary's Garden, where my mother and I had walked our wire-haired terrier, Bonny, when I was still a child. I had a cup of tea at an open-air café and smoked a cigarette.

I walked past Dorset Square, past Marylebone Station and then right into Harewood Avenue, where I stood transfixed by the sight of the new, up-market Blandford Square that held my memories.

I turned and looked and saw St Edward's Convent. If I kicked a tennis ball towards its grey walls, would some pretty Irish novice nun come to the door by the side and say through a grille, 'This is the last time you're getting that ball back today. Have you and Timothy done your homework?'

Powerful emotions swept over me and I walked to Lisson Grove and turned into Bell Street, and a few yards down that once impoverished part of Marylebone stood Christ Church, with its neo-classical façade, great to white pillars, its blue-faced clock with gold numerals.

DOI: 10.4324/9781003375722-20

I stood looking at that de-consecrated building. It looked back, asking why I'd been away for such a long time.

I went to the front entrance and told the receptionist that when I was young, a long time ago, it had been my church. I asked if I could walk around. She said it was now the headquarters of Aspel Communications but yes, of course, I could walk around as long as I didn't touch anything because staff members were busy working. 'You'll find it has changed a bit since you were here,' she said.

I walked down what had been the aisle to the back of the building where we had changed into our white surplices or our full-length server's cassocks. For a moment, the buzz of computers was replaced by the sound of an organ.

The modernisers hadn't changed too much. There was still an upstairs gallery that made the place look like a synagogue in Budapest or Prague. The pulpit, where the rector or Mr Cooper had preached well or badly, according to what my mother felt that day, was no longer there and was replaced by an instant coffee machine.

The organ had gone and so had the communion rail close to where I had sung in my still un-broken voice about a God that so loved the world that he made it possible for even the worst of sinners to live again.

I looked up and Cave's fresco looked down. I hadn't seen it since I was twelve when my mother, full of rage and sorrow about the rector's marriage to Mrs Simpson, had taken me away from this holy place.

I felt a hand on my arm. 'Are you alright?' came a voice. 'You look a bit lost. Would you like a cup of coffee?'

I walked with the girl to where the pulpit had been. 'Hope you don't mind instant,' she said.

She was of West Indian extraction and had an open, kind face. Her sister might have been the nurse with the pasta.

I told her that I was brought up in Marylebone behind the station but now lived in Africa. She said that was funny because her parents were born in Barbados and she lived in Wimbledon.

We finished our coffee and stood up.

I heard a voice singing and wondered if it was a record or radio. But it was a boy's voice. It was loud and clear, and it cut through the dark years which had followed my mother's death, black-cloud years which I felt descend on me so often. I heard it clearly because it was my voice.

O lamb of God
That taketh away the sins of the world
Have mercy upon us.
O lamb of God
That taketh away the sins of the world
Grant us thy peace.

I turned and looked at where the pews had been and saw a group of people moving towards the front of the church. They were staring at the altar and the large gold Cross which stood upon it. Then one of them turned and although I could not see her face clearly, she seemed to be smiling. She knelt at the communion rail and put her hands out. She cupped them, right on top of left, to receive the Lamb of God which the prayer had urged her to take. I moved forward but the picture clouded and once again I heard the low hum of computers.

I looked sideways at the fresco which reminded me of the 'Resurrection' in Sansepolcro in Italy by Piero della Francesca.

I said to the girl, 'I feel sorry for the disciples. I mean, there they are, fast asleep, it's cold and it's raining and they're told to get up and start going again.'

She laughed and said, 'Well, I suppose if you're cold and wet, it's all you can do really, isn't it?'

I shook her hand and thanked her for showing me around. I felt in my pocket to see if I had a business card. Who knows, one day she might fly to Zimbabwe to see the Victoria Falls. Instead, I found the card James gave me after my father's funeral and for a brief moment I heard the sound of marching men and the *rat-a-tat-tat* of drums.

'Have you got a wastepaper basket?' I asked her. 'I need somewhere to put this.'

Five years went by, some full of hope, but others as dead as leaves on a tree in winter.

White supporters of the ANC in Zimbabwe often asked why, of all people, I'd been picked to travel to the Soviet Union as a guest of *Novosti News Agency* in 1987 at the height of Gorbachev's Glasnost and Perestroika. The trip almost coincided with South Africa's decision to drop apartheid, a policy we called Pretoriastroika. Several white officers from Ian Smith's secret police who now worked for Mugabe's special branch called the CIO spread the rumour that I had been a Communist when I was young in England and was more likely than not a well-paid KGB agent.

But most people saw me as a liberal-minded man of good humour but often a fool who drank too much and read books about the First and Second World Wars and British politics and poetry in the 1930s. A bit of an oddball but oddballs are two a penny in Africa.

Most told me I should be happy living such a privileged life, a white who'd come scarless through the Rhodesian war and who wanted to stay on in Robert Mugabe's black-majority-run Zimbabwe.

I moved around central, eastern and southern Africa with a green Zimbabwean passport in my pocket.

I lived on top of a hill at a plush suburb called Borrowdale and was on drinking and nodding terms with diplomats and many of the country's new black leaders.

My wife was young and beautiful. We had two servants, a dog, a swimming pool, two horses and, at weekends, played tennis with rich white friends who built courts and swimming pools for the new black elite.

But I also had masked demons jumping up and down deep inside me, demons angry and eager to show their faces again, demons who rattled their cage when I was asleep and walked step by step next to me in daylight.

The few who knew me well said I drank so much because I was unhappy and unresolved and that I had to get away, return and face who and what that had chased me away from the land of my birth all those years before. The alternative was too ghastly to contemplate, said one close friend who knew nothing about my Mosley past but who did know that drink would do me in unless I took a dangerous, courageous leap into the future.

The alternative was a comfortable but meaningless existence, a life of plenty on a white island set in a deep sea of black poverty.

We sold our house, said goodbye to those we cared about and on October 20, 1996, flew away, landing in London, travelling on to Glasgow and then taking a taxi to a flat we rented for three months in New Town Edinburgh where I knew not a soul other than the ex-Reuters bureau chief in Southern Africa, Fred Bridgland, who I had met and got to know in Lusaka in 1975.

November 16, 1996, was the centenary of Sir Oswald Mosley's birth and an article by his novelist son, Nicholas Mosley, appeared in the *Sunday Telegraph*. In it, he asked if his father was an anti-Semite or if he had been misled on this explosive issue by his followers, which I thought was a strange interpretation of the *Fuhrer Prinzip*.

I was unable to contain my anger.

That night I contacted Fred.

He poured me a couple of large whiskies, which dampened my anger and loosened my tongue. The following week, he put me in touch with a former colleague, Andrew Marr, editor of *The Independent* newspaper in London. Marr said he was interested in the story of a boy brought up in the Mosley Movement and I should travel to London and talk to him.

On November 27, that year, the liberal paper carried a three-page article by me called 'My Childhood.' The following week, I was contacted by an editor at Random House in London, Victoria Hipps, who was a member of the large Anglo-Jewish Montefiore family. In a letter, she asked if I could expand the article into a book. It came out as *Memoir of a Fascist Childhood* in February 1998 and as a paperback the following year. All that led in March 2000 to a sponsored trip to Israel, where I met and spoke to young Israelis, Jews as well as Palestinians, about Fascism and then a trip to various colleges and universities in Britain with a high Jewish student intake. The whole thing ended in Edinburgh, where I addressed a meeting of much older people, some who'd been at the rough end of Mosley meetings after the war, at the home of Sir Malcolm Rifkind, the former foreign secretary and a man who knew parts of Africa well.

We left Scotland a few days before the Millennium and lived for a while in London and then moved to Canterbury and then to a tiny fishing town nearby called Whitstable, once the centre of the British oyster industry.

There, I researched and helped publish a book about the New Zealand-born Christian/liberal Prime Minister of Southern Rhodesia, Sir Garfield Todd. I travelled regularly to Scotland and spent time in London with Commonwealth liberals, who were polite enough not to mention my childhood – not when I was around, at least.

On our thirtieth wedding anniversary in March 2008, we travelled to Prague and promised one another we'd visit the window where some crazy cleric was given the heave-ho, an event which helped start the Thirty Years' War. We toured the Jewish Quarter and went to the home of Kafka, who Alan made me promise not to read until I was at least thirty.

'He loved you,' said Jane.

'I loved him,' I said. 'I think he and Desmond Stewart would have been household names in Britain but for their support for Mosley. We were all mauled in different ways, all apart from bloody Golden Bollocks Max Mosley. Look at him now, a barrister, still married to the policeman's daughter from Brixton, head of Formula One and a multi-millionaire. Max Sodding Mosley. The only one of us who got away scot-free.'

'No one ever gets away scot-free from anything,' she said. 'He probably hides the pain in different ways from you. Ways you don't understand.'

We returned home on Sunday, April 1. I opened up my computer, and there was a one-line message from an old journalist pal in Johannesburg. It said – 'You can take the Nazi out of the Man, but you can't take the man out of the Nazi. See today's News of the World.'

The local newsagent was still open and I bought a copy, and the front-page showed a picture of Max Mosley and various hookers in striped aprons at an SM orgy, which that paper said was Nazi-themed.

Jane said – 'Well, maybe now you'll stop thinking that the only one who escaped without scars was the boy you all called Golden Balls.'

The newspaper placed a black-and-white Formula One finishing flag over the backside of this rich and tragic man, sparing us the sight of anything underneath.

EPILOGUE

Selling, Kent, October 2010

> We have weathered so many journeys, and so many forms of love. Would it have been the same, we ask one another, had we stayed still, in the mill, with the water running under us? There is no way of knowing.
>
> Whereabouts – Notes on Being a Foreigner, by Alastair Reid

Alan Neame died on October 27, 2000.

I didn't know until 2002 when his friend and literary executor, the playwright John Goldsmith, took me to lunch at Alan's old club in Mayfair and then sent me a box full of his unpublished poems, some books, pictures I'd taken of him at the time his first novel was published and a copy of the *Jerusalem Bible*.

Goldsmith said in a letter, 'The Neame family should have let you know. I think they were worried that some of the old Union Movement people would turn up and embarrass them.'

At the bottom of a pile of articles written by Desmond Stewart, who died so many years before Alan, there was a sealed brown envelope with my name on it and a date – April 27, 1966.

It was the letter Alan had placed inside the book *The Lonely African*, a letter which I'd left behind before I flew away to a new life in Africa.

For some deep reason, I was unable to open it and it gathered dust on top of a filing cabinet until the eve of the tenth anniversary of his death in 2010.

I opened it carefully as if I was handling a pin-less hand-grenade. In it was a single sheet of rice paper, a pen portrait of Alan and a copy of the Ezra Pound magazine, *Agenda*. In it, the poem by Alan Neame was dedicated to me on my twentieth birthday. It was called 'Tristan's Leap.'

DOI: 10.4324/9781003375722-21

The letter was short and said –

My dear Trev,

I doubt you ever saw this edition of Agenda but here it is now. You will see that Tristan has to leap because that's what's expected of him. And that is what I long ago expected of you. The courage to jump away from the past and begin again.

Well, there you are now on your way to a new world and a new life. Take my advice. Never return to the Traitor Island. But if you do, you will find nothing the way it was. And one day, you might be the only person on earth that can remember any of the things that happened when you were a child.

How I wish I was joining you. Here I will remain. The claws of ancestors are sharp and don't let go. Never let them get hold of you. Break free, keep running. One day you'll reach the tape and then it will be all over. Like St Paul, you will receive a cup, a lovely one made of Zambian copper, perhaps.

You'll be new to whatever comes your way and no one will know anything at all about your past, your very strange up-bringing in a country that destroyed itself after two European brothers' wars, a country that dare not face the past, yet alone the future.

Try not to drink too much. And try not to over-identify with any particular faction in Africa. That way leads to disaster. Foreigners in Africa and the Middle East are, for the time being, useful royal game. Both Des and I know that full well what happens when people like us get involved in the quarrels of those they neither know and whose ways they fail to understand.

Look what happened to T.E. Lawrence.

But this above all. Always have a hundred pounds spare in a British bank, an up-to-date passport and a valid return air ticket to London.

With love always.

Yer ole pal, Al.

On Wednesday, October 27, 2010, Jane drove me towards Faversham and then down miles of hedge-lined roads towards Selling, past Trafalgar House where Alan lived with his Chinese man-friend, KC, after his parents' death and then down a small leafy road that led to the eleventh-century Church of St Mary the Virgin.

We parked the car and opened a wooden gate that led to the spot that contained his bones.

We sat at the back of the church under a stained-glass window, one of them showing Alan Neame with a group of women farmworkers.

In the foreword to a guide to the church, he'd written, 'Among those many parishioners over the centuries, I think of my own relations, more than sixty of them baptised in this church in the past two hundred years, as I myself was seventy-five years ago and of the more than fifty of them already buried here, as I hope to be.

Through them I have been nourished in the traditions of the place and these have entered my very bones.'

I whispered, 'The Neame family seems to have run this place, landowners, brewers, some of Britain's top military people including a general.'

Jane said she'd try and find the grave. I sat and read the poem he'd written for me over half a century before.

TRISTAN'S LEAP
T.G.
dd.in fest, nat. xx aet.
LOVE works more wonders in the Deep
Than maps can chart or compasses
Encompass. Each day love must sweep
The mines away from Tristan's Leap
Without heroic emphasis.
TRISTAN must leap from cliff to wave
For Ysolt's love he ventures it.
The action looks so bloody brave
That headlong leap from cliff to wave
That though a fool-way to behave
Not one in ninety questions it.
THE WORLD demands the hero leap
Yet lays the mine for his reception
And love will daily dare to keep
The channel free and daily sweep
The minefield – to the world's deception.
The hero shall not fail to leap.
LOVE works great wonders in the Deep
The hero's leap from cliff to wave
From wave to cross, from cross to grave.
Love works great wonders in the Deep,
Works that defy the world's detection,
Works to anticipate and brave
The trials by which the heroes save
And minefield of the Resurrection.

Outside, Jane waved and pointed down. She shouted, 'It's here. Or I think it's here. It's hard to tell. There's grass and weeds all over the place. Someone needs to come and clean things up a bit. You can hardly read the names.'

A voice came from nowhere. 'I'll see that's done. We had someone from the brewery look at it last year but there was no follow-up. I'll let the church-warden know. He isn't here on weekdays.'

First the voice, then the man. He could have been anything between seventy and eighty in a floppy hat and long green mackintosh who'd been laying flowers on a grave behind a small wall. He looked like a pantomime peasant but his voice, and a sniffing and growling Alsatian dog he had on a lead, proved otherwise.

'And you *are*? he queried.

I wanted him to go away, but he said he was a retired solicitor and an old 'acquaintance' of Alan Neame.

'I say *acquaintance* because Mr Neame didn't have close friends in the village. He was a man of what one might call a certain persuasion but my word he was clever. I heard him talk about his role as the official Kent Family Historian. So witty, so amusing, so charming. A Cheltenham College/Oxford University man. Someone told me he had something to do with the Bible being re-written. What will they think of next? But there was always something of a mystery about him. Someone who knew the family said he was a captain or a major in military intelligence during the war. Of course, he never said a word about that. None of the best ever do. But we owe a lot to people like the Neames. They helped make Britain what it is today.'

I exchanged looks with Jane and told him I didn't know anything about Mr Neame's time in the war but that in the early 1960s he'd been my tutor after I left Archbishop Tenison's Grammar School.

'Aha,' he smiled. 'So, you were one of the Neame boys, were you? Well, I never. And you say you're married now?'

I said, 'You sound surprised'

He said, 'Ah, yes well.' And then, 'You know he was a very good man with a soft spot for the world's, what should I say, squashed, down-trodden, abused even? He should have been called Alcinous not Alan. There was poor Ulysseus washed up on the beach and the kindly King Alcinous picked him up, brushed him down, gave him clothes to wear and set him on his way home to Ithica.'

'Al-cinous Neame!' I laughed and said, 'But it was his daughter who saved him. Princess Nausicaa. Without her, the great Greek explorer would have just laid there and rotted away.'

He looked a little downcast and then said with a chirpy look on his face,

'Ah. So, you know the story, do you? And you a grammar school boy. Things change . . . for the better, of course. My word. Alan taught you well. You know, to my way of seeing things there is no holier connection between two people than teacher and pupil. In Hebrew, the word Torah simply means "instruction." Alan Neame didn't tell you that, or did he?'

I looked up at the clock on the church tower. It was exactly noon. Across the road was a woman in a dressing gown watching, binoculars in one hand, a pipe in the other.

The man with the hat and the dog said, 'Ho hum. That's Dorothy. Nothing gets past her. That's why we don't need a policeman in Selling.'

I wanted to say 'please will you go away,' but didn't.

'Well, when Mr Neame was a lot younger, he had all sorts of visitors – mainly young men but some a lot older, more my age. An unusual lot. But towards the end we hardly saw him unless it was in church. Sat there in his pew. Never said a word. Now and again, he'd make a trip to Oxford but always came back depressed. I remember le Carre wrote in one of his books, can't remember which because there were so many. Something about old men going back to Oxford University and finding places and stones reminding them of what they were like when they were young. With some of our literary chaps, it's a disease. All this looking back and regretting.'

I asked, 'And what happened to the Chinese gentleman when Mr Neame died? Did he inherit Trafalgar House where they lived together as man and wife for what was it, thirty years?'

He was aghast. 'Man and wife? KC was Mr Neame's chauffeur, cook, and gardener. As far as I know, the family paid for his return to China. It was purely a business arrangement. Man and wife, indeed.'

He huffed and puffed and walked away but then turned and said, 'If you're hungry, the "White Lion" up the road does a decent steak and kidney pie on Wednesdays.'

It started to rain but before we left, I put a stone on top of the poem and placed it next to his hard-to-read name on the gravestone. I wrote one word – 'Thanks.'

As we drove away, the man with the dog was locked in conversation with the woman with the binoculars.

'What's come over you?' said Jane. 'Considering we've just come out of a graveyard, you're looking remarkably happy for a change.'

ENDS

Ingram Content Group UK Ltd.
Milton Keynes UK
UKHW020618200723
425471UK00024B/421